*To the Memory of Dan
and his appreciation of historical irony*

PREFACE

Two prominent Americans of the early twentieth century offered distinctly opposing interpretations of history. Henry Ford, automobile manufacturer, said that "history is more or less bunk." George Santayana, Harvard philosopher, insisted that "those who cannot remember the past are condemned to repeat it."

As these comments indicate, the value of history has been a much debated issue. In part, the controversial nature of the subject comes from the many interpretations it allows. In simple terms, history is what the historian considers the past to have been. It is an attempt to impose some sort of order or coherence on what, in its own time, may have appeared to be confused, even chaotic. In other words, history is a matter of perspective—what is seen through the mind's eye of the analyst and the writer who is the historian.

Nevertheless, even though there are many perspectives on the past, some understanding of what took place then is important for an understanding of what is occurring now, and what will continue to occur. The human being is a historical being, the only creature aware of his own mortality and, thus, the only creature conscious of the psychological dimensions of time. In the words of the German thinker Martin Heidegger, we live between the not-yet and the no-longer. The study of history provides one line of thought that meaningfully ties these two "times" to the present.

Given such an intellectual condition, we can argue that the study of Modern European History makes good sense. Regardless of our place of origin—or that of our ancestors—we are all part European in our social behavior and our thought patterns.

Over one hundred years ago, the American essayist Ralph Waldo Emerson wrote that "all educated Americans, first or last, go to Europe." This statement is probably a debatable one, but the assertion that every educated American ought to understand the recent European past is a tenable one. Many of the ideals, institutions, and problems that comprise our contemporary life were initially generated in Europe. Capitalism and communism, the stock market and the morning newspaper, soccer and golf, the department store and the two world wars—all were products of modern Europe.

To know something of Europe's history during the last two hundred years is, therefore, to know something of our world today.

The text that follows is designed to assist in such an understanding. An outgrowth of many years of teaching freshman history surveys, this book is addressed to those introductory students who want an overview rather than a heavily detailed account. If the manuscript can be said to have been "urged on," it was by a generation of students at the University of Kentucky who have regularly made teaching a pleasant challenge.

Special thanks are due Gail F. Douglass who was generous in her assistance with the typing of the manuscript, my daughter Susan who helped with the index, and the editorial and production staffs of D. C. Heath and Company who brought this project to a successful conclusion.

Raymond F. Betts

CONTENTS

INTRODUCTION

When Rudyard Kipling jokingly commented that England was not much larger than Yellowstone National Park, he was admitting his admiration for the geographical size of the American Republic, but he was not suggesting that Great Britain had diminished in political status. Kipling recorded his remark in 1899, at the height of English power, when that nation and the several other major states of Europe formed the center of a world system.

During the nineteenth century, European supremacy seemed assured. England prided itself on being the "workshop of the world," and certainly was its financial capital. The French fancied that their culture illuminated the globe, and, indeed, they had reason to think so, for theirs was the language of diplomats as well as of polite society. Germany attracted scholars to its great universities—and exported the Ph.D. to the United States—while at the end of the century its military establishment was the envy of foreign generals. Russia, still exhibiting the appearances of feudalism although the serfs had been freed in 1861, was nonetheless regarded with respect; it was the "sleeping giant." And even the Austro-Hungarian Empire, somewhat dilapidated in political form, was considered a major power and admired for its excellent railway equipment, as well as for its pastries and music. Finally, European flags flew over territories that were thousands of miles from their capital cities: overseas empire made Timbuktu an extension of France and brought the name of the English queen, Victoria, to various cities and physical sites located in Africa, Canada, Australia, and even Hong Kong.

"Eurocentric" is the word employed by historians to describe this unusually favorable world position enjoyed by the states of Europe. And that position today invites the interpretation of nineteenth-century world history in terms of the "Rise of the West" or the "Age of European Predominance."

Perhaps in the future, European history will find its meaningful chronological break, not in the eighteenth century when the Old Order of social privilege was shattered by revolution, but in 1945, amid the rubble of Berlin and before the awesome sight of the Made-In-America atomic bomb. Then, the preeminent role that Europe had played in world affairs for nearly four centuries was disastrously ended. Europe seemed to be reduced in political significance to a size matching the contours of its geographical limits. As before, in the fifteenth century, Western Europe could be regarded as a peninsular extension of the Eurasian land mass, one of the many regions of the world competing for scarce resources, dependent on outside sources of capital, and politically fragmented into units of no grand international consequence.

Reduced to simple analysis, the history of Europe in the last two hundred years is that of the extension and contraction of political power in the world, of the creation and redistribution of a global economic network, of cultural supremacy and cultural relativism. Yet the terms "rise" and "decline," so in fashion a few decades ago, must be guarded against. No historical development is ever neat and smooth. Consider that famine, disease, and economic depression were unfortunate characteristics during the "rise of Europe," just as technological and scientific innovations—radar and penicillin, for instance —were widely evident in Europe's era of "decline." The term "decline" is a particularly inaccurate one. Certainly, Europe's paramount position has been lost, but today most of the nations of that "Old Continent" are richer in goods, more prosperous in income, more educated in population, and more stable in social organization than ever before—and better off than most of those nations now comprising the other continents of the world.

What these up-and-down terms of movement really imply is this: instead of a European-centered world, our world today is polycentric. The military power of China; the industrial power of the United States, Russia, and Japan; the oil wealth of the Arab world—all suggest a new global scope of activities and a new set of regional centers of political-economic importance. No longer can the stereotyped Englishman say with condescension: "The world is divided into two groups: Englishmen and foreigners." In our time, the English are but one of the many international minorities.

Yet such new conditions do not invalidate the assertion that no other civilization at any time in recorded history witnessed such a remarkable transformation from within as did the European: political revolution, social reform, and technological innovation generally changed Europe from an old order of privilege, tradition, and fixed scale to a new order of social mobility, modernity, and expansiveness. Just as the old world appeared to be centered around the church spire and the village pump, the new one was centered around the parliament building, the railroad station, and the stock exchange.

A closer observation of this grand historical sweep, however, will reveal a clutter of persistent old ways. Alongside the great change and progress that restructured certain aspects of society and introduced new daily activities were found time-honored customs and traditions. For example, in the mid-nineteenth century, the English writer Samuel Smiles in his bestseller, *Self-Help*, wrote that the self-made man could rise to any height and stand straight among his fellow citizens. However, at the same time, the farmer in rural England took off his cap when addressed by the country squire, and the courtiers surrounding the emperor of Austria bowed low and curtsied gracefully. While independent citizens were voting for the representatives of their choice in French municipal elections, the king of Prussia was asserting that his political power emanated directly from God. Finally, by way of example, the French railroad system jumped from a total of 17,500 kilometers of track in 1870 to 49,500 in 1910, during which time the average French peasant, who still worked the land with a horse-drawn plow, never traveled farther than fifteen kilometers from home in his lifetime.

Change and continuity—the two conditions that are the foundation of historical analysis—affected every European institution or social practice of this time. The age was one of transition as much as of transformation, the on-going process or movement that has led all of us today to use the expression "What's new?" as a common and casual greeting. Those who were opposed and fearful, as well as those who were excited and hopeful, recognized that the key to an understanding of the age was change. In the words of the great nineteenth-century novelist Charles Dickens, written about the eighteenth century political upheaval known as the French Revolution:

It was the best of times, it was the worst of times. It was the age of wisdom, it was the age of foolishness, it was the epoch of belief, it was the epoch of incredulity, it was the season of light, it was the season of darkness, it was the spring of hope, it was the winter of despair, we had everything before us, we had nothing before us. . . .

The uneven growth of nineteenth-century Europe and the mixed emotions it aroused were intensified in the twentieth century. The earthly happiness that had been promised by eighteenth-century philosophers was turned into living hell for soldiers and civilians involved in the two world wars. Military destruction forced change as civil reform had done before: the social existence of the vast number of Europeans was severely affected by the engines of war. As a result, the naive belief in progress disappeared from the contemporary scene just as had the walking stick and gold-backed currency. Yet, like that famous mythical bird, the phoenix, Europe rose from the ashes of the two world wars to become once again an important, if not the most important, center of the global economy. The standard of living rose in every European country. Television antennas appeared beside chimney pots on copper roofs, and automobiles crowded the narrow streets. The number of automobile fatalities began to rival war losses—as dreadful a sign of the unplanned effects of technological advancement as can be found.

Whether all of this can best be described as the "Americanization of Europe" or as a "New European Renaissance," the important point is that by the late 1950s Western Europe had once-for-all discarded most of the still evident elements of its past and had joined in a transatlantic community, which has as its most common features the Boeing 747 jet airliner, rock music groups, camera-toting tourists, extensive use of drugs, shortages of crude oil, and a variety of blue jeans.

The essay that follows is an introduction to the historical problems of this two-hundred-year-long age that was both "the best of times" and "the worst of times." The approach is cultural, an effort to study major institutions and the values and ideas that formed them—yet with attention also focused on the social environment in which Europeans of the time lived.

Europe
in Retrospect

PART ONE

The Reordering
of Europe:
1789–1871

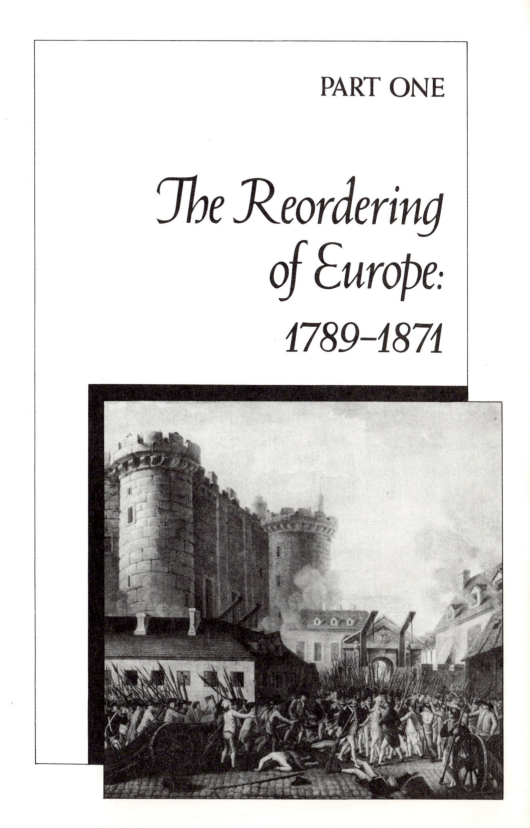

*W*hen Friedrich Engels, Karl Marx's faithful collaborator, said that he and Marx had selected France for the political model of their analysis and England for the economic, he was only stating what his contemporaries and historians since have argued: that the major change in modern Europe came from the political and industrial revolutions that moved society from a relatively fixed, agrarian base to an urban, industrial one in which change was the operating principle.

The fundamental reordering of the social system and the values that supported it did not occur suddenly, nor did it happen dramatically when the Bastille, prison symbol of France's Old Order, was besieged and destroyed on July 14, 1789. Closer to the mark is the metaphysical argument offered by the French romantic author Chateau-briand: the French Revolution was the result of the "slow conspiracy of the ages." There was no conspiracy, of course, just the final eruption of long fomenting problems and social issues that the Old Order could no longer accommodate. And yet that new world, so violently announced in the revolutionary decade of 1789–1799, was not quickly installed. Indeed, the first half of the nineteenth century was an era of turmoil and confusion. Across the years which separated the Revolution of 1789 from the revolutions of 1848 a new society emerged, still an awkwardly constructed affair, combining the principle of liberty and the institution of representative government with industrial inventions and the factory system.

Freedom and steam—a political ideal and a source of energy—these were the forces that drove the new age on.

1

The Old Order

The king was in the counting house counting all his money,
The queen was in the pantry eating bread and honey.

OLD ENGLISH NURSERY RHYME

          The French foreign minister Talleyrand once commented that anyone who had not lived before 1789 did not know how sweet life could be. As an aristocrat, Talleyrand could afford to make such a remark, for his social situation was enjoyed by many court noblemen who found life generally pleasant, even elegant. Dressed in silk, often engaged only in petty intrigue, most often wined and dined to surfeit, they pursued an existence far removed from that of the vast majority of their countrymen and at severe variance with the daily routine of the peasant who was bound by circumstance, if no longer by law, to the land.

    "The plowman homeward plods his weary way," was the poetic description provided by Thomas Gray of the end of daily routine for the early eighteenth-century peasant. His was a severe, monotonous existence, briefly relieved by the conviviality that the warmth of hearth and alcohol could induce, and helped along by young children who participated fully in domestic and field chores. The peasant was the most numerous figure in the Old Regime, the most fixed in social custom and practice, the most ignored by the government.

    Somewhere in between the lofty court gentleman and the lowly country plowman stood another individual, dedicated to trade and the activities of

5

the marketplace, interested in making a good profit, and anxious to rise to higher social station. This was the *bourgeois*, resident of the *bourg* or *burg*, a city dweller who, because of his place in the social order, is also known to us as a member of the "middle class."

The three social groups just mentioned were not so simply separated in reality, nor were they so defined according to social custom. Country nobility often lived no better than the peasants adjacent to them, while the wealthy bourgeoisie sometimes lived as splendidly as did aristocrats. Also, there were rich farmers more like the bourgeoisie in wealth and attitude than the peasants and, therefore, sometimes referred to as a "rural bourgeoisie."

Moreover, these three basic social units did not exactly correspond to the estates system, which had long determined political and legal conditions in the country. The three estates were, in descending order: the clergy, the nobility, and the remainder of the population, but most significantly, the bourgeoisie.

In principle, each estate had a well-determined purpose, as if its members were woven into some medieval tapestry, fixed in time and position. The clergy was responsible for the community's spiritual well-being and therefore interceded by prayer and sacred ceremony with an inscrutable God on behalf of His "creatures here below." The nobility had previously been the knights in shining armor, defending the realm against foreign intruders and local marauders, thereby maintaining some semblance of internal peace. The aristocrats commanded armies and enjoyed the military presence—think only of the Marquis de Lafayette during the American Revolution—but they also played an important role in the administration of government—think only of Lord North at the time of the American Revolution. Last was the "Third Estate," consisting of the vast majority of the population and being the real generator of wealth by which the social system satisfied its basic needs. Agriculture and regional commerce were this estate's major activities, with bread and woolens long having been its basic finished products.

Each of these estates comprised a social state, a self-contained community of custom, prerogative, and purpose. On a most basic level, marriage among them was not sanctioned. Moreover, the language they employed was noticeably different, another obvious mark of distinction. The system of laws, taxes, and privileges varied also from estate to estate, such that the only principle of equality recognized in the Old Regime was the theological one that all human beings were equally important in the eyes of God.

At no time was the estates system more ceremoniously defined than at its last moment of existence. On May 4, 1789, on the occasion of the opening of the Estates-General (the elected representatives of each estate) just before the French Revolution, the participants filed into the chapel of the chateau of Versailles for a *Te Deum*, a religious service of praise to God. The procession inward was brilliant: first came the high clergy in their rich scarlet and purple robes; then followed the nobles splendidly attired in court garb of silk and ruffles; finally came the representatives of the Third Estate, primarily members of the bourgeoisie, dressed in somber black broadcloth.

Such separation in ceremony, dress, and custom was transcended in political theory by the concept of the kingdom. All estates were formally part of one legal and political system, the "realm," over which his serene majesty, the king, reigned.

Ruler, it was said, "by the grace of God," the monarch of the late seventeenth- and eighteenth-century continental state was theoretically absolute in his power. Louis XIV of France was supposed to have said, "I am the state." He certainly ruled as if he were, as did many of his contemporaries. Theirs was deemed to be an authority derived from "Divine Right," the will of God that they should rule and the subjects obey. One of the most influential clergymen during Louis's long reign, Bishop Bossuet, argued: "In order to establish this power, which represents His own, God places on the foreheads of sovereigns and on their visages a mark of divinity."

The Structure of the Old Regime

Pyramidal in abstract form, this old order, the *ancien régime*, which persisted until 1789, still rested principally on tradition, still functioned according to custom, and had long been guided by a world view, a cosmology, that denied mutability—change through time—of both biological and social life. It was held together, beautifully if only imaginatively, by a Great Chain of Being, a series of divinely worked links in which each group of living things was fixed and, by extension, in which each individual was socially set: responsible to individuals in the group above, responsible for individuals in the group below. The well-known expression *noblesse oblige* reveals that the nobleman was "linked" to the peasant below as his responsible superior. The king was answerable only to God.

Today's social scientists, less poetic than the theorists of several centuries ago, call this an "ascriptive society," one in which the individual's socioeconomic function is predetermined, required by the social position traditionally assigned (ascribed) to his family. Birth, not talent; blood, not skill, counted. And so the peasant sowed the field as had his ancestors before him, while the cobbler stitched soles as his children would after him.

For most of the population the regularity of the social order was matched by the routine of daily existence. Time was still measured in seasons, the day marked by the rising and setting of the sun. Wars, by tradition and often in practice, did not begin until after the spring planting and were halted or concluded at the time of the harvest. Winters were lean and long, the time of the year when the term "hearth" truly described the family situation, as one and all crowded around the fireplace that provided light and heat. And even the ermine-enrobed nobility suffered from the tyranny of the season; it is reported that the wine froze at the king's dinner table one wintry day at resplendent Versailles.

Although the overseas expansion of trade and colonies in the seventeenth and eighteenth centuries had greatly stimulated commerce and given rise to new urban centers, the Old Regime remained agrarian and rural, with most of the population engaged in the cultivation of grain crops, in particular—wheat, barley, and oats—that were distributed regionally. Good harvests were critical to social stability. A major source of social discontent was the shortage of bread, which a poor wheat crop was bound to create. The "bread riots" of the eighteenth century, those tense and disorderly moments when urban dwellers rose to raid the bakery and destroy property in protest, suggest that, along with bad harvests, inadequate and irregular distribution of food crops remained a major problem. A local shortage could occur in a country where another part of the land was adequately supplied.

The "bread riot" was therefore not a revolutionary action, not a movement directed to the overthrow of the existing system, but an action taken against bad management. Its objective was immediate: the removal of hunger pangs. No vision of a new world in which everyone lived happily-ever-after appeared before the down-turned eyes of the urban poor or the work-ridden peasantry. Yet if earthly happiness was for the vast majority of the population the subject of fairy tales, change was already taking place that suggested new promise, because of new wealth and economic opportunity.

The estates system, which fit together so well in medieval theory and practice, was coming apart in the seventeenth and eighteenth centuries. Members of the estates were no longer so sharply differentiated in function as they had been. The clergy's concern was, of course, still spiritual, but not all men of the cloth exclusively or particularly prayed or worshiped. More than one prince of the church, like Cardinal Richelieu of France (1585–1642), was primarily an astute politician and most active as a minister of state. The sword still worn by the nobleman suggested that, as a "lord temporal," his particular task was the defense of the realm. The French nobles of the eighteenth century seemed to spend as much time maneuvering on the ballroom floor as on the battlefield, while in England many aristocrats left the battlefield for the marketplace. In the middle of the seventeenth century, for instance, Sir John Weston, son of the Earl of Portland, was the owner of an important soap manufactory. Finally, the bourgeoisie enjoyed a certain social mobility before the revolutionary age. Buying aristocratic titles in the France of Louis XIV, or marrying into noble families throughout Europe, some of them disdainfully left behind their common origins in order to imitate the elegant manners of the class into which they had ascended. Yet a few played important roles in state politics while retaining their middle-class status. The son of a Rheims clothier, Jean-Baptiste Colbert (1619–1683), was the most significant minister of Louis XIV; and a successful Swiss banker named Jacques Necker (1732–1804) served as financial adviser to Louis XVI.

Such examples as these, if exceptional, do indicate that the Old Regime was not so rigid in its social ordering as tradition prescribed. In reviewing the seventeenth century, a group of historians recently declared the age a time of "general crisis," during which the social order was severely disturbed as a result of a major shift from a medieval economy to the first stage of modern capitalism.

This crisis has also been seen as one of irregular growth and development. Population increase and epidemics of the plague, prosperity and depression, the growth of new trade centers and the decline of old ones made for a variegated pattern, not a simple economic design across the European continent. But one sharp line can be traced: the economy moved from a Mediterranean base to an Atlantic one. The scope of European trade was becoming oceanic and worldwide; the cities that now counted were North Atlantic in location or access: London and Bristol in England; Bordeaux and Nantes in France; Amsterdam in Holland.

Economic Growth

A Europe of new dimensions took form, shaped by the ocean-going sailing ship whose hold held goods, precious metals, and cannon. The enlargement of territory, of markets, and of governmental responsibilities marked both the seventeenth and eighteenth centuries. In every sense Europe was expanding.

With the founding of colonial empires in the New World and commercial empires in the Indian Ocean, along the coasts of Southeast Asia and among its islands, Europe exported its politics abroad and imported a variety of goods that enriched national treasuries and satisfied new personal wants. The colonial wars of the seventeenth and eighteenth centuries were fought over political control of territories that had new resources of coveted goods in short supply on the Continent. The silver of Peru, the sugar of Santo Domingo, the furs and timber of Canada, the spices of Indonesia were shipped to Europe where they caused a social and commercial revolution of sorts. The smoking of tobacco altered daily custom, as did the drinking of coffee or tea or cocoa. The potato appeared on the evening table and would be the staple of the diet of the poor in the nineteenth century.

At the base of the Industrial Revolution of the nineteenth century stood the accumulated capital of the seventeenth and eighteenth centuries, many historians have contended. Much of this capital was generated in the regional trade of the Caribbean Sea and the Indian Ocean. Significant quantities also came from the holds of the silver fleets, the ships dispatched annually by the Spanish government to bring the mined silver from the New World. The infamous trade in human kind also worked to Europe's financial benefit. Eighteenth-century commentators said that the city of Liverpool was built on the bones of African slaves. What they thereby indirectly stated was that the shipping industry of that city was directed to the very profitable outfitting of slave ships into which were huddled black Africans destined to work the plantations of the Americas.

While it is true that most continental commerce still moved slowly by ox-cart or horse-drawn coach, the most significant and voluminous activity was now maritime and transatlantic. The new colonial wealth crowded the wharves of bustling ports like Bristol and Bordeaux, from which it was trans-shipped not only to other cities in England and France, but to those European metropolitan areas not directly involved in maritime commerce with the New World and the Far East. This localized transshipment was the means by which the new goods were widely distributed throughout Europe so that—by way of obvious example—the pungent odor of the coffeehouse filled the streets of Berlin and Brussels as well as those of London and Paris. Moreover, such transshipment facilitated inter-European trade, with important raw materials going from their continental neighbors to England and France. England, for instance, obtained Swedish charcoal for its iron-smelting industry in this manner.

The volume of European trade increased impressively in the late eighteenth century, although the effects were far from geographically uniform. Northern Italy, formerly a major center of commercial activity, suffered depression, while Spain assumed a most peculiar economic position as early as the seventeenth century. Here was a kingdom suddenly rich in precious metals and equally poor in economic activity. Thanks to the plentiful gold and silver of New World mines, the Spanish could lavishly purchase what they needed elsewhere. England and France became busy suppliers to the Spanish aristocrats and thus developed an important trade as they accumulated capital. As for Spain, its golden practice inhibited the growth of a commercial middle class, a factor that most historians claim is an important reason for Spain's subsequent economic backwardness.

Yet this continual flow of new gold and silver had a wide, salutary effect on the European economy. The increase in the number and circulation of new coins made capital more easily obtained, thereby causing commercial ventures to be more tempting because of lower interest rates to the borrower. Furthermore, older monetary systems were drastically modified by the introduction of bank notes, promissory statements (in effect, i.o.u.'s that were redeemable) based on a bank's precious-metal reserves and soon having the value of paper money—the forerunner of our contemporary system. With the seventeenth century the rudiments of an international banking system were in place. The Banks of Amsterdam (1609) and of England (1694) were major institutions of exchange, and they were joined by a number of private, family concerns, of which the House of Rothschild was and would remain the most famous.

Commerce, facilitated by banking, was the basis of the wealth of the new major powers of Europe. And with the ascent of commerce, the ways of the world changed. In this new secular atmosphere, the middle class gained new power and prestige. What has been called the "bourgeois ethos" or general commercial outlook came to predominate and was institutionalized. The "clerk" and the "counting house" took their place among social institutions, alongside the bank and the insurance company. Double-entry bookkeeping in heavy ledgers amounted to a new form of language and authorship. Speculation no longer had to do with how many angels could dance on a head of a pin, but rather with the possible price a shipment of tobacco or rum might bring on the London market.

A new interest in capital accumulation developed, and a new respect for mercantile professions was established. What a man was worth was henceforth measured by his bank account, not the content of his soul. The American colonist Benjamin Franklin was praised for his personal industry and frugality which made him sufficiently wealthy at an early age to indulge in other activities, like flying kites. Queen Anne made Josiah Wedgwood, now famous for his chinaware, her official potterer, an honor that helped the talented Wedgwood become one of the foremost—and diversified—capitalists of his day. And the French author Voltaire gained, among his many honors, the reputation for being the first writer of note to earn his keep by his own words—and by some speculation on the market. It was Dr. Samuel Johnson, the eighteenth-century English critic, who summed up the new mood. He stated: "Life is short. The sooner that a man begins to enjoy his wealth the better."

Socially, the bourgeoisie added a new tone to European life. Urban centered, this class began to build handsome townhouses, buy up country estates, send its children to school and advise kings. Although a seventeenth-century playwright like Molière could mock and ridicule this class in his *Bourgeois Gentleman*, the bourgeoisie was already rising to be the most significant element in the new socioeconomic order.

What this class still lacked was political authority: the right to play a political role commensurate with its economic one. It was, therefore, a legally disadvantaged class. When the French historian Georges Lefebvre wrote that "the Revolution of 1789 restored the harmony between fact and law," he was referring to the fact of the bourgeoisie's economic significance and the need for the law to reflect this.

Yet government was not immune to the new spirit of organization. In every major European country the state was increasing its authority. If the king of England had found his power circumscribed when Parliament finally gained control of the "purse strings" in the Glorious Revolution of 1688, the continental monarch was set upon reducing the authority of the nobles and the provinces. The tendency was toward centralization of governmental function and the creation of a bureaucracy to direct it. Much more pronounced in the eighteenth than the seventeenth century, this new state activity did, however, affect the new economic interests.

Mercantilism

A general maxim was repeated in the palaces of Europe: state power depended on economic power. The wealth of the national treasury was a major determinant of the political role the state could play in European affairs. From this maxim developed the theory of mercantilism. Variously practiced and explained from Spain, to France, and on to England, the theory is best summarized in the seventeenth-century phrase "favorable balance of trade." The state should conduct its economic affairs so that it exports more than it imports, so that it is not dependent on the economy of other countries. Once such a favorable balance is achieved, the national treasury will overflow, the industries of the country will be very active, and skilled workmen will be available for those many technical services a state needs both in times of war and peace. Extended to world terms, mercantilism justified colonies: they would be a source of raw materials and a place in which to market finished products. If trade were "exclusive"—bilateral between "mother country" and colony—then the colonial territory was an assured, regular market.

In government as well as in commerce, obviously, power was being defined as wealth, the accumulation of economic resources by which to live more comfortably and to command more authority. When the French king Francis I said in the sixteenth century that he wanted to find some "silver bullets," he was referring metaphorically to the silver mines of Peru which were controlled by his enemy, Spain. Such precious metal in the treasury and goods in the warehouse now counted as much in political calculations as did soldiers in the line. The science of "political economy," or early economics, was a seventeenth-century creation, and an indication of the close relationship now accepted between power and wealth.

The Enlightenment

In retrospect, the ferment and change that appeared to be most noticeable in the eighteenth century and that seemed to be of greatest concern to the then European elite were intellectual, a sort of revolution of the mind, with one universal model displacing another. The paternalistically structured world of the Christian Middle Ages, with God in judgment and the world in constant obedience to Him, persisted through the Renaissance and the Reformation. Even though the unity of the Christian church was shattered and the authority of the priesthood questioned or denied, there continued strong belief in a divinely ordered world, wondrous in its ways and therefore beyond the range of human understanding.

With the so-called Newtonian revolution of the late seventeenth century, the world order was reformed. The world was soon conceived as being a grand clockwork mechanism, with God the master clockmaker. The instrument of His creation operated in set and discernible ways. All physical motion, like the swing of the pendulum which regulated the clock, obeyed certain natural laws. And because these laws were natural—regular, universal, and consistent —they were subject to rational analysis. In brief, the soon widely held assumption was this: man could understand the universe because it was natural and he was rational. Moreover, he might be able to control, even reorder his environment, once he had knowledge of it.

The new scientific attitude of the time depended upon observation, analysis, classification, occasionally experimentation. In the eighteenth century the great Swedish botanist Carl von Linnaeus (1707–1778) began his ordering of the plant kingdom into genus and species. Captain Cook set out on three different expeditions to explore the natural life forms of the Pacific Ocean. Across the Atlantic, Benjamin Franklin engaged in well-known experiments with that curious phenomenon, electricity.

Translated into terms and issues of the social world, the new scientific attitude inspired the thought that human progress was possible. If, as was now asserted, society was a human, not a divine creation, it could be reordered so that mankind could more easily engage in "the pursuit of happiness."

The word "enlightenment" clearly described the new mood of eighteenth-century intellectuals. According to then contemporary philosophers, the shadows of meaningless tradition, the darkness of ignorance and superstition would be dispelled in the light of reason. A "party of humanity," as one historian has described the men of the Enlightenment, sought to know and appraise critically all aspects of earthly existence. These men were the *philosophes*, the popularizers of the new thought, who sought to convince the educated public by means of the written word. Utilizing in particular the essay —the form of writing that attempts formal definition—they set about to define and reform the world in which they lived. Primarily under the editorship of Denis Diderot, the French *philosophes* worked on that monumental undertaking, the *Encyclopédie*, a compendium of all knowledge, practical as well as abstract. Between 1751 and 1772, the work appeared in print, an effort greeted with universal praise.

Even though there were thinkers who were not so optimistic about the possibility of human control of earthly destiny, the men of the Enlightenment were generally in agreement that "men are born free" and have the "right to the pursuit of happiness." What these two catch phrases—which were actually used in French and American revolutionary declarations— meant was a rather new definition of the human condition, of human nature and social purpose.

Environment is the key word, although the eighteenth-century thinkers used the term "experience." Their general argument reads like this: born in ignorance but with the rational proclivity to overcome it, the human being and his mind resemble a clean blackboard, a *tabula rasa*, upon which experiences are inscribed by the senses. This idea was largely derived from the sensationalist psychology of the late seventeenth-century English thinker John Locke (1632–1704), who asserted that our senses, and particularly the sense of sight, are our source of knowledge about reality.

As for the social situation proposed by the *philosophes*, it had a decided utilitarian quality about it. Practical men as well as thinkers, the *philosophes* were, in the main, social reformers. Within their number, it was the Frenchman Claude-Adrien Helvetius (1715–1771) who most clearly developed the notion of utilitarianism—what would later be defined as "the greatest good for the greatest number." According to this thought, programs of reform should be directed toward the betterment of society as a whole; they should be "for the public good."

It is not hard to find in the ideas of the Enlightenment the basic propositions of modern liberal, even democratic, government, notably the ideas of personal freedom and public well-being. But the message of the Enlightenment was not social revolution; it was reform. As aristocrats and bourgeois, the *philosophes* were removed from the harsher conditions of life that the *menu peuple*, the "little people," endured. Some *philosophes* did have a pleasantly rustic view of the common man, but most were both socially and intellectually removed from the daily concerns of the vast majority of the population. In these circumstances, it is not surprising to find that the *philosophes* looked for reform from above, not below.

If they had philosopher-kings, they were the so-called "enlightened despots" of the eighteenth century. These monarchs, who still ruled absolutely with little check on their power, often expressed an interest in bureaucratic, institutional, and even social reform. Before the word gained popularity in the twentieth century, "efficiency" was what they were after: the better management of their lands, the increase in general wealth, the intensification of state control over regional and provincial governments. Furthermore, they sought to break down internal tariff barriers, to introduce new agricultural methods, and even to relieve the worst effects of a still persistent serfdom.

When Peter the Great (1672–1725), the Russian emperor, traveled to Holland to learn shipbuilding techniques and when he forced his noblemen to shave their beards so that they would more resemble their Western European counterparts, he was giving expression to later Enlightenment ideals— if in his own way. Furthermore, when Joseph II (1741–1790), emperor of Austria and one of the most famous enlightened despots, freed his serfs between 1781 and 1789, divided his empire into like-sized administrative units, and required that all his subjects affix house numbers to the outside of their residences, he was also giving full expression to Enlightenment ideals. No doubt the most well-known of the enlightened despots was Frederick the

Great (1712–1786), king of Prussia, who turned his state into a very efficient military and bureaucratic machine, from which the modern caricature of the Prussian as a ramrod-erect executor of orders has been chiefly derived. Frederick once said, "I am the first servant of the state," a far cry from Louis XIV's "I am the state"—and a suggestion of the reforming spirit of the enlightened despots.

Conclusion

Grouping together the many changes of institution and attitude that were discernible in the seventeenth and eighteenth centuries, the contemporary observer of that ancient scene sees the outline or the pattern of the modern world. True, most matters were in sketched form: suggested, vaguely defined, tentatively essayed. The Old Order still held, and to an individual on his way to London or Paris in the spring of 1788 that order seemed secure enough. Only with the revolutionary period of rapid political and industrial change would the alterations be vast and profound.

Still, the pattern of change was there. Economically, the bourgeoisie was assuming primacy, the generator and controller of the nation's wealth. Politically, the state was reforming, with the rudiments of modern bureaucracy in place and with the tendency toward centralization of authority already evident in a country as important as France. Culturally, a new climate of opinion was felt, with the principles of political liberty, of human progress, of social equality in the air. Spatially, the city was moving to the forefront as the attractive center of the "good life" and as the focal point of political activity. Finally, to speak of European affairs, say in 1776, one had to look abroad to the New World or eastward to India and Southeast Asia.

The French Revolution would hurry these changes along, and the Industrial Revolution would add entirely new dimensions to them.

2

The French Revolution

This was the year of the French Revolution. My heart beat high with great swelling sentiments of Liberty.   WILLIAM GODWIN

Few periods of history have been introduced with such drama as was the modern one. Whether historians date its emergence in 1789 or 1815—the beginning of the French Revolution or the end of the Napoleonic Era—they are in agreement that the two decades in which France upset the old European political and social order comprised a uniquely turbulent time that forms a major turning point in world history.

Indeed, when the French historian Georges Lefebvre stated in 1939 that the "ideas of the French Revolution toured the globe," he meant that in ideology and example the actions of 1789 altered the political outlook and inspired new secular hope among the peoples of the world. If the claim is exaggerated, it is so only in a mild way. No revolutionary upheaval caused such anxiety, such excitement. Even the German philosopher Immanuel Kant forwent his daily walk when he learned of what had transpired in Paris in July of 1789. The Revolution interrupted the smallest daily routine, just as it overthrew the most powerful example of the Old Regime.

As with so much drama, the outward play of events began quietly enough at the center of established authority. The news of the fall of the Bastille greeted Louis XVI late in the night of July 14, 1789, after that monarch had retired from a day at the hunt. Once the duke who had carried the news from

Paris finished his statement, the king laconically commented: "Then it's a revolt?" "No, sire," replied the duke, "it's a revolution."

On no other occasion has the French Revolution been described so simply and directly. Yet the distinctions in the conversation between king and noble were not semantic; they were real. The king imagined another bread riot or some such expression of short-lived popular protest. The duke knew that the events in Paris were more fundamental: a challenge to the very existence of the regime.

That challenge was met with equivocation by a king who was indecisive, inadequate rather than cruel, a ruler who was, moreover, supported by courtiers who did not generally appreciate that times were changing. The Old Regime as a political order fell quickly enough. By October, 1789, the royal title had changed from "Louis, by Grace of God, King of France," to "Louis, by Grace of God and the constitutional law of the State, King of the French." But the constructive work of the revolutionaries, the need to build a *novus ordo seculorum*, a new secular order, proved far more difficult than the toppling of the old one.

The French Revolution was, in fact, a series of upheavals, perhaps most aptly described as a major revolution followed by a series of coups d'état. No revolutionary wished to return to the pre-July political condition, but beyond that, there was no clearly determined objective. Moreover, internal resistance to change and later, after 1792, external war between the revolutionary governments and the monarchies of Europe made domestic decisions the more difficult to achieve. Thus, French government between 1789 and 1799 followed the sweep of a pendulum, going from absolutism in 1789 to constitutional monarchy in 1790, on to radical republicanism in 1792–1794 (with the Terror as the most dreadful aspect), then back to a middle position with the Directory of 1795–1799, and finally on to the right with Napoleon, "first consul" in 1799 and emperor in 1804. In outward appearance, this imaginary pendulum sweep seemed to bring the French people back to the absolutism they had discarded in 1789.

THE PHASES OF THE REVOLUTION

1789–1791: The National Constituent Assembly

Beginning in June 1789 the Third Estate of the Estates-General, called by King Louis XVI to repair France's finances, seized the political initiative and made the demand for fundamental governmental reform. The "Constituent" forced through a series of reforms that converted France into a constitutional monarchy, abolished feudal privileges and created a representative (but not democratic) electorate. Its most famous piece of legislation is the Declaration of the Rights of Man and Citizen, roughly the equivalent of the American Bill of Rights.

1791–1792: The Legislative Assembly

The Constituent provided France with a unicameral parliament called the Legislative Assembly. The king governed in conjunction with this body, but his own waivering vis-à-vis the Revolution, the machinations of his wife, Marie Antoinette, and a growing desire for republicanism worked to undermine the regime. On August 10, 1792, a Parisian mob marched on the Tuileries (the royal residence in the Louvre Palace) and forced the king to flee to the safety of the Legislative Assembly. De facto, the monarchy was now through. The most notable action of the Legislative Assembly was its declaration of war against Austria and Prussia in April 1792. (From this date until Napoleon's abdication in 1814, with the exception of a brief period in 1802–1803, France was at war.)

1792–1795: The First Republic and the Terror

This period, during which the Revolution reached its height, witnessed the establishment of the Terror as a governmental device to extinguish enemies of the regime, and produced its two greatest figures, Danton and Robespierre. In September 1792 France was declared a republic, and an elected Convention (in imitation of Philadelphia) set out to give France a republican constitution. Although a very liberal and democratic constitution was introduced in June 1793, it was shelved and revolutionary government was continued. A political struggle between the two major groups, the Girondins (moderates) and Jacobins (radicals) was won by the Jacobins, of whom Robespierre was the most famous. Actually, France was ruled by the Committee of Public Safety, a twelve-man body of which Danton was the first acknowledged leader and then after Danton's execution, Robespierre. The Revolution became more frenzied in the spring of 1794 and began to "devour its own," that is, to execute revolutionaries who were in opposition to the Committee's program. Finally, Robespierre was arrested and executed in July (Thermidor in the revolutionary calendar) of 1794.

1794–1795: The Thermidorian Reaction

After Robespierre's execution, a reaction against the Terror and governmental stringencies took place. A new constitution was created, and the Revolution entered its final phase.

1795–1799: The Directory

In these years a weak and unpopular government known as the Directory (executive power was held by five directors) attempted to rule France. Attempted coups d'état from Left and Right occurred, and the Directory came more and more to rely on the military. The most famous of the coups occurred on the 18th of Brumaire (November 9) 1799 when Napoleon overthrew the government.

Voltaire, master of epigrams, once cynically remarked that "the more things change, the more they are the same." He seemed to have a point that could be applied to the activities of the French Revolution. However, if political instability between extremes was one obvious characteristic of the Revolution, a new ideological structure was another. The French established a new realm of politics.

It is not too much to say that the ideas of the French Revolution became the measure of what later characterized modern European society, both in principle and in institution. Most obviously, the Revolution established the principle of popular sovereignty in the place of absolutism, thus replacing the dynasty with the nation. Providing the first major nation in Europe with a written constitution and a code of political behavior—this was the Declaration of the Rights of Man and Citizen—the revolutionaries, in the summer of the year 1789, had already converted the king's subject into the nation's citizen. Representative, parliamentary government now rested on the principle that the people's needs, not the king's will or whims, would direct the affairs of the state. What the eighteenth-century French political theorist Jean-Jacques Rousseau (1712–1778) called "civic virtue," the right and responsibility of the citizen to participate in the affairs of the state, was most obviously recognized in the vote. Universal manhood suffrage first appeared in 1792, but it did not become a permanent feature of French political life until 1848.

On a grander scale, the effect of revolutionary credo and action was to make the nation the major social unit. Heretofore, the loyalty of the subject was to his king, of the countryman to his province. That there was a Nation (duly capitalized), a community of like-minded citizens, motivated by common ideals and remembering a common past to which individual loyalty should be primarily directed, was a concept the French Revolution sharply outlined, if it did not originate. Again, during the revolutionary decade, the notions of a "nation in arms," of the "motherland in danger," were popularized, with the citizen army and the concept of the draft reinforcing the authority of the state and preparing the way for modern warfare. The "defense of the sacred soil of the homeland," became a primary duty of the citizen; and that homeland took on fixed frontiers, within which the national community lived, separated from its neighbors.

The new secular state, which the Revolution defined, created a community ambivalent in purpose: first, the state was in theory designed to serve the individual, to assure his rights; second, the individual was to serve the state, to defend it, uphold its ideals. The relationship might have been reciprocal, and, in fact, it eventually came close to that in England, the most democratic of the European nations in the nineteenth century. But on the Continent, the citizen more served the state, than the state the citizen. The rise of democratic government was slow, interrupted, still incomplete on the eve of World War I. Here, as in so many other areas of influence, the results of the French Revolution extended across the century.

The Ideology of the French Revolution

Culturally, the French Revolution provided the world with its first meaningful experience with political ideology. The word, and the concept it expressed, were revolutionary in origin. Indeed, it was Napoleon, a man who had no truck with idle thought, who called the intellectual system-makers of the late eighteenth century *idéologues*, abstractionists, or, as we have heard in recent years, "eggheads." The father of the DuPont who founded the famous American chemical company was called an *idéologue* by Napoleon. And this Pierre-Samuel DuPont de Nemours (1739–1817) spent half a lifetime drawing up constitutions, writing letters, while also finding time to offer a learned paper to the American Philosophical Society on the language of ants, and to inform his son that gout was the disease of the intellectual.

However, DuPont was not a brilliant mind, and Napoleon was an opinionated soul. Despite these two figures, ideology triumphed; it directed the French Revolution, and it soon grew, like roses on a bush or the heads of hydra—a matter of outlook, of course—to provide the nineteenth century with an unusual number of competing theoretical social systems.

What was ideology? It was and remains a system of ideas that are usually goal-directed. Thus, it is a theoretical explanation of the world's situation and a prescription for improvement or radical change of that situation. In this sense, ideology is rooted in historical consciousness, in an awareness of mankind's progress through time and how that progress might be redirected toward an alternate objective. Most ideologies are, therefore, fundamentally political, bright descriptions of the means and methods by which the instruments of revolution, party, or government ought be used for the purpose of social change.

Ideology is, in a way, the secular equivalent of theology. It directs the believer's attention to a perfected future when present woes will have dissipated and social harmony will reign. The future, therefore, holds the promise for the ideologue that heaven holds for the devout, religious-minded individual.

The introduction of ideology into the modern world was one major effect of the new secular spirit of the eighteenth century. Once society was deemed to be man-made—and here the influence of the Enlightenment is noticeable —then it could be changed. Ideology was the prescription for that change. And the force of ideology was felt throughout the modern era.

In sum, the French Revolution did many things, unleashed new forces, destroyed old ideas, offered new promises. Not the Revolution itself, of course, but the people who made it.

Many historians have described the French Revolution as the encounter of competing classes. In such an appraisal the Revolution is seen to begin with aristocratic protest against the absolute monarchy bequeathed by Louis XIV, then to enlarge in scope as a bourgeois movement seeking fundamental political change, and, finally, to take on popular dimensions with working-class participation, particularly in Paris.

Certainly a most notable development of eighteenth-century political life was the reassertion of the French nobility. During the reign of Louis XIV it had lost power and had become noticeable only in show, in attendance at court and in participation in the elaborate rituals that Louis XIV seemed to enjoy. After that monarch's death in 1715, the nobility mustered its forces, with leadership now coming from the "nobility of the robe," the legal and judicial sections, whose members wore the robes of magistrates, and who raised matters of principle and law that reaffirmed the ancient rights of the nobility and questioned the authority of the absolute monarchy.

In its first and nonactivist phase, from 1787 to 1789, the Revolution therefore amounted to a legal debate between monarchy and aristocracy over the financing of the state and the political authority which each claimed to enjoy and exercise. It was the near bankruptcy of the state, largely caused by aid to the American revolutionaries, that served as the immediate provocation for aristocratic opposition in 1787, when an Assembly of Notables (consisting of aristocrats), called by the king and his finance minister, demanded political authority in return for tax reform. This assembly achieved nothing but further aggravation between monarch and aristocracy. However, if the aristocracy now presumed to speak in the name of the "nation," it certainly made no request to extend the political base of the nation.

Such an extension was demanded and obtained by the bourgeoisie, who ushered in the major phase of the French Revolution. To quote again the words of Georges Lefebvre, "The Revolution of 1789 restored the harmony between fact and law." The fact was that the bourgeoisie were the most significant economic element within France. The wealth they generated and the professions they filled were far more important than the political role they were allowed by tradition and law to play. Through revolutionary ideology and institutional change, the bourgeoisie gained a political authority not known before in any European country. In this sense, the French Revolution was a bourgeois revolution. The abolition of aristocratic privileges, the confiscation of church and aristocratic lands and their purchase by the bourgeoisie, and the removal of internal obstacles to trade and commerce allowed the middle class greater economic and social mobility.

In rhetoric and institution, the French Revolution was a liberal revolution, in which the liberty of the individual was proclaimed, private property was respected. Later, when Napoleon announced his doctrine of "careers open to talent," he was following revolutionary thought and also anticipating the Horatio Alger theme of "pulling yourself up by your own bootstraps." In truth, the ideology of the Revolution amounted to extended praise of the "self-made man."

Yet it should not be assumed that revolutionary practice directly followed revolutionary principle. The exigencies of the time—war, counterrevolution, factionalism within the various governments—combined to tempt the revolutionary leaders to shelve most of the ideals until peace and calm were restored. The most influential factor in this decision was the war which the French began, out of fear of foreign invasion, on April 20, 1792. As the "Declaration of Revolutionary Government," issued on October 10, 1793, succinctly stated: "The provisional government of France is revolutionary until the peace." Put otherwise, revolutionary times required revolutionary, not democratic, government. The now familiar arguments about "national security" were then new, but no less disturbing.

The problem of war against France—England had joined Prussia and Austria in April of 1793—and the problem of provisioning the home population with sufficient staples—again the issue of "bread"—complicated government and allowed another social element to play an important role in the Revolution. This element was the multitude, variously called the "crowd," "the mob," or the "rabble." Thomas Carlyle, trying to paint a fiery-bright picture of the Revolution, described Paris in the second week of July 1789 as already a city in which "the streets are a living foam-sea. . . . Mad Paris is abandoned altogether to itself." From his mid-nineteenth-century perspective, Carlyle viewed the crowd as an uncontrolled mob, blood-thirsty and wild-eyed.

Recent scholarship has disputed and abandoned this view. Today we know the so-called "mob" was composed primarily of lower middle-class artisans, that their initial behavior was no more disorderly than that of protest movements we witness with great frequency in our own age. Far from wishing to be part of a "spontaneous anarchy," as a French contemporary of Carlyle's saw the situation, the Parisian crowds were set upon relieving the unsatisfactory living conditions they felt had resulted from a government both mismanaged and insensitive.

This urban crowd was made up of the *sans-culottes*, the craftsmen, skilled and semi-skilled workers who wore no knee breeches (*culottes*), hence who enjoyed few of the benefits of the wealthy and the aristocratic. They were interested in having their immediate grievances righted; high-flung ideological considerations were of no concern to them.

In a way, therefore, the revolutionary forces that disturbed France in the summer of 1789 were coincidental: the coming together at a particular time of people protesting their economic plight and people seeking fundamental governmental reform. As many critics have asserted, it was the weight of the urban crowds and the direction of the reform-minded bourgeoisie that gave the French Revolution its force. At no time was the importance of the *sans-culottes* more obvious than in the years 1792 and 1793, in that extended moment of transition from constitutional monarchy to republican government. According to the eminent French historian Albert Soboul, the *sans-culottes* were representative of popular democracy. They disdained the aristocrats and viewed with contempt the airs and manners of the rich and well-born. In a public display without precedent in Paris, they strolled the fashionable boulevards where before would have been seen only the knee-breech-ered gentleman with gold-headed walking stick and fair-headed companion in hand.

As the Revolution became more popular in support, it also became more intolerant; this dual situation occurring in the years 1793 and 1794, when the Jacobin faction, that most closely identified with the people of Paris and with democracy, was supreme. (The Jacobins were named after their meeting place in a monastery in the rue St. Jacob.) In June 1793 the Jacobins effectively removed their political opposition and proclaimed a "republic one and indivisible," in which legislative power would be predominant. The ascendancy of the legislative assembly had begun earlier and had reached an important stage in April 1793, when the Committee of Public Safety was established. This twelve-man group was, as its title suggests, responsible for the well-being of the state. But by the summer of 1793, when the Jacobins had reorganized the Committee and effectively controlled the government, the revolutionaries were exhibiting a political ruthlessness unlike any seen before. As they set out to eliminate their enemies, they seemed to follow the cynical imperative coined at the time: "Be my friend, or I will kill you."

It was during the Reign of Terror, 1793–1794, that revolutionary tribunals meted out hasty justice. Opponents of the regime, revolutionaries themselves, fell beneath the blade of the guillotine. This was the awful period in which "the Revolution devoured its own." Some eleven thousand individuals died as enemies of the state, and their deaths added up to a new, horrendous activity of modern Western civilization: institutionalized violence, the harsh elimination of political opposition by the state. Later, Stalinist Russia and Nazi Germany would cause the figures of the French Revolution to seem small. Unfortunately, the mass age would also mean mass annihilation.

The Terror was spent by the summer of 1794, when reaction against it set in. The end was reached at the moment the individual most frequently identified with the harshness of revolutionary retribution, Maximilien Robespierre (1758–1794), was himself beheaded on July 28, 1794. It is important to note that Robespierre came closest to being the revolutionary "hero." A lawyer and one of the first declared republicans, Robespierre was a man of determination, anxious to see the Revolution realized according to his lights. Many say that Robespierre was Rousseau's translator, taking the philosopher's ideas on equality and civil government and making them public policy. Yet Robespierre's political behavior was far from democratic. Elected to the Committee of Public Safety in July 1793, he soon came to dominate that group, hence dominate the revolutionary government. He exhibited himself as a ruthless individual, incorruptible, dictatorial, impersonal, and determined to sweep away all who opposed the Revolution. He urged the war on against the monarchical powers of France, and he encouraged the Reign of Terror. He was feared and unloved. He was the image of the modern revolutionary whose profession and passion are political.

But for all this, Robespierre was not of the heroic dimensions of a George

Washington or a V. I. Lenin. The French Revolution did not support such a person. It almost seemed as if individuals followed the Revolution, did not lead it. Some French historians of a romantic bent have insisted that the real hero of the revolutionary decade was the French people, a collectivity then acting with one mind, feeling with one heart.

Certainly, the French Revolution had a quality of spontaneity, of accident, that later revolutions would not have. There was no clearly defined revolutionary party or conspiratorial group that initially plotted the Revolution, and the contending factions that followed after the Revolution had occurred never gained a firm grip on the nation's imagination or its institutions. The Jacobins came closest, but their unchallenged period of rule was limited, lasting only a year.

It must be remembered that the French Revolution was the first major social revolution, of far greater dimensions and of deeper purpose than the American Revolution that had preceded it. Only the Russian Revolution of November 1917, the one that ushered in modern Communism, would rival in world importance what occurred in France between 1789 and 1799. Underlying this extended dramatic development was the new belief that revolution was the most effective means to achieve political and, consequently, social change. Not reform from within, but overthrow from without appeared to be the new law of political physics.

The ten years of the French Revolution have since been reviewed in terms of the old historical concern with change and continuity. To the revolutionary demand for a "new secular order" came the conservative response that society can never be built anew. According to this interpretation, we are all inescapably part of our own age—historically determined, hence socially indebted to previous generations. The usual analogy made to support this argument was that of a house: the present occupant can renovate, alter, add new wings; but if an attempt is made to remove the foundation, the whole structure will collapse.

At the basis of the debate over what the French Revolution could and did accomplish is to be found the nineteenth-century concern with liberalism and conservatism. To sweep away the old and begin the new was the liberal solution; it was predicated upon the assumption that human nature was essentially good, mankind essentially rational, and the purpose of life the "pursuit of earthly happiness." To respect the past, to work within the social structure that now exists so that it is modified, not destroyed, was the conservative solution; it was predicated upon the assumption that human nature was weak, mankind essentially selfish, and the purpose of life the search for social stability and order.

Equally enduring as a historical problem was the position of the French Revolution on the time scale: was the Revolution the end of one era or was it the beginning of another? It seems to have been both: it ended a world based on tradition, on blood-right, on fixed social status. In principle and by legislation, it made the individual citizen the center of a new social order. The social order should, therefore, be designed to maximize this freedom, this personal liberty.

The Age of Napoleon

The ideal of a social order that provided personal liberty remained far off. It soon could not even be heard enunciated in France, where the sound of trumpets and the beat of drums now suggested that any march forward by humanity was to be of a military sort. Napoleon turned the Revolution to his own uses—and they were not democratic.

Napoleon has been called the "French Revolution on Horseback," a title which has considerable validity if his actions and his program are considered.

A military hero who had won spectacular battles in the Italian peninsula against the Austrians, who had ventured to Egypt in 1798 and fought a "Battle of the Pyramids" there, Napoleon was of heroic proportions, if of diminutive physical stature. He was a man of great ambition and of great self-control and calculation. (He once remarked that his mind was arranged the way a set of file drawers would be, everything in its proper place and accessible.) But he was ruthless as well, for he determined to make fate his mistress.

At one of the several moments when the pendulum motion of the French Revolution swung the nation toward internal chaos again, the desire for strong government, for public order, was loudly expressed. The government of the Directory was by the summer of 1799 faced with growing popular opposition and was publicly challenged by street riots. Napoleon had already been called in during the year 1797 to put down one such upheaval, which he claimed to have eliminated "with a whiff of grapeshot," and now he eyed the opportunity to do more than give an order to a group of musketeers.

With the aid of his brother Lucien, then a senator, Napoleon staged a coup d'état; he dispersed the weak government and seized power with the backing of his troops. Thus on the ninth of November 1799, the day of the coup d'état, the Napoleonic Era began.

THE NAPOLEONIC ERA

1799–1804: The Consulate
In imitation of the Roman system, the Consulate had three consuls elected to office for a period of ten years. As First Consul, Napoleon controlled all the power. Some of his more spectacular reforms were effected during this period. Of great interest is the Concordat of 1801 by which France and the

Catholic Church came to an understanding. (The Church had been forced underground during the Revolution.) Catholicism was reestablished in France, not officially, however, but only as "the religion of the majority of Frenchmen." Napoleon retained effective control of the Church by having the authority to nominate all high church officials. In 1802 Napoleon exploited his military popularity by having himself elected Consul for Life.

1804–1814: The Empire

In 1804 France was given a new constitution through which "the government of the Republic is confided to an Emperor." By plebiscite (the great Napoleonic political device) the purple mantle fell easily on Napoleon's shoulders. While Napoleon had created an array of parliamentary bodies grouped under the name *Corps legislatif*, he ruled as an absolute monarch. His mother, a Corsican of pessimistic hue, was wont to remark, *"Pourvu que ça dure"* (If it only lasts). It did, until 1813 when, at Leipzig, in the "Battle of Nations," Napoleon was defeated by a combined Russian, Prussian, and Austrian force. (His grave military mistake had been the invasion of Russia in 1812, an invasion which extended his army and its supply lines beyond endurance.) Napoleon abdicated at Fontainebleau on April 6, 1814, and was sent to the island of Elba.

1815: The Hundred Days

Napoleon grew impatient, detected dissension among the allied powers who had defeated him, and surreptitiously returned to France in March of 1815. He marched triumphantly on the capital, while the newly returned Bourbon monarchy of Louis XVIII fled to Belgium. In Paris, Napoleon gathered together an army and set out to meet the allied army under the Duke of Wellington, who was marching on France. Napoleon met defeat at Waterloo on June 18, 1815. Exiled to St. Helena, he died in 1821.

Napoleon's titles varied—from "First Consul" to "Consul for Life" to "Emperor"—but these variations were only outward modifications in the consolidation of personal power. When he assumed the imperial dignity as "Emperor of the French," he explained this somewhat-less-than-humble action by saying that in a Europe of kings, he had to be a "crowned Washington." In the greater scheme of things, the title and the garb Napoleon fancied were far less important than the changes he brought about in his real capacity of "enlightened despot."

Napoleon was a popular ruler who initially provided stability to a politically weary nation and who obtained widespread support by his many astonishing military victories. In his role of military strongman, Napoleon presented something of the appearance of the modern dictator, and some historians see him as the first in that dismal line leading down to Hitler and Stalin. Yet there is no denying that Napoleon institutionalized many of the ideals and institutions that the French revolutionaries had never got beyond paper. In this sense it was in the Napoleonic Era that the administrative structure of modern France acquired clear definition. Napoleon reorganized regional government, making it directly responsible to central authority. He thereby furthered the Jacobin ideal of "one republic, indivisible," by making the Parisian ministries the seat of all national power. Furthermore, he reformed the university system, established the Bank of France, and had drawn up the *Code Napoléon*, the most important legal codification since Justinian's effort a good milennium before. Each of these actions enhanced the power of the central government and, in turn, further secured Napoleon's hold on public authority.

Yet the Napoleonic regime rested less on institutions than on public acclaim. Napoleon was the first ruler to make effective use of the plebiscite— that special national election in which the voting public is required to decide one important issue. In 1802 the French people were asked, "Shall Napoleon Bonaparte be consul for life?" The results of the ballot boxes showed that 3,568,885 voted in the affirmative, while only 8,374 responded "no." Then in November 1804 the voting public was again asked for its collective opinion, this time on whether the Bonaparte family should inherit the imperial title. Again, the response was impressive, with 3,572,329 agreeing, and only 2,759 opposing. Such figures tell nothing of the seriousness or freedom of the voting, but they say much about state control of elections. Modern dictators have followed the Napoleonic precedent with equally impressive results. Here is an important example of the twisted use of democratic electoral devices to assure dictatorship.

But the battlefield remained the political campaign field for Napoleon. Victory meant popularity. And then came final defeat. On June 18, 1815, outside the little town of Waterloo, not far from Brussels, Napoleon fought and lost his last major battle. He retreated by coach in sullen disgust and was soon thereafter shipped by his victors to the island of St. Helena, off the coast of South Africa, where he lingered and died in 1821—at the age of fifty-two. Napoleon once said his career was like that of a meteor, briefly lighting the night sky of history.

It was more than that. For this brilliant, ambitious man, who directed the destinies of France and Europe for some fifteen years, emerged as a historical "hero," not a person doing good, but a person altering the course of history. No other figure, save Jesus Christ, has been the subject of more biographies than Napoleon. Such a raw statistic says much. Napoleon was the model of the "self-made man," the individual, both lonely and aloof, who courted history, who sought fame and endured ignominy. There would be others like him, yet none so successful and none so respected historically. Napoleon ended the French Revolution. He completed it by giving its ideals administrative structure; he destroyed it by denying the French people the very liberty they had waged revolution for.

Conclusion

Some English wit during the era of the French Revolution said that the French revolutionaries were like the man who was asked if he could play the clavichord. "I don't know," he replied, "but I am willing to try." And so the French people were willing to try the first major experiment in self-government that Europe witnessed. The only analogous contemporary experiment was, of course, in the new United States.

Yet what sets the French effort off by itself was the enormity of the change. The major absolute monarchy in Europe, the strongest military power of the time, the most populous country in Europe—this was France of 1789. If the royal government verged on bankruptcy, no one doubted the importance and strength of the French nation. That such a nation should succumb to a change so radical as that of the Revolution was momentous.

Perhaps more important was the hope offered by the revolutionaries. Liberty was the magic word that raced around Europe, exciting the middle classes and frightening the aristocracy. Tradition had in principle and in fact been replaced by popular sovereignty. The French Revolution unsettled the Old Order, as it ruthlessly prepared the way for a new secular age.

3

International Order and Domestic Strife

I am told that, because there is no visible disorder on the surface of society, there is no revolution at hand. . . . True, there is no actual disorder; but it has entered deeply into men's minds.

ALEXIS DE TOCQUEVILLE
1847

When Napoleon boarded ship as a prisoner of the English, he did not carry in his baggage the problems he had produced on the European continent. The year 1815 is, therefore, not so much a turning point in modern history as it is a dramatic moment in a period of political turmoil. And so the hero departed a broken man, but the revolutionary age went on.

Nevertheless, the imperial expansion and military conquest that were the brutal characteristics of the Napoleonic Era were not continued. Indeed, the period extending between the last volley fired at Waterloo and the first fired in World War I was marked by an unusual absence of European-wide war. This is not to say that the military was given no opportunity to exercise its talents or that there were no significant political altercations. The direction of turbulence was inward. The revolutionary political and economic activities of the first half of the nineteenth century were particularly of a domestic and civil sort. They were communal concerns more than diplomatic affairs. Their effect was therefore greater on social structure than on international organization.

The European State System

The few dramatic changes made in this period were territorial, not operational. The European state system retained a remarkable consistency in its operating principles since it issued forth in the Thirty Years War (1618–1648). First, in general structure it was pentagonal in shape: five major states in competition. France, England, and Austria were the ones that persisted in general state form throughout the period; but the other two varied. Prussia was enlarged and transformed into Germany during the nineteenth century, while Spain, of major European significance in the sixteenth and seventeenth centuries, was replaced by Russia in the nineteenth century.

The international behavior of these competing states was regulated by a simple theory consonant with the general thinking of the day. "Balance of power," as the principle of European diplomacy was called, seemed to be a translation of basic mechanics, as described in Newtonian physics, to the world of international politics. Likened to a scale, but of obviously enormous proportions, Europe was theoretically assured a condition of equilibrium if the contending forces were properly balanced against one another. By the calculated weighing of the four major continental powers, just such a state of equilibrium might be reached. Or so it was posited in diplomatic circles.

As might be guessed, the one power most capable of shifting its weight around, of moving from one side of the diplomatic scale to the other, whenever politics seemed to tip precariously, was Great Britain. And, indeed, not only did British diplomats adhere to the concept, but they also frequently used their nation as balancer, particularly in the late eighteenth and nineteenth centuries when the commerce and the navy of Great Britain predominated in world affairs, and when the island kingdom had no continental territorial interests.

Balance of power was thus primarily a status quo form of politics, the attempt or the tendency of the European state system to maintain international affairs much as they were and to check any single power from reestablishing its hegemony, its dominance, over the Continent. That Great Britain was the main force behind the three major military coalitions that fought the armies of the French Revolution and Napoleon is an indication of how the balance of power system worked. Some critics have suggested that the balance was so well maintained that major war was averted after Napoleon; and they equally argue that the balance had become so delicate in the first years of the twentieth century, when Europe was divided into rival alliance groups, that the slightest jar would upset the entire system.

Credit for the one hundred years in which wars were restrained and peace most often maintained has been granted to the diplomats who gathered at Vienna to arrange their world after Napoleon had been forced to leave it. The Congress of Vienna, which extended through the winter of 1814–1815, was a glittering affair—and an immediate source of Vienna's later reputation

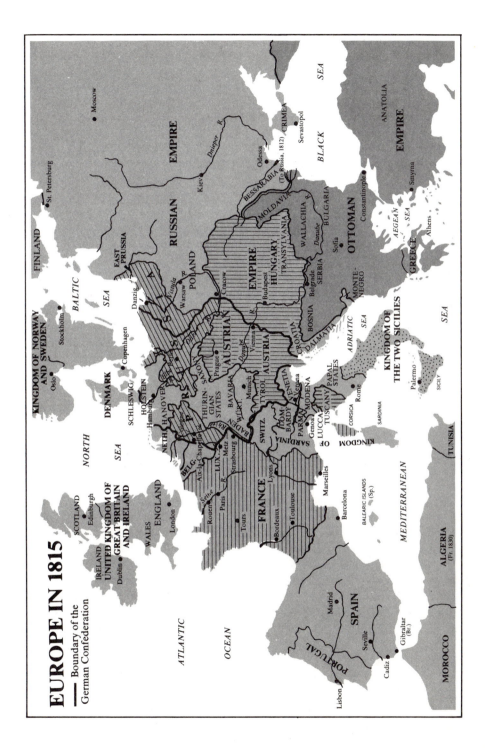

EUROPE IN 1815

— Boundary of the
German Confederation

ATLANTIC

OCEAN

IRELAND

Dublin

SCOTLAND
Edinburgh

UNITED KINGDOM OF
GREAT BRITAIN
AND IRELAND

WALES

ENGLAND

London

KINGDOM OF NORWAY
AND SWEDEN

FINLAND

St. Petersburg

Oslo

Stockholm

Copenhagen

DENMARK

SCHLESWIG

HOLSTEIN

Hamburg

NORTH

SEA

BALTIC

SEA

Moscow

RUSSIAN

EMPIRE

Dnieper R.

Kiev

Odessa

(To Russia, 1812)

BESSARABIA

MOLDAVIA

WALLACHIA

Danube R.

Sofia

BULGARIA

SERBIA

Belgrade

BOSNIA

MONTE-
NEGRO

CROATIA

DALMATIA

ADRIATIC

SEA

BLACK

SEA

CRIMEA

Sevastopol

Constantinople

OTTOMAN

EMPIRE

ANATOLIA

Smyrna

AEGEAN

SEA

Athens

GREECE

EAST
PRUSSIA

Danzig

Vistula R.

POLAND

Warsaw

Cracow

AUSTRIAN

EMPIRE

HUNGARY

Budapest

TRANSYLVANIA

Vienna

Prague

SAXONY

THURIN-
GIAN
STATES

BAVARIA

Munich

WÜRT.

TYROL

VENETIA

LOM-
BARDY

Verona

PARMA

MODENA

LUCCA

Genoa

TUSCANY

PAPAL
STATES

Rome

KINGDOM OF
THE TWO SICILIES

Palermo

SICILY

SARDINIA

CORSICA

KINGDOM
OF
SARDINIA

SWITZ.

BADEN

Strasbourg

Metz

Aix-la-Chapelle

BELG.

LUX.

NETH.

HANOVER

Oldenburg

Rhine R.

Seine R.

Paris

Rouen

FRANCE

Tours

Bordeaux

Lyons

Toulouse

Marseilles

MEDITERRANEAN

SEA

Barcelona

BALEARIC ISLANDS
(Sp.)

SPAIN

Madrid

Seville

Cadiz

Gibraltar
(Br.)

PORTUGAL

Lisbon

MOROCCO

ALGERIA
(Fr. 1830)

TUNISIA

P R U S S I A

PRUSSIA

AUSTRIA

Elbe R.

Oder R.

Berlin

as the city of "wine, women, and song." Although there was a great deal of reveling, the participants soberly attempted to reassemble a Europe shattered by twenty years of military activity.

The work of the diplomats was far-ranging, but particularly fixed on assurance that the expansionist tendencies attributed to France would be held in place. The first order of business was the containment of France, and this was achieved by surrounding that nation with enlarged or new states, like Prussia and the Netherlands, that might serve as buffers. Equally important was the effort to find a maintainable balance. It has been suggested that the work of the Congress was carried out with such wise consideration that no single nation was so generously satisfied and no single nation so badly abused that resentment or desire for retaliation led to grand war.

Yet the results of the Congress would also be called reactionary by later critics, for the peacemakers opposed the ideology of the French Revolution and the political effects caused by it. It was Klemens von Metternich (1773–1859), minister of the Hapsburg Empire and the major architect of the Congress of Vienna, who particularly feared revolution and was determined to see that it did not again inflame Europe. Metternich wished to maintain a "Concert of Europe," a system of international conferences held when needed for the purpose of cooperative regulation of international affairs. Following upon the Congress of Vienna, there was a series of additional conferences held between 1818 and 1822 that gave some semblance of reality to his plan. Of them all, the conference of 1820, held at Troppau in Austria, was the most significant, for it upheld the right of international intervention into the domestic affairs of a nation in order to check revolution.

Broadly sketched, the international affairs of the era 1815–1848 were directed by a coalition of conservative states against the liberal sentiment, institutions, and practices exported by the French revolutionaries. Nationalism, republicanism, constitutionalism: these were the clearly related ideologies undermining the foundations of monarchical Europe.

The Age of Revolution

"When France sneezes, Europe catches cold," Metternich once remarked. His homely metaphor summed up the dominant characteristic of the years 1815–1848, when revolution frequently occurred along lines originally drawn by France. In 1819 there was a brief, liberal revolution in Spain; another occurred in Italy in 1820. Then there was the Greek revolution for independence from Turkey in 1821, an activity that inspired the English poet Lord Byron to participate. Russia endured a short and confused revolt in 1825 when liberal, aristocratic factions attempted to influence the succession to the throne. And then in July 1830, France underwent another revolution, this one joined in the same year by a revolution in Holland. Finally, in 1848, a series of revolutions erupted throughout all of Western Europe with the notable exception of Great Britain.

THE REVOLUTIONS OF 1848

France

France underwent two revolutions in 1848. The first, in February, was led by the bourgeoisie who desired governmental reform. Middle classes and workers cooperated in Paris, but, for the first time, the Socialists made clear demands. Workers wanted the "right to work," and this was duly inscribed on the program of the Provisional Government. To placate workers' and Socialists' demands, the government established the Luxemburg Commission (so-called because it met in the Luxemburg Palace in Paris), headed by the Socialist Louis Blanc and charged with the task of reviewing the labor problem in France. The government also established the National Workshops by which unemployed workers would be paid to engage in public works projects. The tenuous alliance between bourgeoisie and proletariat was threatened in the spring of 1848, but the provisional government's abolition of the workshops in June 1848 was a signal for the revolt of the Parisian workers.

The second revolution of that year, described as the "Bloody June Days," saw the bourgeois pitted against the workers who had raised the red flag on the barricades and who were giving evidence of class conflict. With the aid of the military, the workers' revolt was pitilessly put down. The Constitution of the Second Republic, created by the Provisional Government, afforded France the first opportunity to elect a president directly and by universal manhood suffrage. Among the candidates, one easily carried the field in the December election, Louis-Napoleon, the nephew of Napoleon I, who blandly stated that his name was his program.

Germany

Throughout Germany, revolutionary agitation followed in the wake of the news from Paris, and liberal ministries were installed in many German states. Riots occurred in Berlin on March 15, and the king, Frederick William IV, vacillated about what to do. On March 18, the Berliners were told of the king's intention to grant Prussia a constitution and to use his influence in the constitutional revision of Germany as a whole. On March 21 the king issued another statement announcing his leadership of the German people and his willingness to merge Prussia into Germany. German liberal nationalists assumed the initiative in German politics by establishing a *Vorparlament* (preliminary parliament) which was to prepare for the election of an all-German constituent assembly. This latter body, known as the Frankfurt National Assembly, was composed of elected representatives from the German states and proceeded to provide Germany with a liberal, federal constitution. Excluding Austria, the Assembly offered the newly created imperial crown to Frederick William in 1849. That monarch, again master in his own house thanks to the Prussian troops, was reported to have said that he would not accept a crown from the gutter. The king's refusal caused the Assembly to be split by factionalism and its efforts to be dissipated. By 1849, with little visible success, the revolutionary movement had died in Germany.

The Austrian Empire

Throughout the Austrian Empire, in Vienna, Budapest, Milan, and Venice, revolts broke out, both liberal and national in nature. News of the Parisian revolt inspired agitation by students, supported by workers in Vienna. On March 13, as a result of these demonstrations, the Emperor Ferdinand forced Metternich to resign, and that gentleman followed Louis-Philippe to London. The emperor promised to summon the Diet (Assembly) with the purpose of discussing constitutional reforms. In Hungary, Louis Kossuth demanded national autonomy, which the Austrian government had to momentarily grant. In Italy, the ruthless military policies of General Radetsky checked the revolutionary agitation. In fact, the Austrian military leadership was largely responsible for squashing the revolutions.

Metternich's medical metaphor may therefore seem quite appropriate, but he also used another one more in keeping with subsequent analysis. He described the revolutions as "earthquakes," a term suggesting that revolutions are natural occurrences, meteorological phenomena like floods—or to use Tocqueville's choice—volcanoes.

Viewed at a historical distance, this revolutionary activity did seem to surge forth, often without direction or control and as if irresistible in origin. There was a decided element of spontaneity in much of it. Immediate causes included the painful ones of unemployment, poverty, and starvation—as well as the political ones of extended suffrage and more responsible government. No revolution occurred in a political vacuum or simply emerged out of deeply felt idealism. Nor did any revolution break out solely for reasons of economic strain. If there was a general cause, it was the government's unwillingness or inability to respond to the new conditions of a changing economy and an altering social situation. The increase in the number of wage earners and the resettlement of the population in cities were strikingly evident in the early century. And yet government continued almost as if only the middle classes required some accommodation. "Do you hear them [the working classes] repeating incessantly that all who are above them are incapable and unworthy of governing them?" asked Tocqueville in 1847.

In the nearly two decades extending from the French revolution of July 1830 to the European-wide revolutions of 1848, economic conditions gravely affected political decisions. Skilled workers in Paris were more numerous than the bourgeois elements in the July Revolution that ushered in the "Bourgeois Monarchy." Textile workers in Lyons, France, in 1831, and in Silesia, in 1844, complained of the decreases in wages, resulting from a decline in the purchase price of the goods they sold to merchants. These workers then rose in revolt. Later, in 1846 and 1847, bad harvests and the dreadful potato famine—the latter brought on by a blight that turned the potatoes black—led to economic stress that strained European society. Finally, economic depression in the industrial sector increased unemployment and intensified the discontent of the urban poor.

These were the underlying conditions that made Europe so susceptible to revolution. For working classes as well as for middle classes the governments of the day were not effectively responsive. When the first of the two revolutions that France endured in 1848 broke out in late February, the workers were demanding, in their slogan, "the right to work." The bourgeoisie also were making demands, but principally for more liberal government.

The revolutions of the first half of the nineteenth century were political, with two objectives: first and most universal, the establishment of liberal, parliamentary government; second, and most evident in countries north and east of France, the creation of a nation-state.

The liberal objective was an extension of what the English considered as their historic rights, and what the French proclaimed were the rights of man: personal freedom. This freedom was most easily defined as the right to vote, to decide one's political destiny at the ballot box. But in the early century, heavy property requirements restricted the suffrage to rather small numbers. In the Restoration Monarchy of France that followed Napoleon and spanned the years 1815–1830, only about 100,000 out of a population of some 25 million had the privilege of voting. And in England similarly low participation was gradually corrected by a series of "reform bills," the first of which was passed in 1832, and the last, all but granting universal manhood suffrage, was introduced in 1884. It has often been said that what the English reluctantly legislated, the continental governments were forced to concede in the streets. With the Revolutions of 1848, the French were the first to get universal manhood suffrage in Europe.

For many liberal thinkers the most promising means by which to achieve constitutional, therefore responsible, government was within a national framework. Once the nation as a social and political community was established, harmony, not dissension, would prevail. The great mid-century liberal thinker John Stuart Mill, in his *Representative Government* (1861), defined the sentiment of nationalism as follows: "A portion of mankind may be said to constitute a nation if they are united among themselves by common sympathies which do not exist between them and others." It was this union of "common sympathies" that suggested nationalism would lead to domestic peace and mutual understanding. Beyond England and France, which did exist as nation-states, the sentiment enjoyed wide favor.

In seeking a national community, many theorists developed a line of thought that has subsequently been called "romantic nationalism." Mill was not the only person who argued that historical experience was the most powerful basis for a sense of common purpose and destiny. The romantic nationalists often combined the myth of past communal happiness with the promise of meaningful future political unity. This was a historic exercise in which a disunited people were often told to seek their purpose and collective identity in another age, some heroic moment when life was simpler or more glorious or more dramatic. Thus looking backward, the disunited people might also look forward to a new age in which they would form a cultural and political community. For the first time scholars rummaged around the past to find the blocks that would form the foundations of contemporary national unification.

In Italy, still divided into several kingdoms and also containing provinces ruled by Austria, reflection on former Roman greatness led to hope for a "New Rome," once the land was unified.

In Germany, a number of scholars went to the common people, the *Volk*, to find there, among the folkways and customs, a "pure" Germany, untainted by foreign influence. The fairy tales associated with the Grimm brothers were gathered as these two linguists sought to find the roots of the German language and those enduring qualities that existed in the customs of the peasantry.

Such romantic nationalism complemented liberal thought, also concerned with self-identification. Both the individual and the community were to determine their own destinies according to their own lights: reason and history. Constitutionalism was therefore easily equated with nationalism.

At no time did the possibility of European political reorganization along national and liberal lines seem so imminently possible as in the revolutionary year of 1848. Between February and June of that year, Paris, Vienna, Berlin, Prague, Budapest, Rome, and Milan were the settings of revolutionary upheavals that toppled governments or urged them to introduce hastily contrived reform. Bourgeois and worker fought on the same barricades, where they were joined by university students, making their first significant appearance as a group of radical reformers.

Most of these revolutions were as ill-directed as they were poorly met by the established forces. For a brief moment, however, it did appear that the old order was about to collapse. But governmental promises to introduce constitutional rule, the lack of coordinated revolutionary leadership, the growing bourgeois concern that the revolutions would go too far, and the reorganization of the established military forces, all were elements that combined in each country to bring 1848 to a relatively quiet and unsuccessful close. The year 1848 was the turning point when European history did not turn, according to the English historian J. M. Trevelyan.

Liberal nationalism did not triumph. Rather, the monarchs of Prussia and Austria readjusted their crowns, while in France the new president was the nephew of Napoleon. By 1852 this "prince-president," who had said that his political program was his name, upheld his questionable inheritance by a coup d'état. France was then governed by Napoleon III under the Second Empire (1852–1870).

The dissipation of liberal hopes did not result in the end of national unification movements, however.

The National Unification of Italy and Germany

Perhaps the key to what subsequently happened is found in the now famous words expressed by Otto von Bismarck, the Prussian minister, in a speech he made before the budget commission of the Prussian Chamber of Deputies in 1862. "The great questions of the day," he sternly stated, "will not be decided by speeches or by majority decisions . . . but by blood and iron." The national unification of Germany and Italy occurred in a manner quite different from what the romantic nationalists had in mind. Not the will of the people, but the strength of the armies and the cunning of diplomacy turned the trick.

The series of events by which Italy and Germany were unified have long allowed for historical comparison. One state was the principal agent of unification: Piedmont in Italy, Prussia in Germany. One man was the guiding genius: Camillo Cavour (1810–1861) in Italy, Otto von Bismarck (1815–1898) in Germany. In both instances, several minor wars were the major catalysts leading to unification. And finally, the pivotal war in the process of unification was directed against Austria, because Austria intruded into both Italian and German territory as a foreign dominator. In 1859, with the support of France, Piedmont engaged Austria in war. Although the French suddenly pulled out of the war, Piedmont did gain Lombardy, the large northern province, as a result. In 1866 Prussia defeated Austria and thereupon formed the North German Confederation (1867), a loose political system that assured its dominance of Germany. In sum, then, the multinational Hapsburg Empire was an obstacle to and a cause of Italian and German unification. Austria was forced to relinquish its territorial hold and political dominance in these countries, an action which coincided with the rise of Piedmont and Prussia as the major unifying power in each.

One further point should be emphasized. Italian and German unification was made at the expense of France, as well as of Austria. It was in the Franco-Prussian War of 1870 that Bismarck manipulated the remaining German states into a military alliance with his North German Confederation. The successful outcome of that war was followed by the creation of the German Empire. In the Hall of Mirrors at the palace of Versailles, the king of Bavaria proclaimed the king of Prussia to be the emperor of Germany on January 18, 1871. While the French and Germans were fighting, Piedmontese troops occupied Rome, heretofore papal territory under the protection of France, and the final step in Italian unification was made: Rome became the capital of the Kingdom of Italy.

As historians are generally concerned with the unusual and the irregular

—the "fact"—the variations in details by which the unification of Germany and Italy took place are very important to a close understanding of diplomatic and political developments of the time. What is significant in a historical review of a broad sort, however, is this: the unification of both countries was neither achieved by liberal politics nor by liberal philosophy. While Cavour was a liberal who supported the idea of a written constitution, both he and Bismarck were believers in strong state authority and endorsed the monarchical system of the day. They placed national unity above constitutionalism, which they actually abused.

Even this last statement is open to historical contention, for what both men consciously assured was the dominant position of their own state in the newly unified Germany and Italy. Hence, some historians have argued that what was achieved was the Prussianization of Germany and the Piedmontization of Italy. The two new nations resulted from imposed national unification, not from a spirit of popular nationalism. And it was therefore Prussian and Piedmontese policies and institutions which dominated in the new nations. The result was a constitutional form that did not respect or respond to liberal desires.

In particular, the unification of Germany changed many conditions in continental political life. First, it meant a shift from a French-centered to a German-centered Europe. The largest, most populous, most industrially efficient state of Western Europe, Germany was paramount before the century was out. Moreover, its social and political structures were not of the liberal sort that the ideals of the French Revolution had proposed. An effective alliance existed between German big business, the aristocracy, and the military. As there was no room for real democracy in Bismarck's "blood and iron" theory, so there was none in the new German Empire. Finally, even in Bismarck's time, but primarily during the reign of Emperor Wilhelm II (1888–1918), many influential Germans sought for Germany a new role in the world. The idea of *Weltpolitik*, of world politics, was appealing. Along with this new attitude came a militant mood.

Conclusion

The better part of the nineteenth century was given to the working out of the political and social problems left by the French Revolution. Until the defeat of Napoleon in 1815, European political and military affairs were directed against his vast imperial system. Thereafter, certainly to 1848, the fear of liberal revolution occupied the minds of conservative European statesmen. And from 1848 to 1871 the last major problems concerning national unification were solved by "blood and iron." By 1871, therefore, a European nation-state system had been elaborated, fixed until the shattering effects of the First World War.

Within the confines of the nation-state, whether it was newly-formed Imperial Germany or long-established monarchical England, the social issues generated in the early nineteenth century continued to intensify.

If, for a brief period, the international scene had an unusually serene appearance about it, the social order was still in a state of turbulence. The major states of Europe were either formed or reformed politically, and nationalism seemed to have triumphed—although not in the form expected by the liberals of an earlier era.

Political revolution had abated, but the Industrial Revolution was generating a new social order.

4

The Age of Power

Here we have, in the place of the isolated machine, a mechanical monster whose body fills whole factories, and whose demon power, at first veiled under the slow and measured motion of his giant limbs, at length breaks out into the fast and furious whirl of his countless working organs.
KARL MARX

The Duke of Wellington, fierce adversary of Napoleon on the continental battlefield, feared in old age that the railroad would serve to move revolutionaries around. His concern was not misplaced: in 1848 a group of Belgian revolutionaries did attempt to return to Brussels from Paris by way of the railroad; however, they were switched to a side-track by two railroad engineers, and thus were greeted by the army, not by flag-waving compatriots.

This minor incident in a year of great political events is important for its symbolic value. It suggests that the industrial process manufactured social change as well as machine products. For the first time in history people could move about easily and quickly: across continents, around class barriers, and on to a future of greater material comfort.

Mobility came to be a term useful in the description of social relationships as well as of geographical ones. By train and steamboat the most incredible voluntary migration took place, with millions of Europeans moving from countryside to city, from Old Europe to the New World, from American coastal cities inland to prairies and plains. Moreover, new population centers dotted Europe. Manufacturing cities like Manchester and Birmingham in England, or Dusseldorf in Germany, and Lyons in France grew in size and economic importance, spawning in the process a new class of factory "hands." In such locations new industries like steel, locomotive construction, and cotton textiles, required the services of a new professional figure: the engineer. Not only was he trained in a new type of school, the technical institute, but also he quickly figured as the hero of much science fiction, such as that written in quantity by Jules Verne in the 1860s and 1870s.

Finally, technological innovation inspired social reorganization—what later would be called "social engineering"—as well. Model communities were planned complete with mass-transportation systems; the concept of urban zoning was introduced; and the department store—a French "invention" of 1852—appeared as an organized replacement for clusters of shops. As if anticipating the industrialization of every phase of life, a French urban planner of the 1860s proposed that a grand necropolis—a city of the dead—be built north of Paris and joined by railroads which would have their stations conveniently located in the old cemeteries of the city. Coffins and mourners could thus be transported on schedule to the site of eternal rest so that space in the capital would be reserved for more lively uses.

Another Kind of Revolution

The radical change in life's pace, purposes, and organization is reason enough to accept the term "Industrial Revolution." What had heretofore remained constant in daily social existence was now thrust into a state of flux and change. In effect, nearly two thousand years of social behavior went up in a cloud of steam. Consider the following facts: (1) When news of the Battle of Waterloo was brought to London, it traveled no faster overland than had news of Caesar's defeat of the Gauls; (2) When the English Romantic poet William Wordsworth wrote his lyrical odes, he did so at night in light that provided no better illumination than that available to Charlemagne's scribes; (3) When Louis XIV was operated on in 1686 for the removal of a fistula, he endured the pain due to surgical techniques that the physicians attending the pharaohs of Egypt would have known.

In a short time, all of that changed. Railroad trains moved a mile a minute by the 1850s. Shortly thereafter anesthesia was employed in operating rooms, while epidemical diseases, like smallpox, were beginning to be controlled by inoculation. In the same period, gaslights illuminated poets' verse, and the words of poet and politician alike could be read daily at the breakfast table, thanks to newspapers printed on fast-production rotary presses. On the occasion of the Diamond Jubilee of her rule in 1897, Queen Victoria telegraphed a brief message to the people of her empire, and that message was received in Australia, Canada, India, and Central Africa within a few hours.

These rapid changes were made possible by technology. It was not pure science as such, but applied science that triumphed in the nineteenth century. Practical invention and mass production were the key activities of the industrializing world of Europe. They were, furthermore, set in a new social environment: the factory. There, thousands of workers streamed in at dawn and drifted out at dusk. They performed specialized functions, by attending to a stamping machine or assembling a part, such that the final product was not the result of individual creativity, but of group effort. Cotton clothing, footware, kitchen cutlery, railroad engines, telegraph keys, cast iron fences— these were but a few of the items in the lengthening inventory of factory-produced goods that were marketed in Europe and exported around the world.

However, the age of mass production, even though distinguished by its dramatic appearance, was rooted in the past. The availability of mechanical power certainly goes back to the medieval windmill, used for grinding meal. Small-scaled factories were constructed on the banks of fast-moving streams in France and England in the early eighteenth century. Well-contrived mechanical inventions existed for over a century in the form of pocket watches, music boxes, and even spring-powered automatons that could write or play a tune.

What brought together diverse mechanisms such as these and composed them into the industrial system were practical men seeking answers to practical needs. The first clear movements of modern industrialization were seen in the rocking beam of the piston-driven steam engine contrived by the iron manufacturer Thomas Newcomen in the first decade of the eighteenth century. Newcomen's device helped pump water out of iron mines in England, but it was a very inefficient instrument and remained so until the wit of the Scotsman James Watt improved its efficiency by altering its form late in the century. Watt's machines were soon pumping water out of coal mines as well as iron mines, thus allowing for an increase in coal production and, conversely, in the use of steam power soon to be generated more by coal than wood. By the 1780s, John Wilkinson, an iron manufacturer and skilled technician, had applied steam power to his manufacturing. Between the American and French Revolutions, the Industrial Revolution made its first disturbing, clanking sounds, as iron machinery was driven by the hiss of steam within the confines of the factory.

A few decades later, when the stationary engine was set on wheels, when the wheels were placed on two parallel rails of iron, and when these rails were extended between one city and another, the industrial age moved into clear view. In 1825 the Stockton-Darlington Railroad, all of twenty-five miles long, was in business, the first of its kind in Europe.

> *Soon shall thy arm, Unconquer'd Steam, afar*
> *Drive the slow barge and move the rapid car.*

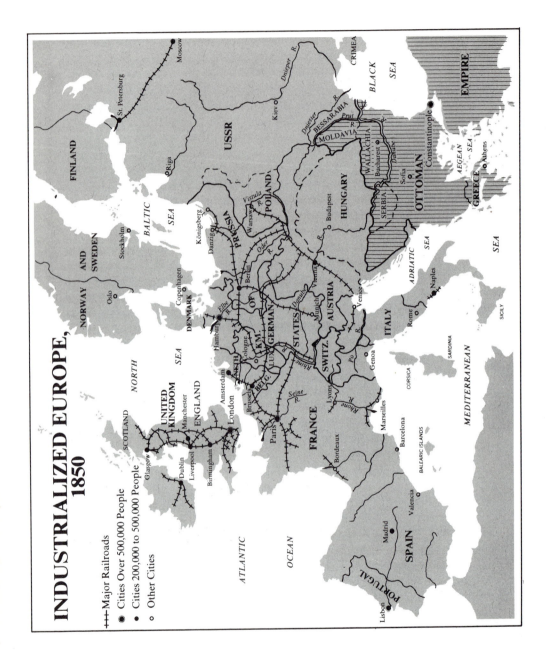

INDUSTRIALIZED EUROPE, 1850

+++ Major Railroads

● Cities Over 500,000 People

• Cities 200,000 to 500,000 People

○ Other Cities

ATLANTIC OCEAN

UNITED KINGDOM

SCOTLAND

Glasgow

Dublin

Liverpool

Manchester

Birmingham

ENGLAND

London

NORTH SEA

NORWAY AND SWEDEN

FINLAND

Oslo

Stockholm

St. Petersburg

Moscow

Riga

BALTIC SEA

DENMARK

Copenhagen

Königsberg

Danzig

Hamburg

Elbe R.

Amsterdam

Brussels

BELG.

LUX.

Cologne

Rhine R.

KM.

STATES

OF

GERMAN

Berlin

Oder R.

Vistula R.

PRUSSIA

Warsaw

POLAND

Kiev

Dnieper R.

USSR

Dniester R.

BESSARABIA

MOLDAVIA

Prut R.

WALLACHIA

Bucharest

Danube R.

SERBIA

Sofia

OTTOMAN

Constantinople

CRIMEA

BLACK SEA

HUNGARY

Budapest

Vienna

AUSTRIA

Munich

SWITZ.

Danube R.

Venice

ADRIATIC SEA

ITALY

Rome

Genoa

Po R.

Naples

SICILY

SARDINIA

CORSICA

MEDITERRANEAN SEA

FRANCE

Paris

Seine R.

Lyons

Rhône R.

Bordeaux

Marseilles

Barcelona

BALEARIC ISLANDS

SPAIN

Madrid

Valencia

PORTUGAL

Lisbon

GREECE

Athens

AEGEAN SEA

SEA

EMPIRE

This heroic couplet was written by Erasmus Darwin, grandfather of Charles, at the end of the eighteenth century. If not elegant, it was timely. Steam was the motivating force that generated the Industrial Revolution. It utilized the major fossil fuel, coal, and allowed production to proceed regularly and tirelessly. For the first time in history, energy was not subjected to animal fatigue or the vagaries of the weather. Wilkinson's steam-driven hammer, in operation in 1782, moved at a pace of 150 blows a minute, far exceeding anything the village smithy ever wildly dreamed of achieving.

By the middle of the nineteenth century, this industrial process of coal mining, iron manufacturing, and steam application had reached most of Western Europe to a very noticeable degree. Its most obvious measurement of success was the railroad. In 1832 the French built their first railroad; the Germans and Belgians followed in 1835, and Italy in 1848. Later, the impressive Trans-Siberian Railroad was completed in 1903; while the Berlin to Baghdad Railroad, a romantic and political venture, begun in the 1890s was still uncompleted in 1914. Not only did the mania for railroad building increase iron production and thus speed up industrialization, but the railroad also became the most convenient means of carrying bulk items, like coal and iron, thus making industrialization all the more feasible. Although the railroad train ran on straight lines, it provided the circular economic motion of consumption and transportation that accounts for the great productivity of the first industrial age. Railroading was an impressive technological development, but one matched by a distinctive economic organization emerging at the time.

Capitalism and Entrepreneurs

The modern European industrial system was capitalist in mode. Its principal figure was the entrepreneur—a French term seldom translated because it literally means "undertaker," and in American usage that word has little to do with constructive effort. The entrepreneur had the capital or borrowed it. In some instances, commercial banking families that had grown wealthy on the colonial trade of the eighteenth century now turned to manufacturing. In other instances, such banking firms were able to loan money at attractive interest rates below 10 percent and thus induce risk-taking by entrepreneurs beginning new industries. Lastly, intrepid manufacturers saw the wisdom of utilizing new devices and struck out in new industrial ways themselves. It was Matthew Boulton, a Birmingham manufacturer of metal art objects, who recognized the value of Watt's steam engines and financed their manufacture. The combination of Boulton and Watt was an important, but not unusual, one. Entrepreneur and inventor worked together now as patron and artist had in the Renaissance.

The entrepreneur's principal social function was organizational. He brought together the factors of production: resources, equipment, and laborers, by the use of his capital. And he combined them all into a workable unit housed within the factory.

This he did with the clear purpose of accumulating wealth. The industrial system was production-oriented, but profit-motivated. Furthermore, it proceeded from the assumption that the market of consumers was infinitely expandable: the demand for more products and new products would be large enough to absorb all that could be manufactured. The new society, according to more than one economist, was the acquisitive society, in which material comfort and personal possessions were the easily measured components of happiness. As the ruthless and crass industrialist in Charles Dickens' *Hard Times* (1854) says to the one worker he considers different from the rest: "You don't expect . . . to be fed on turtle soup and venison with a gold spoon, as a good many of 'em do!" This industrialist, of course, was made by Dickens to impute his own lust for worldly possessions to his employees. But the attitude was a widespread one. As the French philosopher Alexis de Tocqueville remarked in *Democracy in America* (1835), "The passion for physical comforts is essentially a passion of the middle classes." What Tocqueville and Dickens both observed was a new materialism made possible by industrial productivity.

As never before, wealth also meant power. The captain of industry replaced the captain of infantry as the man of the hour. The House of Krupp, manufacturers of cannon, was more important than the House of Wittelsbach, monarchs of Bavaria. The great shipowner Albert Ballin, founder of the Hamburg-America Line, was a friend and counselor of Kaiser Wilhelm II. And Cecil Rhodes, who mined diamonds and gold in South Africa, meddled in the politics of imperialism to the point that two African colonies—Northern and Southern Rhodesia—were named after him. It was Rhodes who offered what might be considered the slogan of the new age: "Philanthropy is good, but philanthropy at 5 percent is better."

Such philanthropy only trickled down, without much interest of any kind, to the lower classes who were more crushed than uplifted by the early development of industrialization. A new class of urban working poor appeared, those unskilled workers labeled by Karl Marx as the "proletariat." In its early days the industrial process was labor-intensive, requiring large numbers of individuals—"hands"—to both supply and superintend the machines. Such labor had no job security; pay and length of employment were determined by the needs and interests of the entrepreneur or the fluctuations of the market. Frequently, wages were set by that hidden law of "marginal subsistence," with the worker's income barely allowing him to take care of the basic needs of his family—and more than occasionally not reaching that modest goal.

Initially, the hours in the factory were long, the work oppressive. A fourteen-hour workday, maintained six days a week, was not unusual in the textile factories; and more than a half-hour for refreshment was unheard of. Young children worked at a grueling pace in the mines where their small bodies allowed for rather easy passage and in the textile factories where their nimble fingers could keep pace with the weaving machinery. More important was the new female labor force, upon which the textile industry was so dependent. As for the men employed in mine and forge, they were spent at an early age, broken in spirit and body before they turned thirty. A governmental report of 1842 showed that the average age of death for "mechanics, labourers, and their families" in Manchester was seventeen. The hazards of factory employment were high, with industrial accidents a serious cause of injury and dismemberment, and with a new urban-industrial disease, tuberculosis, working its dreadful effects.

Protests Against Industrialism

The working classes in the industrial cities were situated in an appalling environment that bred disease, despair, discontent—and the clamor for reform. While it is true that not every industrial city presented the bleak picture associated with Manchester, England, of the 1830s and 1840s, the general dehumanization of factory labor was the subject of widespread denunciation. Some of the sharpest critics, Charles Dickens, Alexis de Tocqueville, and Friedrich Engels (Marx's collaborator), generalized from their observations of Manchester; yet what they stated was at worst exaggerated, not falsified.

Concomitant with early industrial development, therefore, was a movement of protest urged by reformers and revolutionaries alike. Karl Marx (1818–1883) was foremost among them, and his short tract (co-authored by Friedrich Engels), *The Communist Manifesto* (1848), provided the most awesome picture of future developments: a class war between the "haves" and the "have-nots."

Marx was both critic and prophet. He provided a form of social analysis structured on the notion of competing social classes that has remained a major contribution to sociological and political theory. But as a mid-Victorian, reviewing the plight of the worker in Manchester or London, Marx prophesied that only class warfare and the overthrow of the capitalist would assure an equitable society. He singled out private property as the root of all social evil, considering the capitalist to be both parasite and thief: it was the capitalist who lived off the sweat of the proletariat, stealing the fruits of their labor by paying them much less than they were worth and taking the difference in the form of profits. This arithmetical difference between wage and worth, between money and value, accounted for the capital by which industrialization took place and would continue, according to Marx. Only when private property was prohibited, hence individual capital accumulation was checked, would an equitable society emerge. The important point is this: Marx objected to the ownership, but not the management, of the system.

However, he was opposed to those social reformers who imagined that the best way to change the situation was through the establishment of new and idyllic working communities far from the site of the belching red-brick chimneys. These efforts were dismissed by Marx as "utopian," both unrealistic and unhistorical. It was necessary to be part of the historical process of class struggle, to engage in the fight against the capitalists on their own urban ground. "Workers of the world, unite!" is the stirring command with which the *Communist Manifesto* ends. For Marx, consciousness of their plight would create unity among the working classes, and at that point their combined strength would allow for the forceful overthrow of the capitalist system. Class war was the only means by which the social order could be changed, for the government was, in Marx's opinion, "the executive committee of the bourgeoisie," that is, its chief agency for retention of control.

In the postrevolutionary age he sanguinely imagined, Marx assumed that private property would be restricted to needed personal possessions, and wealth would be equitably redistributed—"from each according to his ability, to each according to his need" would be the slogan and reality. The state would "wither away," for its primary purpose of protecting private property would no longer exist. An ideal world, a world characterized by social harmony, not conflict, would finally come into existence.

Although history was not played out as Marx had hoped, he was not alone in the dire predictions he made in mid-nineteenth century. At that time the worst effects of the new industrialism were everywhere to be seen. Even the century's most famous conservative, Benjamin Disraeli, who became prime minister of Great Britain, arrived at the same conclusion as Marx. Actually, it was the other way around, for Disraeli expressed his views before Marx. Disraeli's novel, *Sibyl*, published in 1845, bears the suggestive subtitle: *The Two Nations*. These are defined by Disraeli as the rich and the poor. One of Disraeli's fictional heroes is bold enough to allow that they really are two nations in harsh opposition.

Urban Growth

This unresolved tension between entrepreneur and worker, which was such a significant fact of mid-nineteenth-century social existence, was matched by another new condition equally obvious at the time: the mushrooming of urban growth. Most critics concur that urbanization was a concomitant feature of industrialization. Just as the factory system mobilized large numbers of workers, so its location close to a center of transport or a supply of natural resources, created new urban space: cities quickly spread around the mills and factories which themselves were often clustered together in large number. The result was dreadful residential congestion, blanketed in polluted air.

By contrast, the city in the preindustrial era lay within the immediate circumference of the countryside. The cock's crow awakened the merchant almost as often as it did the farmer; and the weekly market brought country-folk from a few miles around to the central square where they mingled and bartered with their urban counterparts. Few of Europe's cities were enormously large, and within their confines it was not unusual to see small gardens cultivated for the purpose of raising daily staples, or to encounter pigs roaming the streets and acting as useful scavengers. Even as late as 1830 strawberries were grown in large quantities within the city limits of London.

There should, however, be no attempt made to romanticize the preindustrial city. London of the eighteenth century wallowed in filth, endured great crime, and allowed the thriving trade of gin shops where children as young as five could drink poorly distilled alcohol at a tragic cost to their well-being. Epidemic diseases played havoc with the cities, as typhoid and dysentery produced high annual death rates. Fire, too, was awesomely destructive, with the Great Fire of London in 1666 destroying some 450 acres of housing. And the ghetto, so tragically familiar in contemporary society, suggested in the preindustrial city the existence of sectional discrimination, with Jews shunted off, isolated in one quarter.

What immediately distinguishes the industrial city is the rapidity of its growth, a quantitative leap that had dire qualitative results. Manchester, the first major industrial city, had a population of 70,000 in 1801; yet by 1831 that population had grown to 142,000. Roubaix in France was hardly more than a village of 8,000 in 1831; however, ten years later its population stood at 34,000. The most spectacular change was in London, where the population of 988,000 in 1801, bulged outward at 2,363,000 in 1851. Behind these statistics is found a series of social problems that perplexed governmental authorities, irritated social reformers, and provided the raw material for the many novels of social realism that then appeared.

The best way to describe the new urban form is by the familiar word "sprawl." An English urbanist, Patrick Geddes, writing in the early twentieth century, looked back on London's growth and suggested that it was "without previous parallel in the world of life—perhaps likest to the spreading of a great coral reef." The haphazard nature of urban development, dictated only by the needs of the marketplace and the rabid speculation of the real estate owner and the builder, soon led to an inadequacy of basic facilities—like water and sewers—to overcrowding, and to the practice of scalping rents. In sum, the urban worker not only suffered the indignity of being mastered by the machine, but also endured the debasement of an existence in the "slum."

Mid-nineteenth-century Europe was thus the setting of great industrial progress and social discontent. The age was suspended between two worlds: the old of order, the new of change.

Conclusion

The historian's appreciation of irony easily inclines him to the conclusion that the French Revolution promised liberty to the self-sufficient individual, while the Industrial Revolution provided a form of enslavement to the person who was needed for a particular function, not because of his basic humanity. If, therefore, the two "revolutions" seemed to combine poorly in their achievement of immediate results, in the long run they forced a new definition of the social being, of the individual in his or her social situation.

In theory, both asserted that the individual was a free agent, to make of a life what he (or she) could. (For the sake of historical accuracy, the personal pronoun must remain "he": women had little say and few rights in nineteenth-century society.) Again, Napoleon's phrase "careers open to talent" summarized the idea nicely. In the political arena and in the marketplace, the citizen could express his mind and sell his labor as he saw fit. This was the theoretical nature of liberty: the social freedom to do what you wished so long as you did not interfere with the liberty of others.

But, in fact, the liberty of others was often denied or trampled upon. The cynical comment that some men are free and some are freer than others approaches nineteenth-century political reality and suggests why the first half of the century was so revolutionary. Underprivileged segments of society also wished to enjoy the political rights granted only some. Introduction of a written constitution and extension of the suffrage were, therefore, major political objectives.

Such demands as these were being registered at the time the hierarchy of the old social order was disappearing. No longer were there the traditional three estates; in their stead appeared a set of social classes, dominated by the bourgeoisie, middle class in name, perhaps, but top class in economic fact. It is true that the aristocracy still continued to direct the major political affairs of the state through much of the nineteenth century. However, society was, as Marx had perceived, being redefined in terms of the new industrial system. Yet, even so, entrepreneur and worker did not stand in a simple and fixed opposition as "bourgeoisie" and "proletariat." The stark adversary relationship outlined in Marx's thought never left the pages of his works. In reality, there was no single middle class, but rather several strata in which, for instance, small merchant was easily distinguished from industrialist capitalist. Moreover, worker and factory owner were more often given to cooperation than to class struggle in the thousands of small industrial enterprises that dotted the French and German landscape.

Yet the factory complex in the large city was the setting in which class confrontations and outright conflict did take place. Fear of class warfare may have been out of proportion to its probability, but there was sufficient industrial violence to give currency to Marx's prediction that the capitalist system would be overthrown from within. Industrial sabotage—the destruction of machines, for instance—was one device employed, as was absenteeism, the quiet form of protest. However, the strike was developed as the most effective form, used more in the twentieth century than in the nineteenth, it is true, but the most forceful expression of labor's demands created in the nineteenth century.

Even with these manifestations of industrial discontent, the second half of the nineteenth century witnessed no series of revolutionary activities comparable to those that had occurred in the first half of the century. Reform seemed to be more the order of the day. The point is that the European political system, with its parliamentary processes, was sufficiently flexible in structure and promising enough in democratic purpose to accommodate and attract new social interests. The legally recognized organization of labor unions is one example of this flexibility, as is the development of new socialist political parties pledged to change the industrial system at the ballot box, not on the barricade.

None of these various social and economic activities worked well, but the general system worked well enough to allow for consolidation and expansion in the second half of the century.

Portrait of George Arnold *by* W. *Hogarth. Reproduced by Permission of the Syndics of the Fitzwilliam Museum, Cambridge (England).*

The Bourgeoisie Portrayed

No more significant testimony to the importance of the European middle classes is to be found than the extensive artistic representation of these modern citizens over the last several centuries.

In much eighteenth- and early nineteenth-century painting, the bourgeois appears as the *honnête homme*, the man of public virtue, who

Portrait of Sir Joseph Paxton *by S. W. Reynolds, after O. Oakley. Reproduced by Permission of the National Portrait Gallery, London (England).*

realized the importance of "good health, good sense, and good conscience" (an eighteenth-century French summary of bourgeois values).

The bourgeois was the man of his time: self-made, progressive, and businesslike. As the "captain of industry," he directed the activities of the new world. Perhaps no individual better represented this new figure than Sir Joseph Paxton, whose portrait was done in a popular nineteenth-century style. Best known for the design of the Crystal Palace, Paxton began his career humbly, first as gatekeeper, then as gardener to the duke of Devonshire. Ambitious, talented, and determined, Paxton used his unschooled ability to build greenhouses, then the Crystal Palace, and, in the meantime, a fortune.

Sunday in the Botanical
Gardens *by Daumier.*
Babcock bequest, 63. 1993.
Courtesy of the Museum
of Fine Arts, Boston.

*Le mariage de convenance by Sir William Q. Orchardson. Reproduced by
Permission of the Glasgow Art Gallery.*

Nevertheless, the talents of a Paxton were contrasted with the
dull calculations and petty pretensions that social critics saw as the
qualities of the bourgeoisie. By the mid-nineteenth century, Charles
Dickens had created "Scrooge," and the humor magazines were printing
sketches mocking the middle classes. The most famous cartoonist of
that era was Honoré Daumier. Called the "Molière of the Pencil" because of his wit, Daumier walked the streets of Paris in the 1840s and
1850s, memorized what he saw, and returned to his apartment to trans-
late his critical impressions on to paper. His drawing "Sunday in the
Botanical Gardens" starkly captures the leisure activity of the bourgeoisie, but shows this activity to be regulated by convention and undertaken without much genuine enjoyment.

In a far more stylized way, the English painter Sir William Orchardson revealed another "slice of life" from the times, the "Mariage de
convenance" (1883), in which the young woman who has married into
wealth in order to climb above her social station finds dullness of existence her real reward.

Sunday Afternoon on the Island of La Grande Jatte *by Georges Seurat.*
Helen Birch Bartlett Memorial Collection, Courtesy of The Art Institute
of Chicago.

However criticized, the bourgeoisie had attained a position of prominence and security in Europe at the turn of the twentieth century. This was the French era of *La Belle Epoque,* and the artist Georges Seurat captured something of its solidity and form. Like Daumier before him, he depicted a Sunday afternoon, warm and uneventful, marked only by the appearance of many bourgeois, properly attired and equally proper in their behavior. Outward appearances were what counted.

The inner experience of the First World War played havoc with the gentility and manners of European society. The polite veneer of the bourgeois world was hopelessly scarred. It was the German artist George Grosz who bitterly exposed the harshness of this new era. His sketches of German society in the 1920s describe a cruel and calloused world, and so they have been taken as visual intimations of the Nazi regime

Evening Rush Hour in Saxony by George Grosz. Courtesy of the Estate of George Grosz, Princeton, New Jersey.

that would soon follow. In "Evening Rush Hour in Saxony," Grosz sketched a street scene in which individuals go their separate ways, oblivious to one another. It is a spiritless world, hurried on by routine and selfish desire, not by a sense of civic pride or communal involvement.

If Grosz's artistic criticisms were the most severe of the era, they were not unique. Moreover, they would reappear in a different form after World War II in the genre of "pop art." Essentially an American art form, the subject of which was often presented in a humorous or sarcastic mood, pop art reflected American materialism and the advertising industry that promoted it. With photographic accuracy, the pop artists expressed the emptiness or flat dimension of modern domestic life.

Tourists (1970) by Duane Hanson. Photograph by Eric Pollitzer.
Reproduced by Permission of the O. K. Harris Gallery, New
York.

The contemporary American sculptor Duane Hanson, in a lifelike
work (what the French call *trompe d'œil*, or visual deception), places a
bourgeois couple in a vulgar pose. His "Tourists" represent a recent
social phenomenon. Armed with a camera and often decked out in
ridiculous attire, they gape at the wonders of the world, now made
available to them by means of rapid communication, retirement benefits, and the successful effort of most nations to foster tourism as a

Unfruitful Search for the Planet Leverrier by *Daumier*.
3rd state lithograph. Babcock Bequest, Del. 1531.
Courtesy of the Museum of Fine Arts, Boston.

major, contemporary industry.

And yet, Hanson's interpretation is but a new variation on an older theme, treated earlier by Honoré Daumier. His "Unfruitful Search for the Planet," shows an elderly middle-class couple from the last century also gaping at something they do not quite understand.

Respected and ridiculed, the bourgeoisie has provided an important subject for artistic treatment in the Western world.

PART TWO

Expansion and Explosion: 1871–1918

$\mathcal{I}$n 1889 the Eiffel Tower rose nearly one thousand feet into the Parisian sky; in 1912 the ocean liner Titanic, nearly nine hundred feet in length, set out on its maiden voyage to America. Both structures were the wonders of their age, proof of European technological success and expressions of the unusual power that the late nineteenth-century European world had amassed.

Belief in ever-increasing material progress as a condition of modern life was widespread in Europe, and this belief had as its corollary the assertion that material progress was in itself a moral benefit. Already in mid-century, a little troupe of idealists, known after their leader Count Claude-Henri de Saint-Simon as the Saint-Simonians, entertained the glorious ideal that good things would come from great works—the world would be made one and harmonious if bound together by iron rails or connected by waterways. Ferdinand de Lesseps, who built the Suez Canal, was of this persuasion, as were several of the most important French railway engineers. Across the Atlantic, the poet of the new age was Walt Whitman, who captured the exalted spirit in the following lines from "Passage to India":

> Lo, soul, seest thou not God's purpose from the
>   first?
> The earth to be spann'd, connected by network,
> The races, neighbors, to marry and be given in
>   marriage,
> The oceans to be cross'd, the distant brought
>   near,
> The lands to be welded together.

This spirit of industrial expansion, evidenced throughout most of the century, was both modified and greatly enlarged in the last three decades, when political expansion in the form of overseas imperialism was evident from tropical Africa to the frigid Arctic.

Yet late nineteenth-century expansion, whatever its form, did not move along the poetic lines expressed by Whitman. There was little visible harmony, no welding together of interests or purposes. Europe had become economically and politically competitive, with national rivalry taken as the norm. The long years of relative peace had encouraged many people to assume that in this self-styled "century of progress," a major war was not possible. It also led a few people to a different conclusion: that peace was enervating, productive only of complacency. When the Prussian general Helmuth von Moltke stated in 1880 that "everlasting peace is a dream, and not even a beautiful one," he expressed more than his own opinion.

War came in 1914, and with a ferocity and interminable length that few had dared anticipate. And with the war, nineteenth-century Europe would be shattered. Good-Bye to All That was the title of one of the most popular personal accounts of the war experience.

5

Concentration

It is the age that forms the man, not the man that forms the age.
THOMAS B. MACAULAY

The international exposition—what we today call a "world's fair"—was a mid-nineteenth-century European innovation designed primarily to display the hardware of the continent's industrial technology in an architectural setting of grandeur and fantasy. First defined in the impressive setting of the Crystal Palace of the London International Exhibition of 1851, such international fairs temporarily rose in many European cities in the last four decades of the century.

In its assemblage of a wide variety of the century's ever-increasing products, the international exposition was a symbol of the general concentration of contemporary European culture. Throughout the second half of the 1800s, populations were concentrating in the cities, industry was concentrating in a few geographical areas and nations, wealth was increasingly concentrated in the hands of a capitalist elite, labor was slowly concentrating in unions so as to better its condition, power was more effectively concentrated in a central government and increasingly in a permanent bureaucracy, and, finally, as the century ended, large numbers of men were drafted and concentrated in regular standing armies.

The older European pattern of scattered populations, small-scaled industry, and competing sources of political power, was now transforming into a pattern both more structured and monolithic in appearance. The term "mass," heretofore part of the vocabulary of physics, acquired a new social meaning even before the century ended. Moreover, this realignment of people in space—so easily seen on the production line of the large factory or at the central telephone switchboards in the major cities in the 1890s—was part of a new process of "rationalization": organization structured along orderly lines and with efficiency of effort the purpose in mind.

Only during World War I, when so much of national effort was directed to running the war machine, were the effects of such social concentration and rationalization imprinted on almost every aspect of European life. But a half-century before, the trend had clearly been established.

The New Productivity

When the London Exhibition of 1851 opened, a Scottish preacher gave the invocation which contained the lines: "Produce! Produce! Were it the pitifullest infinitesimal fraction of a product, produce it in God's name!" Productivity thus seemed to enter European life as an admonition, an imperative of both an economic and a cultural sort. Work became a good in itself. Value and quality soon were correlated. Good came to mean big; better to mean bigger; and best to mean biggest. Statistics, until then of little cultural consequence, assumed the state of a science and the function of a social regulator. Voltaire had once quipped that God was on the side with the larger number of regiments. In the new industrial era variations on this statement were accepted as truth. By the twentieth century the measure of a nation's annual steel production was taken as the most convenient measure of that state's power. Moreover, the brief supremacy that Europe enjoyed throughout the world was based on the decidedly favorable balance of trade that the Continent enjoyed throughout the nineteenth century.

Great Britain, Germany, and France were the great producers and exporters, matched only by the United States and not excelled by it until the first years of the twentieth century. Thus the statement that Europe was the "world's workshop" was not an exaggerated one. Increased production was generated by a combination of new industrial technologies and new business techniques.

The last quarter of the nineteenth century has frequently been considered the era of the second phase of the Industrial Revolution. Just as iron and coal had characterized the first phase, now steel and electricity came to the fore, joined in the early twentieth century by oil. Such a distinction is, however, one of emphasis or intensity, not one of kind or quality. Technological change was an underlying characteristic of all nineteenth-century industrialization, with new inventions and improved processes accelerating production and increasing its range.

Yet the core industry was metallurgical. First iron, then its offspring, steel, were the materials upon which modern industry was structured. And no manufacturing was more concentrated than that of coal and iron. The late eighteenth-century method of converting coal to coke improved the iron smelting process and later was important to steel production where high temperatures were so necessary. Thus, a new economic geography of industrialization appeared, running along short transportation axes that brought coal and iron to the factory. The Midlands of England, where Manchester and Sheffield are situated; the Ruhr Valley, where Dusseldorf and Essen are situated; and the Saar Valley, where Metz and Mannheim are situated—these became the major factory regions.

After a number of refinements in production, primarily designed to reduce impurities, steel replaced iron as the basic industrial metal. Both less brittle than iron and inherently stronger, steel soon stood everywhere around the Continent: on the grocer's shelf in the form of the "tin can," in the Parisian sky in the form of the Eiffel Tower, and out of the arsenals of Krupp in the form of cannon.

COMBINED STEEL PRODUCTION OF
GREAT BRITAIN, FRANCE, AND GERMANY

Period	Annual Average in Metric Tons
1880–84	3,270,000
1890–04	6,850,000
1900–04	14,450,000
1900–13	27,260,000

Other industries appeared, with chemical and electrical products now adding a new dimension to the international market, and with an entirely new industrial product—individual transportation—first making its appearance with the bicycle. The machine tool industry also took on major proportions thanks to the refinement of steel (the Bessemer process) and the new device of interchangeability of parts—both developments American in origin. Thus, in the second half of the nineteenth century, industrial production was refined, diversified, and increased so that even the most rural or poverty-ridden family might exhibit one of its products, whether a Sheffield knife, a kerosene lamp, or a spool of thread.

But beyond the smallest product was amassed new business techniques which represented the new scale of social life as well. No less an opponent of the capitalist system than V. I. (Nikolai) Lenin (1870–1924), leader of the Russian Communist Revolution of 1917, explained it this way: "The enormous growth of industry and the remarkably rapid process of concentration of production in ever-larger enterprises represent one of the most characteristic features of capitalism."

The "ever-larger enterprise" was best defined as the corporation. An outgrowth of the older joint-stock company that had served seventeenth- and eighteenth-century commercial development so well, the modern corporation made its appearance in the nineteenth century but only became the prevalent business form in the second half. Enjoying the advantage of limited liability (the stockholder could legally lose no more than his invested share in the corporation; hence the English expression "Limited" or "Ltd.") and provided with the means of amassing great quantities of capital for investment purposes (by the device of the stock issue), the corporation not only suited best the needs of private industrial development but also encouraged that development with the money it pumped into equipment, factories, and inventions. It was the expensive requirements of railroad construction more than any other economic development that provided the impetus to the use of corporate structure.

With the corporation's financial flexibility and expansive power, and with the increasing complexity of industrial productivity and marketing, the process of economic concentration intensified just before World War I. In every European country new forms of combination were tried, but the most famous, and commented on, was the cartel. Legalized and well practiced in Germany above all other countries, the cartel was an effective means by which to control the marketing of goods; it was a mutually arrived at agreement among producers in a given industry either to (1) regulate production (determine the amount and the percentage of goods that each member concern would produce); (2) regulate the market (geographically divide the market among the member concerns and/or regulate prices). The two great German cartels were the Rhenish-Westphalian Coal Syndicate (1893) and the Steelworks Union (1904).

The concentration of the means of production was paralleled, but in no way as sharply, by the organization of large banks. Lenin later interpreted their appearance as marking the advent of the age of finance capitalism. According to him, this was the period in which the financial interests gained control of the economy, with bankers sitting on the boards of directors of large corporations, and with the major lending banks providing the immense sums of capital needed for further industrial expansion. The financier, no longer the entrepreneur, was the "captain of industry," and he sailed a straight course to wherever high interest rates existed.

Lenin's argument has been severely criticized for being grossly simplistic, even anachronistic—that is, offering a description of a situation that did not yet exist. But there was also evidence to support his general assertion. As industrial development grew more complicated, the need for even greater capital financing was felt, and it was primarily through bank loans and stock issuance that the entrepreneur was able to finance his activities. In this sense, therefore, individual private ownership declined; corporate ownership increased; and bank investment portfolios contained increasing amounts of stocks and bonds of a corporate nature. As one critic has remarked, Europe was held together by a thread of gold in the early twentieth century.

Toward a New Social Order

As never before, the dimensions of the European world were altering and expanding, bringing the excitement of possible material prosperity for some, the anxiety of industrial unemployment and overcrowded living for many more. Economic and political power were concentrating in the city and, accordingly, the most obvious social change of the time was the decline of the rural base of European society. The pronounced industrial advantage of England was measurable by mid-century when half of that nation's total population lived in cities. By the end of the century the same could be said of Belgium, Holland, and Germany. Only France persisted in its old rural ways, not reaching a comparable urban percentage until between the world wars.

This demographic shift was the result of both general population increase and internal migration. First, the tendency toward marriage at an earlier age and the reduction of infant mortality through new medical techniques were important factors in the expansion of the European population. Second, the factory replaced the farm as the center of manpower. With the commercialization of farming, the use of chemical fertilizers and, later in the century, the employment of mechanical devices, increased productivity made the small-scale farm a marginal operation and the individual farmer rather obsolete. For many youth, opportunity seemed to be situated in the city. Whereas 21.2 percent of the English working population was engaged in agriculture in 1871, only 11.5 percent was in 1911.

The passing of country life was a condition that did not go unnoticed and unregretted by contemporary Europeans. In England, the decline of the self-sufficient farmer, the yeoman, was cause for nostalgic reflection and romantic writing. In Germany, youth movements took to the woods and the mountains to pursue a brief existence in the out-of-doors and to find mystical communion with the soil. And in France, a small number of individuals who found urban, bourgeois life stultifying looked to the colonial world, but North Africa in particular, as a "school of energy" similar to the American Far West.

Moreover, social thinkers expressed concern over the social polarity they now detected: the concept of "community" (the German *Gemeinschaft*), of a small-scaled rural social order held together by religion, tradition, trust, and mutual interdependence, was placed in opposition with "society" (*Gesellschaft*), a large-scaled urban social order, held together by money, rational structure, and competition. For many literary figures and social critics the city came to mean corruption, not inspiration.

It was true that the awesome dimensions of the urban scene were frightening to many. Crowds gave way to masses, large and undifferentiated numbers of people, related only by place of work and need of wages. Charles Dickens had described this new, concentrated order in *Hard Times*, where

Coketown appeared as a number of streets all alike and "inhabited by people equally like one another, who all went in and out at the same hours, with the same sound on the pavements."

As a result of their population density, the masses presented a new set of problems for local government. In the first place, none of the European municipal governments was initially prepared to leave the limited, eighteenth-century legal base of their authority to encounter the new and pressing demands: effective sanitation systems, pure water supplies, sufficient housing. Government had to be reformed and extended so that its functions went beyond public order to public services.

Notable reforms directed against urban blight were undertaken in the second half of the century. During the reign of Napoleon III, the city of Paris was provided with an incredibly efficient sewage system—a visitor to Paris can still travel through a portion of it without the slightest offense to his or her nose—that was greeted with enthusiasm and awe. Joseph Chamberlain, mayor of Birmingham, England between 1873 and 1875, introduced a series of reforms that were referred to as "municipal socialism." The gas and water supplies were made public services, controlled by the government. The clearance of slums and the introduction of a city park system were also hallmarks of Chamberlain's administration.

Municipal reform was one of the most important activities of the very late nineteenth century, at which time most European governments provided legislation to grant the city power to raise the monies necessary to offer a range of local services. Gas, water, garbage collection were in the forefront, but so were new experiments in municipal housing, with the city of Vienna in the lead. Imperial Germany became a model of municipal reform and efficiency, a major result of the rise of the Social Democratic party there.

New Responses

From an olympian perspective, what was witnessed is this: the movement away from earlier liberalism, with its stress on laissez-faire in public matters, an attitude captured in the slogan, "the least government is the best government." Concomitant with this political liberalism had been the emphasis on individualism. Now, public welfare grew in political importance, and this necessarily involved the government and stressed communal interest.

It was municipal government in which the initially striking changes occurred. The term "municipal socialism" comes close to describing the new attitude. Welfare democracy it was, in which government was called upon to assist in the accommodation of the new urban masses.

The problem that municipal government now set out to solve in a practical way had been considered in theory before the late nineteenth century. If there is a pivotal figure in the theory justifying the shift from the laissez-faire ("hands off") state to the regulatory one, it is Jeremy Bentham (1748–1832). A curious personality, with a practical and occasionally whimsical turn of mind, Bentham popularized the Enlightenment notion of utilitarianism, which he broadly defined as the greatest good for the greatest number, and which he predicated upon his "felicific calculus," the belief that the possible good and pain—the degree of "usefulness"—in any undertaking could be mathematically measured. (In one equation in this felicific calculus, Bentham asserted that "push-pin," the forerunner of pinball, yielded greater pleasure than poetry.) Bentham's thought pointed in the direction of the substitution of democracy for liberalism. Not the good of the individual, but of the collectivity or, to be more accurate, of the majority, should be respected. Here in theory, as later somewhat in practice, government by the few, government "of the rich and the wellborn," gave way to government for the masses. Both in the United States and Europe, the new times were heralded as the "century of the common man."

As political democracy spread in the late nineteenth century, so did a new form of concentration: the trade and labor unions. The trade union was well installed by mid-century and was designed to protect skilled workers. Flourishing in the building trades, among railroad engineers, printers, and textile workers, these unions were not so removed from their guild predecessors. They were mutual aid societies, offering health and death benefits; and they were guardians, attempting to control the numbers of individuals wishing to enter a particular trade so that members of that trade could command a good wage because of their relative scarcity. The labor union was not organized around a particular trade, but was broader in scope, covering the labor interests of entire industries, like iron and steel, and directed toward labor issues of a national sort. As these significant self-interest groups grew in size, they also grew in influence; to the governments of the day, they were a source of concern and worry.

GROWTH OF LABOR UNIONS

Country	Year	Union Membership
Great Britain	1892	1,576,000
	1913	4,135,000
Germany	1891	344,000
	1913	3,074,000

The immediate objectives of union agitation were better working conditions—more pay and less hours. But there was also a demand for further and more fundamental reform. In the late nineteenth century a number of socialist parties were formed so as to use the electoral process to gain control of the state and then initiate social change.

In their early years the unions and the political activists had generally gone in separate ways. The first major effort at some form of public forum was Karl Marx's First International of Working Men's Associations, convened in London in 1866. Because it consisted of a number of groups with contradictory political purposes, the First International did not succeed. As evidenced shortly thereafter, the major split within socialist ranks centered on strategy: revolution versus reform. The Marxists looked to the overthrow of the state from without, by revolution; the reformers assumed the best approach was to play the parliamentary game, that is, to gain control by becoming the majority party, and then effecting reform from within.

It was in the 1870s and 1880s that reformist or revisionist socialism became a major political force in Europe. Within the German Empire the Social Democratic party, a combination of two smaller groups, was formed in 1875. It soon became a major political instrument, with over one million members and the largest number of seats in the *Reichstag*, the lower house, by 1914.

Slower in political success was the French socialist movement, which had been initially set back by the Paris Commune. This short-lived municipal government, ruling Paris from March to May 1871 during the political instability resulting from French defeat in the Franco-Prussian War, had given the outward appearance of being radical, run by revolutionaries and workers. Marx praised it in his *Civil War in France* (1871), wherein he called it the first experiment in communism. In point of fact, it was neither radical nor communist, but some of its measures (a moratorium on rents, for instance), were denounced, and its resistance to an army sent in by the provisional French republic led to a brief but tragic civil war. The new French republic exiled some of the socialists involved in the Commune, and not until amnesty was granted in 1879 did French socialism begin to be an effective political force.

Yet even to speak of a French socialist party at the time is an inaccuracy. French socialism was split into several competing groups and was only united in 1901 under the skillful leadership of Jean Jaurès (1859–1914), schoolteacher, orator, and humanist. By 1914, this unified party, the SFIO (French Section of the Workers International), was also a major element in parliament, and it appeared that Jaurès would soon become premier. He was, unfortunately, the victim of an assassin's bullet at the outbreak of World War I.

Other socialist parties appeared in Belgium (1885), Austria (1888), Italy (1892), and in Great Britain the Independent Labour party was established in 1893. All of these parties demonstrated, by their very existence, two important facts: the growing success of reformist, or parliamentary socialism, and the increasing importance of the labor issue. Political democratic devices were now being used to achieve social democracy, particularly change in the direction of the improvement of the laboring class's condition.

The most noticeable institution of the labor movement, however, was the strike. Collective protest was designed to assure collective bargaining. Behind the movement lay the simple contention that singly the worker was helpless against the complicated and strong structure of the capitalist corporation and the government that seemed to support it. Collectively, however, the worker was deemed to be omnipotent. And so the thought was even entertained that a "general strike" could paralyze the industrial nation by bringing its public services to a halt and, thereby, forcing quick capitulation from governmental authorities and business executives. For different reasons, some political and some economic, such general strikes occurred in Belgium in 1893 and 1902, Holland in 1903, Italy in 1904, and France in 1904. None attained its ultimate objective, but they were all effective enough to suggest that the industrial system was not operating smoothly. To employ a social science concept, there was a problem of dysfunction, a failure of the social system to allow easy accommodation of new interest groups and to solve new problems in ideological as well as practical terms. Put quite simply, the social structure was out of whack, in need of adjustment or reassembly.

This dysfunctional condition was most evident in terms of cyclical unemployment, a condition that was the direct result of economic slumps or depressions throughout the century, but most attenuated during the so-called "Long Depression" that cut from around 1873 until nearly the end of the century. The "social question," as the European ruling classes called the problems of unemployment and consequent labor unrest, taxed the abilities of the governmental authorities and frightened the psyches of the middle class.

There were attempts to find solutions. Emigration was a partial answer. In 1854, some 427,000 Europeans had left for the United States; in 1882, the number had risen to nearly 789,000; and in 1907, the figure was a staggering 1,285,349. Imperialism was advertised as a possible solution, the means by which to find new markets and hence new jobs.* And then there were individual pieces of legislation indicating either growing state responsibility or growing political anxiety. Bismarck's outstanding reforms, the insurance acts, were a particular example: sickness insurance legislated in 1883; workmen's compensation against unemployment in 1884; old age and social insurance in 1889.

From within the working community itself a number of social combinations designed for group betterment were introduced. These "voluntary associations," as they would later be called by social scientists, or "friendly societies," as they were frequently called by contemporaries, called for mutual cooperation and stood in opposition to the competitive nature of so much of early capitalist-industrialist organization. Among the first manifestations of such effort were the consumer co-operatives that sprang up in the late nineteenth century, first defined by the English Co-operative Wholesale Society of 1863. Then the most popular of the "friendly societies" emerged, the

---

* See the following chapter for a fuller explanation.

insurance companies, run for workers' protection, not private profit. Lastly, in the field of education great strides at self-improvement were taken, as evidenced with the establishment of the Workers' Education Association in England in 1903.

Concentration of industry and population thus effected new political and social combinations, all designed to improve or regulate the worst excesses of an industrial market system which, according to its critics, placed production before humanity.

Even on the international level there was concern with an uncontrolled economy. This was expressed in the tendency toward protectionism in the last three decades of the century. Worried about a glut of goods accumulating through increased domestic production and an influx of foreign imports, most European nations sought to protect the home market by introducing protective tariffs. This policy was strongly pursued in France and Germany. Only England still valiantly upheld the principle of free trade, but even some of that nation's politicians, like Joseph Chamberlain, spoke of the need for an "imperial tariff league," uniting Great Britain and her colonial possessions in a defensive and mutually beneficial economic system, and thus keeping out of this transoceanic trade system most foreign goods by means of heavy import duties. The plan never succeeded, but in principle it represented the contemporary mood about the dangers of uncontrolled growth and intensifying concentration.

Beyond the marketplace and the factory, the setting of economic difficulties still unresolved at the end of the nineteenth century, was another world newly organized and generally exciting, that realm we today call "popular culture."

Cultural Implications of Mass Society

For the masses, and in part because of them, an interesting social quantification took place. New services and new distractions appeared in amazing number and with amazing rapidity. Most obvious was the mass transportation system. An American engineer, appropriately named Train, constructed the first tramway in England in 1860. Within twenty years all of the major cities of Western Europe had such urban rail systems, and the Germans, first in the world with electrical developments, electrified their lines in the 1880s, beginning in Frankfurt, the first city to have overhead electrical wires for power. But before such overhead developments, the London underground (subway) system had been initiated in 1863, with electrification added in 1890. Later, the Paris *Métro* (metropolitan line), inaugurated in 1900, provided Europe with one of its finest underground transportation systems. Such short-range commuting altered city spatial patterns, as place of residence and place of work were no longer adjacent. Thus, the tendency toward sectoralization, of dividing the city into units of work, administration, and residence, was accentuated by this new mass mobility.

Mass education also approached reality with the establishment of public educational systems. Within the decade of the 1870s, England, Austria, Hungary, Italy, Switzerland, The Netherlands, and Belgium all introduced state-controlled, secular elementary education. Most such educational reform and expansion of services was predicated upon the liberal belief that the modern citizen needed a basic education to assume the civic responsibilities and handle the new tasks that an industrializing world generated. But elementary education was considered sufficient enough, so that the universities remained the privilege of the aristocratic and the wealthy.

Increased literacy meant increased reading. Mass-circulation newspapers, emblazoned with sensational headlines, made astonishing gains. The English *Daily Mirror* had a circulation of over one million copies a day in 1911; and the French *Le Petit Journal* had a daily run of two million in 1900. Cheap pulp fiction—particularly the so-called "penny dreadfuls"—provided a form of escape into realms of mystery and mayhem. Such books, along with newspapers, could be purchased at newsstands, soon a familiar sight in railroad stations and on streetcorners. Or they might be obtained at lending libraries, another late nineteenth-century institutional innovation.

The concentration of population and wealth in the cities allowed for the flourishing of professional entertainment. In London, certainly the theatrical capital of Europe, ten major theaters were constructed in the twenty-year period 1876–1896. Elsewhere in Europe theaters catering to a wide variety of audiences increased, with eleven large theaters constructed in Germany between 1878 and 1895. As early as 1846 Covent Garden in London had been expanded to seat 4,000. And that essentially English institution, the music hall, appeared in quantity in the 1870s. There, the young and the poor congregated to enjoy popular entertainment. "It was a jam—not a crowd— when one boy coughed it shook the thousands wedged in and around him," remarked George R. Sims of the music hall audience in his satirical *Ally Sloper's Half-Holiday* (1888).

Even organized sports acquired a mass appeal at this time, thus leaving their narrow aristocratic base. The bicycle was the first industrial product used in competitive racing, except, of course, the steamboat. The famous *Tour de France* was an established institution in the first decade of the twentieth century. More significantly, football (soccer) became the first mass spectator sport, with its major professional clubs situated in industrial cities like Manchester. In 1901, for instance, 110,000 persons attended the Football Cup Final held in England.

Thus, as the old century expired, a significant tertiary, or service, sector joined the primary sector (agriculture) and secondary sector (industry) of the European economy. New professional activities, like public education, professional entertainment, publishing, were made possible in large measure because of the wealth generated by industrialization and because of the rapid communications created by it.

Conclusion

The Russian author Leo Tolstoy argued at the end of the century that "money is a new form of slavery, and distinguishable from the old simply by the fact that it is impersonal—that there is no human relation between master and slave." His statement was a severe indictment of contemporary conditions and at some variance with the facts.

The most dreadful aspects of industrialism, those which formed so much of Marx's thinking, had been mitigated. The general standard of living was rising throughout Western Europe, and the working classes were beginning to partake of some of the benefits that their efforts had generated. Better health and recreational services, the extension of public parks and sewers, the use of gas and electric lighting made the city a safer place than it had ever been before—if not still an aesthetically pleasing place. Yet much of Victorian architecture was based on the principle of whimsy as well as on stern utilitarianism. Railroad stations often looked like cathedrals or chateaux, and the British Houses of Parliament at Westminster were grandly gothic in appearance.

Above all, this was the era of the bourgeois, praised in the manuals of etiquette and self-improvement, often damned in the drama and fiction of the literary world. From a middle-class perspective, Europe at this time was at the pinnacle of power, in large measure controller of the world's destinies. There was some concern publicly expressed that Russia and the United States would one day displace Europe from its lofty position, but, as the century turned, Europe's future still looked bright to most, and its authority could be seen as extending to the four corners of the world.

6

Expansion

I would annex the planets if I could.   CECIL RHODES

One of the most dramatic, morally debatable, and significant activities of the nineteenth-century European social order was its outward movement into a dominant position on several continents and among many islands cast about the earth. Of course, empire was hardly a new institution. It has been a rather constant characteristic of the Western world since well before the days when Roman legions sallied forth to make alien peoples bow beneath standards surmounted by bronze eagles. And even the first years of the nineteenth century were witnesses to Napoleon's effort at surpassing imperial Rome. But never before the end of the century were there so many expressions of imperialism, with rival colonial systems competing in so many areas of the world. Great Britain, France, Holland, Belgium, Italy, Germany, Spain, Portugal, even Russia (not to mention the United States and Japan outside of Europe) intruded forcefully into Africa, or Asia, the Middle East, or the South Pacific—and finally sought the North and South Poles in the early years of this century. As an American senator of the time remarked, the Western world had an acute case of land hunger.

The intensity of this activity has led it to be called a "scramble," more specifically a scramble for Africa and Oceania (the islands of the South Pacific). Because it appeared to be so sudden and so competitive, and yet so much a part of late nineteenth-century political and economic power, this particular phase of overseas expansion has been labeled the "New Imperialism" in order to distinguish it from the "Old Colonialism" that supposedly ended in the late eighteenth century. Between the two, according to an older school of historians, existed a hiatus, a lull, during which Europe remained at home.

Today there is rather common agreement that European overseas expansion was a constant factor of the nineteenth century, with British commercial activities the most obvious aspect, but with both Great Britain and France seeking new trade outlets, strategic sites, and—on more than one occasion—a political advantage of one over the other. At the end of the century political annexation was the dominant characteristic of imperialism. If one considers that the major European land holdings in Africa before 1870 were Algeria (France) and South Africa (England), and then regards the political map of 1914 when only Liberia and Ethiopia were independent African states, one can appreciate the rapidity of the political change.

Why?

The Causes of Modern European Imperialism

Along with the French and Industrial Revolutions, imperialism has been a mine of causes picked at by many generations of historians. The Marxist-Leninist argument would have it that an ever-increasing capitalism needed new places for financial investment and for markets of its goods in order to avoid its necessary collapse. This is the analysis contained in the title of Lenin's most famous work, *Imperialism, the Highest Stage of Capitalism,* published first in 1917. "Highest" here has reference to a scale of historical progression: it is the last stage beyond which capitalism cannot go because it can find no other outlets to relieve the pressure that capital accumulation has generated. Thereafter the system (in today's parlance) will self-destruct.

Even the pro-imperialists of the late nineteenth century used a somewhat similar argument, but not to condemn capitalism. A famous French supporter of empire referred to colonies as the safety valve of the industrial steam engine, without which it would explode. And more than one publicist exclaimed, "No exportation without colonies." Thus, in the minds of contemporaries imperialism was the process of expansion by which to assist the industrial system in its search for new markets and, consequently, new profits. But where the imperialists considered this process a commercial policy, Lenin deemed it a historical necessity, a particular phase of capitalism, when financial interests controlled industry and were helpless to do anything but place their gold overseas, if they did not want an overwhelming glut.

The distinctions between the two economic approaches to imperialism may seem highly refined at first glance. Yet what the imperialists were urging as policy—a conscious state decision to better the society's economy—Lenin was analyzing as part of an unavoidable, necessary, or fated historical process; for him it was not policy, but inevitability: it could not be reversed or changed, and beyond this "highest" stage lay the necessary fall of the entire capitalist system.

This particular argument is stressed somewhat, not because it effectively accounted for the European history of the moment, but because Lenin's thesis grew in historical importance in the twentieth century to become the most popular explanation of modern imperialism, and one still vehemently proclaimed today.

Yet the commercial argument was and remains an important one, particularly if it is not reduced to a simple correlation between the amount of colonial territory acquired and the amount of goods and money exported. Europe's traditional and then current areas of principal export were the Americas and Europe itself. Very little money or goods went to tropical Africa or the islands of the Pacific. If anything in the commercial domain, the newly acquired colonial territories were "claims" "pegged out" for the future, as Lord Rosebery, late nineteenth-century British prime minister, described them in a consciously chosen mining metaphor.

What this idea suggests is the growing political consciousness of the competitive European industrial system. With the United States and Germany added to the great producing nations of the world—alongside England, France, and Belgium—there was concern that national industries would be disadvantaged, that national treasuries would suffer accordingly. Add to this concern another dimension, that stemming from the "social question." The so-called Long Depression of 1873–1896 was a downward trend in cyclical economics which meant chronic unemployment and possible social unrest. When Cecil Rhodes said that imperialism was a "bread-and-butter" question, it was this problem that he had in mind: new markets overseas would relieve the economic slump at home by generating the need for more products, hence reemployment of workers. Modern analysts, following the thought of an outstanding English imperialist of the turn of the century, Lord Alfred Milner, have called this "social imperialism."

Alongside the economic argument sturdily stands a political one, as old and as much discussed. In brief, it would read: imperialism is overseas nationalism. The rivalry traditionally demonstrated by European states was extended overseas in the late nineteenth century, as it had been earlier in the seventeenth and eighteenth centuries. In the later instance, it was Africa and Oceania that were the fields of political and military maneuver, as it had been North America and India earlier.

The coincidence between the political establishment of modern Europe —with the unification of Italy and Germany in 1870–1871—and the dramatic acquisition of new territory—say that of Tunisia by France in 1881 or Egypt by England in 1882—tempts the conclusion that the old diplomatic grounds of Europe, Germany, and Italy, where the major powers struggled and bickered, were now gone and had to be replaced elsewhere. In this argument Africa was of no European interest in and of itself; it was an area in which European diplomatic negotiation could be played out. But there is more to the thesis than this.

Nationalism must be considered. As has frequently been asserted, nationalism had the qualities of a secularized religion; it suggested the purposes and the destiny of the society upholding it. In the United States the idea of "Manifest Destiny," of the belief that divine purpose directed this nation westward to the Pacific, is a well-known expression of this sentiment. The German soldiers who wore belt buckles in World War I with the words *Gott mit uns* on them is a less significant, but no less telling example. Each western nation tended to develop a grand national myth about its unique and destined goals. In broad and poetic terms, these myths were all translated to the colonial world in variations of Kipling's famous words: "the white man's burden."

France, Great Britain, and the other colonizers had a duty to bring the benefits of their advanced civilization to the world beyond their geographical limits. Here is a smug and simple argument, but one of great appeal in the late nineteenth century when European technological superiority could be measured. It was easy to conclude that the steam engine was a manifestation of European cultural superiority in all domains. As one French cynic put it: the Chinese were supposedly inferior because they had no machine guns or generals like Moltke, the Prussian who directed the stunning German military defeat of France in 1870. This failure or unwillingness to distinguish wisely between technology and culture allowed the Europeans to be arrogant, and, moreover, to assume that in any arrangement of the world they were at the head or in the center.

Buttressing this contention was a pseudo-scientific attitude known by the name "Social Darwinism." Darwin's theory of evolution, first espoused in his famous book *On the Origin of Species*, published in 1859, was extended and distorted to include social organisms as well as biological ones. Not Darwin, but lesser minds and less cautious ones, suggested that the state or society was like a biological organism: it grew or it died—the alternatives were that stark. In a world already described by capitalist economics as being "competitive," the biological contentions that all species "struggle for survival" and that the strongest would survive could be and easily were made social laws.

Nationalism now carried the striking corollary that the state needed to expand, to grow in size as proof of its vitality and as confirmation of its historical destiny. Given the fact that this was the age in which bigness had already acquired qualitative value, it was easy for nationalists to conclude that the bigger the state in size, the greater it was in culture or civilization. The terms "Greater Britain," "Greater France," and even "Greater Germany" were bandied about as expressions of national pride in overseas political enterprises. The notion that the "sun never sets on the British Empire" was a comforting thought for the late nineteenth-century English. When the German foreign minister, Prince von Bulow, asserted that Germany seeks "her place in the sun," he was hoping for a similar condition.

These new perceptions of the place of European nations in the world suggest that an age of global politics was emerging. Naval power was then at its zenith: the Americans sent the "Great White Fleet" around the world during the administration of President Theodore Roosevelt; the British launched the latest in battleship design with the *Dreadnought* in 1906. And the Germans, hoping to threaten, if not compete equally with the British, began a large navy in 1898 under the watchful eye of Admiral Tirpitz and the proud gaze of Kaiser Wilhelm II. To support these new oceanic fleets in their world mission, coaling stations and naval ports were deemed necessary. The port of Singapore, the city of Dakar in Senegal, the base at San Diego—and many other lesser known geographical locations—were linked into grand "lifelines of empire," of which the British "red line" was the most famous: going from England, past Gibraltar, through the Suez Canal, beyond Aden to India. And the new canals—the Panama and the Kiel—were manifestly assets in this naval age, the means by which to move fleets quickly from one body of water to another. Thus, a strategic component was added to the many reasons, or justifications, for imperialism.

The causal pattern of modern imperialism was complicated and extensive. Equally important, it was not all Eurocentric. The explanations adduced above clearly suggest that imperialism radiated from its center in Europe out to the peripheries of the non-Western world. However, historical patterns are neither so symmetrical nor so singularly directed. Beyond the grand generalizations concerning an expansionist capitalism or a glory-seeking nationalism are the vexing peculiarities of the "local scene": the activities carried on by merchant, adventurer, soldier, or missionary, far from the capitals of Europe —and often equally far from the thinking taking place in them.

Many contemporary historians are persuaded that the periphery often acted on the center: in terms of physics, the activity was centripetal as well as centrifugal. A local revolt, coastal competition among vying European merchants, problems with local rulers or local pirates, all were factors upsetting the local balance of power and necessitating the intervention of the home country, if the position of its local nationals—again the merchant, missionary, adventurer, and soldier—was to be maintained. As the peculiarities of regional history are examined, the simple pattern of a Eurocentric imperialism is found wanting. The activity occurring on the local scene in Africa or Asia may have propelled an unwilling or unprepared government into imperialist activity it really had no national interest in. In this respect, imperialism can be considered national reaction to local "accidents."

What remains important, regardless of the causes that inspired it, is the acquisition of such incredibly large and varied colonial empires throughout the world.

Europe's Imperial Age

On the occasion of Queen Victoria's Diamond Jubilee in 1897, a grand parade brought onto the streets of London the panoply of empire. Soldiers and residents from all parts of the far-flung British Empire moved in colorful array, a living tableau depicting the grandeur of empire. It was a glorious moment—for the British, of course—and the last of such magnitude before the apparent solidity of the imperial foundation was found truly defective. Across the Channel, a few years before, the French celebrated the anniversary of their great revolution in 1889 with an international exhibition, at which products and peoples from the French overseas empire were displayed for Parisians to admire. Far away from all this, and a few years later, Kaiser Wilhelm II appeared in 1898 in the Holy Land. He assumed the role of a latter-day Teutonic knight, his handsome military uniform encircled in a magnificent white cape, and his head crowned with an eagle-guarded helmet.

These separate acts, amusing and pretentious when seen in retrospect, can be understood as nationally satisfying when set in their own times and among the people for whom they were performed. Beyond or behind the pageantry of empire was the reality of Europe's political domination of the world.

It was a flimsy, ill-conceived domination, however. The working principle upon which the operation of empire was maintained was this: the colonies should cost the colonizing country little or nothing. Empire "on the cheap" was the English phrase to describe the condition. And so, very little of striking innovation or permanence was introduced. The chief purpose was to guarantee an administrative system capable of providing peaceful conditions in which trade could flourish and revenues be sufficiently collected so that the administration would be self-supporting. (There was something rather circular about it.)

The effects on the indigenous populations were generally disruptive. Older cultural systems were jarred by the European presence with its different set of values and purposes. Perhaps the most revolutionary of European changes was that of the global market economic system. Not only did this system tend to destroy the sustenance economies that still existed in many parts of the world by substituting cash crops for local food crops, but also it introduced the monied wage that tended to break down the older family and communally centered societies in which work was divided on the basis of need, not organized around income. Moreover, the requirements of the new market economy were not parallel with those of local needs. Cash crops frequently meant the creation of monocultures: agriculture based on a single crop or a dominant crop, such as peanuts in Senegal, tea in Ceylon, cocoa in the Gold Coast. Through such a system many of the basic food needs of the colony were often not locally produced. For instance, the importation of rice from Indochina into West Africa became a common practice of the later French colonial empire.

If, then, colonial empires had a jarring effect on local cultures, what were their effects on Europe proper? First, it must be stressed that empire was not an exceptionally popular business; it was more often than not greeted simply with national acceptance, except on those grand occasions of state, like Victoria's jubilees, or those dramatic moments as when the English General Charles Gordon was killed by the dervishes, religious militants, at Khartoum in the Sudan in 1885. For the most part, imperialism was viewed as an understandable part of a modern nation's activities, further proof of the state's energies or "vocation." In the cabinet meetings, where state policies were generally formulated, empire was secondary to continental considerations. Or, put otherwise, it was an extension, not a totally different realm, of foreign policy. The many colonial entanglements between France and Great Britain toward the end of the century were measured in terms of the national rivalry that had long existed between these two nations. That no major international conflict broke out between European nations over a colonial matter is partial proof of the secondary nature of imperialism to European politics, as it also is partial proof that the "concert system" still had some life in it: negotiation was preferred to military engagement.

Yet in another sense, imperialism both expressed and gave further rise to the inflated thinking and bombastic rhetoric of the late nineteenth century. It was scarcely a modest age, and it was becoming less and less a rational one, if newspaper headlines and public oratory were to be believed. There was a lot of diplomatic swagger and sword rattling, but in no country more than Germany. Well before the World War broke out, German talk of *Weltpolitik*, of establishing a world role and a world politics by which England could be challenged, was common. And some of the French were obviously anxious to test their manhood in the colonies, far away from a stolid and stultifying middleclassdom that they deprecated. Morocco was soon described as a "school of energy," where, through pursuit of an active, outdoor life, the youth of the day would be prepared for the arduous national tasks of the morrow.

What we today recognize as a spirit of machismo complicated the continental political situation by enhancing popular receptivity to an aggressive mood. It was already there for some time, frozen in the British term "jingoism."

We don't want to fight but by jingo if we do,
We've got the ships, we've got the men, we've got the money too.

These lines date back to the 1870s and represent a popular English reaction to possible war with Russia over the fate of Constantinople. But they have come to explain the chauvinistic nationalism that ran throughout Europe at the end of the century. And so, in the popular thought of then contemporary Europe, imperialism was expressive of an expansionist mood, of a sense of pride over national effort and also of a fear of competing neighbors that conditioned all too many Europeans to the possibility, indeed the excitement, of possible war, while they still pursued their peaceful ways, generally confident in their collective national purposes.

Conclusion

In its formative and reformative phases, the European state system rapidly extended outward to include overseas empire. With the rise of the dynastic or monarchical state of Western Europe in the sixteenth and seventeenth centuries, the first European empires were founded; they coincided rather neatly with the reign of the "new monarchs" like Queen Elizabeth I or King Louis XIV. Then, two centuries later, with the reformation of that state system and the successful establishment of a collection of nation-states, now including Germany and Italy, another wave of major expansion took place. More than coincidence seems to have existed between these two sets of occurrences.

The close correlation between national power and economic development has been frequently commented upon. The mercantilism of the earlier period has been revisited in the later period with the term "neo-mercantilism," used to describe the protectionist tariffs of the late nineteenth century and the search for new and "safe" colonial markets and sources of raw materials. In both historical situations, major technological breakthroughs help explain the success of empire: in the first instance, new sailing techniques and instruments, the perfection of the ship-located cannon, capable of firing a broadside against other ships and coastal defenses; in the second instance, the steam engine and the machine gun were the generators of imperial power.

However, in the late nineteenth century, the mood of imperialism was part of a larger mood of expansiveness, of increasingly generated power in the factory, in the laboratory, on the battlefield. Power was real in a reading of a nation's steel index. And power was symbolically and historically displayed in the national flags that were solemnly raised and lowered in all the parts of the world where Europe was present.

For those who believed in and practiced it, imperialism can now be seen as a preface to the dramatic summer of 1914 when young men, bent upon heroic action and dedicated to the pursuit of national glory, rushed from both sides to the western front.

7

Discontent and Tension

At the present rate of progression . . . it will not need another century or half century to turn thoughts upside down. Law in that case would disappear . . . and give place to force. Morality would become police. Explosives would reach cosmic violence.

HENRY ADAMS
1905

       In French history the years at the turn of the twentieth century are called *La Belle Epoque*, that delightful time when bourgeois life seemed at its richest and fullest. The comforts of earthly existence were everywhere apparent: top hats, electricity, interior plumbing, telephones, spacious boulevards in growing cities. More significantly, the franc was as good as gold because it was minted in that metal and therefore readily acceptable and well invested around the world. Perhaps the most opulent development of the time was the elevation of the ancient Roman custom of the banquet to a grand bourgeois art. Tables groaned under magnificent gastronomic creations, and middle-class stomachs frequently displayed the roundness of overcontentment. It was during this era that Maxim's became an internationally renowned dining spot, and that the *cordon bleu*, originally a royal award of chivalry, was widely recognized as the sign of excellent cooking.

       What has been said of France could equally be said of England, Austria, Germany, or Italy. The middle classes were well satisfied, the world in which they circulated seemed settled and secure. "An excessive value on the placidity of existence," was the way the English philosopher Alfred North White-head once described this situation.

Yet that placidity was seen by many critics as only a surface condition. Beneath the routine of daily life they found indications of weak supports: false beliefs, wrong goals, unwarranted smugness. Doubt and disdain about the very nature of modern civilization were attitudes assumed by some intellectuals and social activists. The growing materialism of the age, the seemingly excessive concern with physical comfort, and the social hypocrisy of the middle classes—these were subjects that figured in so much contemporary art: the plays of Henrik Ibsen and George Bernard Shaw, the novels of Samuel Butler and André Gide, the cartoons in the English publication *Punch* and the German publication *Simplissimus*.

Moreover, some of the sentiments of social critics ran through darker and deeper currents. There was an undercurrent of discontent and fear. Like the hero in Robert Louis Stevenson's *The Strange Case of Dr. Jekyll and Mr. Hyde*—a novel appearing in 1886—European society seemed to be creating an unpleasant and uncontrollable nature, the direct outcome of its own conceit. How long modern civilization could maintain the peaceful balance achieved by the forward motion generated by science and industry was a question asked long before the outbreak of World War I.

Beneath and Beyond Calculation and Reason

In 1878 Thomas Masaryk, future founding president of the Republic of Czechoslovakia, completed his study, *Suicide and the Meaning of Civilization*. The study was one of the first on a subject that was of growing public interest. Masaryk estimated that some fifty thousand people took their own lives annually in Europe. This dreadful social phenomenon led him to want "to show how suicide as a general or 'mass' phenomenon had developed out of and is part of modern culture." Although Masaryk has been proven wrong in his assumption that suicide is an outgrowth of modernity, his general concern with the underlying disorder of his age was not misplaced. To many of his contemporaries the world was something less—or more—than a rational place.

Since the Enlightenment, the principle of reason had provided the norm for human behavior. Democratic politics and scientific investigation were based upon it. And so was the market system, which assumed that everyone calculated to his own benefit. The prevailing intellectual attitude of the century was, in effect, a combination of Hegel's premise that "all which is real is rational, and all which is rational is real," and the empirical approach to scientific observation, an approach that basically considered the rational mind to be informed by the sense of sight. What is seen can be scientifically assessed—this was a nineteenth-century postulate. In such a view of things man was considered not to be an actor or doer, but primarily a dispassionate observer on the sidelines of the world, a thinking creature who only notes what happens around him.

Dissent from this interpretation was strong toward the end of the century, although the Romantics of the early century had raised objections chiefly of a literary sort. Contrary to the scientific belief in external reality, the Romantics only saw outer appearances and inner truth. For them the imagination transcended the sense of sight; it alone provided meaning, hence understanding. Put otherwise, it was insight that determined outlook. Later, the English playwright Oscar Wilde expressed this thought when he asserted that life imitates art, that the artist teaches us to see, to appreciate, and—above all—to value. In this way human beings impose their feelings and inspirations upon reality. The world is shaped by the imagination.

Such thought harbored spiritual qualities that the scientific positivism of the later century ignored or denied. For Masaryk this was the key to an understanding of contemporary suicide. He argued (in italics): *"In our schools, large and small, only the intellect is cultivated."* A struggle between learning and religion thus ensues, with the result that *"no perfect character can be created, only an intellectual and moral chaos."*

The incomplete or disjointed psyche of modern man, which Masaryk singled out as the root cause of suicidal tendencies, was one that appeared in many contemporary assessments. The French author Emile Durkheim, author of another and far more important study on suicide published in 1897, found the modern cultural condition to be one of anomie, of rootlessness or unrelatedness. Without well-articulated and arranged values, the individual could not relate to the world, could not find a satisfactory place in it, and thus was lost. The anomic condition was one of cultural despair. On a more popular level, critics argued that the whole person was only found when the individual engaged in acts of commitment, in personal self-assertion.

A new mysticism, a blend of action and devotion, appeared in religion, in nationalism, and in imperialism. If there was a key word that figured in the vocabulary of many writers, it was "will." "Will" was clearly a metaphysical term, beyond any simple means of scientific measurement. It was even enshrouded in further ambiguity in the phrase "will-to-power," coined by the German philosopher Friedrich Nietzsche (1844–1900). Taken out of its author's context, the term was soon popularized to mean forceful assertion, domination, even rule of the weak by the strong and thus disrespect, or contempt for the common man. Nietzsche perhaps intended none of this, but his writing lent itself well to brief excerpts, and he was thereby more often quoted than read, and made something of a prophet in the early twentieth century.

It is worth noting that Nietzsche, along with a considerable number of other contemporary writers, used the word "energy" as a synonym for "will." Both industrial power and human power were related; the nineteenth century concluded on a theme of force, as well as on a theme of peaceful progress. For the American Henry Adams, the "dynamo" had replaced the "Virgin" as the symbol of the times. It was energy, not contemplation; force, not beauty, that he saw prevailing.

These attitudes, if suddenly pronounced, had been forming for several decades. They certainly found an early focal point in Charles Darwin's work. His publication of *On the Origin of Species* was a moment of excitement in 1859. The book had the quality of being "timely": it appeared when educated people were toying with the ideas of change and evolution, of what one author has described as "the historical articulation of nature." The interest in change-through-time was a keen nineteenth-century one and helps explain the popularity then enjoyed by history. But Darwin added a scientific authority which had hitherto been lacking to the subject.

On the Origin of Species was a scientific explanation of animal evolution. Darwin offered as the operating principle of change the idea of "natural selection," a process through which certain forms of life adapted better— more efficiently—to their environment and thus survived. Darwin's thought revolutionized biology, aroused religious controversy, and inspired a reinterpretation of social science.

Within two decades of the book's publication, Social Darwinism—the application, extension, and distortion of Darwin's biological analysis to social behavior—had spread throughout Europe. Society was now conceived as being an extended organism, with its own life-cycle, its own competitive principles, its own collective desire to survive. "Struggle for survival" and "survival of the fittest," terms earlier employed by Darwin to explain his biological theories, now became thrilling slogans for an age of commercial and political competition. Thus Social Darwinism provided a pseudo-scientific justification for imperial expansion, for military aggression, and for the forceful assertion of the nation as well as of the individual. One of the most popular social commentators in late nineteenth-century France, Gustave Le Bon, stated: "The right of the strongest! This is the only law which is always imposed, and it is also the one which has allowed humanity to progress the most." The statement appeared in Le Bon's *The First Civilizations*, published in 1889, a century after the French revolutionaries had issued The Declaration of the Rights of Man and Citizen.

This pessimistic and deterministic mood washed over the democratic principles which had been the hope of thinkers in the early century. A new conservatism, unrestrained by an older aristocratic base, added a new ideological component to European thought. The forerunner of what would be known in our times as "The Radical Right," this conservatism combined, often in a clumsy but appealing way, several points of view.

First, there was virulent or chauvinistic nationalism, trumpeted about in phrases asserting the "blood-bond" of the community, its unique historical position, and the glories of war as a manifestation of the nation's strength and power. Nationalism, hitherto generous in its acceptance of the idea that all peoples had the right to define themselves and to live together harmoniously, now became exclusive and bellicose. An oppositional relationship, one expressing the virtues of one people or nation and the weaknesses of another, quickened the spirit of international rivalry and fear. The German historian Heinrich von Treitschke (1834–1896), one of the most influential academic figures of his day, excited his students with statements like this: "Again and again, it has been proven that it is war which turns a people into a nation." And Houston Stewart Chamberlain, English son-in-law of the German composer Richard Wagner and an important theorist of the German racial cult, wrote in 1910: "We are left with the simple and clear view that our whole civilization and culture of today is the work of one definite race of men, the Teutonic." Nationalism distorted history into the forceful triumph of one group of people who were culturally, and frequently racially, made to appear as strikingly different from their neighbors.

Second, there was a contempt for parliamentary practices. As democracy triumphed in political fact—with the extension of the franchise—its distractors found it weak and indecisive, not assertive. A French author, Emile Faguet, wrote a book entitled *The Cult of Incompetence* (1910), the subject of which was democracy, and the theme of which was the mediocrity of democratic rule. Moreover, political process was given a new interpretation with the idea of the "elite." The concept was formulated by the Italian philosopher Vilfredo Pareto in his work *Socialist Systems* (1902). It was not classes in opposition, he argued—and thereby dismissed Marx and his theory —but elites, groupings of superior men itching for power, who contended with one another to gain control of society by using the masses as tools to support their struggle. The autonomous individual of liberal philosophy was now replaced by the manipulated masses of the new conservative philosophy. It is interesting to note that Benito Mussolini would later state that he learned much from Pareto.

The mind that accepted this new conservatism rejected the social results of both the French and the Industrial Revolutions. Authoritarian, it mocked parliamentary procedures and described them as ineffective. Elitist, it treated the urban, industrial masses with contempt, as objects to be directed or dominated. And, somewhat romantically, it turned to view the countryside, where it claimed the real people resided. These, supposedly, were the folk sturdily attached to the soil and leading a life of simple devotion and vigorous action, while their city brethren calculated and rationalized for their own selfish advantage. Anti-semitism, which grew virulently in the late nineteenth century, was greatly reinforced by the notion of the Jew as the true city dweller, an individual without a soul or compassion—a schemer.

If such opinion as this was only mildly disturbing—if noticed at all—to most members of the middle classes or the growing proletariat who lived in those sunlit years of *La Belle Epoque*, it was soon to be of major importance. The darkly hued thoughts expressed at the turn of the twentieth century, those briefly reviewed above, marked a transition between two differing concepts of the human condition. In the seventeenth century Descartes had proclaimed, "I think therefore I am." In the twentieth century the Nazi philosopher Alfred Rosenberg claimed, "We think with our blood."

Moreover, the changing mood was itself formed by a number of social groupings, some in protest against bourgeois comfort and democratic purposes, others against oppressive authority. Youth, an influential social category throughout the nineteenth century, now contained a pronounced element that was illiberal, given to desperate action, revolutionary or militant or both. In Russia, student riots grew more violent and anarchistic, directed toward the paralysis, if not the overthrow, of the autocratic regime. Political assassination appeared as an accepted tactic, with Tsar Alexander II, one of the most prominent victims of the thrown bomb in 1881. Often conspiratorial in nature, actionist in purpose, and fatalistic in mood—a sense of foreboding, of inevitable death, characterized the thought of many youthful anarchists—these individuals were dedicated terrorists, modern political figures who expected acts of violence to change the social order of things.

Peace was no longer accepted as a good in-and-of-itself by some Western European youth of middle-class origin. In Italy of the early twentieth century, the "Futurist" movement, both artistic and political in form, grouped a number of young intellectuals yearning for action. The writer Filippo Marinetti (1876–1944), chief figure in the movement, offered what amounted to a manifesto: "We want to glorify war, the world's only hygiene." In France a collection of ardent imperialists looked upon the sands of Africa as the environment in which to rejuvenate their old nation. There, in the words of Hubert Lyautey, future marshal of France, "our race is being retempered and recast as if in a crucible." From England, Lord Baden-Powell, founder of the Boy Scouts, offered this remark: "Better than football, better than any other game, is man-hunting."

Thus, to the growing complexities of European international politics was added the volatile element of a new cultural discontent. It was to have a conditioning effect, making some youth anxious for war and inspired to serve happily when it came, making some statesmen impatient with the practice of diplomatic compromise and somewhat reckless in their plans, and making many citizens all too willing to sacrifice their newly gained liberties when some mystical national destiny was held before them.

When the diplomats failed at their task and the militarists were allowed to display their grand plans for battle, a generation of young people willingly went to war, and a generation of middle-aged people cheered them on.

The Delicate Balance of Diplomacy

Behind such a mood was the detailed map of Europe. By 1914 the political lines were ensnarled with criss-crossing lines of alliance. Never before in European history had there been such extensive and long-formed alliances of military defense in a period of peace. The older balance of power, predicated upon the principle of individual state initiative and diplomatic flexibility, was replaced by blocs of alliances and alignments, holding Europe together politically, much like a suspension bridge between two opposing foundations, in a state of tension.

It would, however, be a grave historical error to imagine that the alliance system was neatly and concretely erected as if a simple problem in political engineering. The process, if it can even be called that, was hesitant, complex, and incomplete. For, indeed, the one side, gravitating around Germany, was well bound by carefully worked out defensive military alliances, while the other side, gravitating around France, was held more by general agreements or "understandings."

The history of the alliance systems begins with the dramatic shift in European political power dating from 1870 and Germany's defeat of France in the Franco-Prussian War of that year. Since the days of Louis XIV, France had been the dominant European power, her army the most effective and generally threatening. That French was the language of European diplomats is one obvious indication of the significance France enjoyed in the political world. Now an age of Germanic hegemony began, one that would last through the days of Adolf Hitler. With its large population (approaching 60 million at the turn of the century), its new and well-organized industrial machine, and its successfully battle-tested army, Germany dominated the Continent.

The historical vision we today have of Germany was not the contemporary view of those who witnessed the fall of France. France had long been the European troublemaker, the expansionist state whose most recent ruler, Napoleon III (1852–1870), was the nephew of the great Napoleon. From the perspective of the European chancelleries, Napoleon III was a *parvenu*, a political opportunist, both muddle-headed and deluded by grandeur. His defeat by Prussia/Germany was not generally lamented.

Equally important was the diplomatic finesse with which Bismarck conducted German affairs. Under him Germany was a satisfied nation, pleased to enjoy a status quo—after 1870, of course—in which its interests were respected and secure. Germany was now united, and Bismarck was not pressing for further territorial aggrandizement. It was in this general context that Bismarck could play the role of "honest broker," a term he applied to himself during the Congress of Berlin, 1878, when the European powers joined to regulate the peace terms following a brief Russo-Turkish War. Germany therefore appeared as no threat, but as a responsible member of the European community.

From across the Rhine, on the French side, no such observation was made, as might be expected. On the contrary, the condition of national hatred that the French now generated for the Germans was even constructed into a grand historical myth, forced back in time to the Gauls, when the Germanic tribes supposedly were aggressors against France. Now, the German annexation of the French provinces of Alsace and Lorraine, the financial indemnity imposed by Germany, and the severe hurt to national pride suffered when the French army ignominiously collapsed, made the leaders of the French nation bitterly attentive to Germany.

Conversely, Bismarck feared the possibility of a war of revenge on the part of the French, and French propagandists even called for one. The fear was not taken lightly, for Bismarck knew that France had not been gravely weakened by the recent military encounter. That the financial indemnity was paid off in less than three years was proof that France was still a very powerful nation.

Bismarck's military concerns shaped his diplomatic actions. He feared what he called a "nightmare of coalitions," one that would bring France and Russia together and thus leave Germany open to double attack. Both German diplomats and soldiers wished ardently to avoid a two-front war, one that they knew Germany could not successfully wage. Geography had denied Germany any meaningful natural boundaries against military attack, and nature had made her a nation dependent on many imports to sustain her humming industrial machine. All of this clearly in his mind, Bismarck sought the military security of Germany and the diplomatic isolation of France.

The Bismarckian alliance system came to rest on two major defensive alliances. The first was the Dual Alliance of 1879 that joined Austria to Germany in case of a military attack by Russia. Put simply, the terms stated that if one of the two states was attacked by Russia, the other would offer military support. The second alliance was the Triple Alliance of 1882, now joining Italy with Austria and Germany, and extending the defensive arrangement against France as well as Russia. By these two alliances, Germany was assured of diplomatic and military support should a war break out.

Against these alliances appeared another system, perhaps better defined as a loose confederation. It was inspired by France, and the year 1890 is its initial point. That was the year Wilhelm II "dropped the pilot"—*Punch* magazine published a cartoon describing Wilhelm's dismissal of Bismarck in this manner, thereby suggesting a ship of state without guidance. Now France took the diplomatic initiative, both because of the relative tranquility of her domestic situation and the growing concern over German foreign policy.

Historians have argued that Wilhelm II and his advisers were reckless in their handling of diplomatic matters. The emperor frequently used bombastic rhetoric, speaking of Teutonic crusaders and harping on Germany's greatness. The foreign policy of his government was directed to a new *Weltpolitik*, a world political policy of searching after places in the sun, or, less metaphorically, an effort to break out of what Germans considered their continental confinement. To play a world role commensurate with the nation's new industrial and military stature, Germany would necessarily encounter England basking in the sun. To many Germans, England was the chief source of German political confinement. As for France, the Germans made some threatening gestures, precipitating two crises, in 1905 and 1911, over Morocco, where the French had laid tentative claims to empire. German bluster soon turned out to be diplomatic blunder, and that state was cast in an isolated position, only resulting in further German frustration.

Hastily sketched, these are the conditions which both explain the French effort at international alliance and, in turn, explain the diplomatic setbacks of Germany. In 1894 France succeeded in her pursuit of Russia, and the two states signed a defensive military alliance, each assuring the other of military support in case of attack from Germany. The Franco-Russian Alliance, this improbable alliance between the most revolutionary and the most reactionary country of Europe of the time, was signed, and, with it, the possibility of a two-front war became a German probability. Then in 1904 the French and the English reconciled their long-smouldering colonial differences and signed the Entente Cordiale, a diplomatic gentleman's agreement, reducing friction, arranging political differences in North Africa, and preparing for the exchange of military views. This was no alliance, but a step toward one and an assurance of further cooperation in times of international stress. In 1907 England and Russia drew up a similar entente, settling their major points of contention in Persia, and, again, leading to the possibility of military understanding.

There were the two camps: the German, holding to it Austria and Italy in alliance; the French, holding to it Russia in alliance, and England in "understanding." With the exception of the Italian shift to the French camp in 1915, the major European belligerents of World War I were grouped together, and in opposition by 1907. But this did not necessarily mean war.

War Clouds

Europe underwent a series of crises in the first decade of the twentieth century, in Morocco, in the Balkans, in the Far East. None disrupted the European state system, but each and all suggested the growing spirit of belligerency and the decline of moderation in diplomatic affairs. The mood of the intellectuals, described earlier in this chapter, now expanded to more popular dimensions. Both French and German military theorists taught their soldiers the glories of the offensive, preached about the manliness of the charge, and about the anticipated heroics to be obtained by the use of the bayonet. War was claimed to be the crucible in which the metal (and mettle) of the nation would be tested. The metaphor is a mawkish one, but it was often used. In the most popular novel to emerge from World War I, Erich Maria Remarque's *All Quiet on the Western Front*, the high school youth are told—by a history teacher, ironically—that they are the "Iron Youth" who must gloriously fight and conquer for the Fatherland.

Matching this increasingly strident tone of nationalism, in which the clash of steel was converted into a poetry of noble endeavor, was the increasing armaments race. The first decade of the twentieth century was one in which the Germans created a navy designed not to defeat but to thwart the navy of Great Britain. Initiated with the naval acts of 1898 and 1900, this navy was constructed to conform with Admiral Tirpitz's "risk theory." The "risk" was to Great Britain, which would be sufficiently matched by the German navy to risk in a war the loss of enough of its ships so that the British "two-power standard"—maintenance of a fleet capable of encountering any two others—would be destroyed. In sum, the German navy would so reduce the British navy that Germany and her allies would master the sea. The English did not rejoice at the sight of German vessels being launched. With the introduction of the Dreadnought series in 1906, England reemphasized her naval position and went the way of even bigger, more heavily armed battleships, another display of European fascination with size and power.

Standing armies also reached impressive proportions: Germany had about a half million men under arms in peacetime, and France was not far behind. Each nation devised new weapons, and each concentrated seriously on strategy. In this new industrial age, even strategy was forced to conform to timetables: the Germans meticulously planned out an offensive, with arrival times in various parts of Belgium and France calculated nearly with the exactness of the schedules maintained by crack express trains.

The German plan was named after its creator, Count von Schlieffen (1833–1913). Schlieffen reasoned as had Bismarck and all other major German strategists since that time: Germany could not wage a successful two-front war. With the Franco-Russian alliance a stark reality after 1894, he had to choose which state he would attempt to knock out of the future war first. France was selected for this dubious honor, but for clear reasons. The mobilization of Russia would be slower, the military potential of France was greater. Better catch the stronger, better prepared state offguard first; such was the essence of the thought behind the Schlieffen Plan. Translated into military terms, it meant that the Germans would maintain a holding action on the eastern front against Russia, while they would move rapidly and daringly against France. What the Germans needed was the element of surprise; what they counted on was the precision of their military maneuvers.

Like a hinged door, with its hinge situated around Metz, the German armies would move through the lowlands, violating Belgian neutrality, and invade France from the Northwest. If all went well, these armies would penetrate south of Paris, thus isolating the capital and cutting off the French armies from support deep in France. Here was a brilliant military plan, requiring the courage of keeping the "hinged" area of the German front rather weak so that the concentration of troops at the "swinging door" portion to the Northwest would be strong and therefore assure a rapid "swing." Schlieffen himself said the plan would require a Frederick the Great to achieve its success. No such general was available on either side in 1914.

Without further excursion through the sandtables upon which the Germans played out their plans, one can see that the Schlieffen Plan was not one that could be accommodated to slow diplomacy and careful political deliberation. If the conditions of war were at hand, the plan could only work if it were seized upon and acted upon readily. In sum, German military planning had placed diplomatic considerations in the rear. The anxiety of war was only compounded by the rapidity of enactment that the Schlieffen Plan presupposed.

No other nation had concocted anything from the chemistry of war that matched the German plan, but all were convinced that the offensive was the necessary posture to assume. Why? The answer is disarmingly simple. Almost all strategists thought that modern warfare was bound to be short. First, the industrial state was too sensitive to endure a war of long duration, a war of attrition. Second, and clearly related to the first argument, the expenses of modern warfare would be too much for any state to endure. Third, there was historical confirmation of the "short-war" thesis. Both of the recent major European wars were effectively over in a matter of a few weeks; such was the interpretation of the Franco-Prussian War of 1870 and the Russo-Japanese War of 1904–1905. A "summer war," this is what generals, politicians, and the public at large thought would happen. Hence the war would be fought and won by the standing armies with no need for the reserves. The entire argument conspired to place an emphasis on the offensive. Whoever moved first and swiftest would no doubt win.

That such thought as this could have been received with equanimity by many Europeans is proof of the fascination with war that then held the imagination. Many historians have commented that the long period of peace and comfort Europe had enjoyed led to the romanticism of war. Removed from actual life, warfare had become the stuff of early science fiction with Jules Verne and H. G. Wells commenting on it. Wells wrote as a prophet, his message a warning; but to many of his readers, his words were thrilling fictions, producing a slight chill of the spine just before retirement to an eiderdown-covered bed.

Conclusion

In the two decades before the outbreak of World War I, there were dramatic signs that the European mood and the international political condition were changing drastically. Prophets of doom and heralds of elitism had scornfully dismissed the virtues of democracy and the results of industrialism. The older "concert" of Europe had given way to the noisy confusion of nations jostling against one another and into new alliances. How easy it is for us to see this as a period preparatory to destruction. But it was not so perceived by most people living at the time.

All of these signs of impending doom were not clearly noticed by the masses of Europeans who still thought they were living in a "century of progress." Indeed, the impressive number of turn-of-the-century commemorative books, forerunners of our "coffee table editions," were lavishly illustrated with the wonders of the age, and the prose in which they were couched painted a purple word picture of greater wonders yet to come.

The age clearly has its element of drama, of impending tragedy and general unawareness. European civilization was at its pinnacle, at a height never again to be attained. In almost all fields of human endeavor, the Europeans were in the forefront, perhaps already being surpassed by the Americans in industrial prowess, but nonetheless visibly the center of a world system. The war would slowly grind this position down and leave behind a multitude of problems, many of which were never solved.

The complacency of the age was in its own greatness and in a disinclination to believe seriously that one war could possibly destroy it all. The guns that opened fire on the western front in August of 1914 shattered all dreams and all delusions.

8

The War

On the idle hill of summer,
  Sleepy with the flow of streams,
Far I hear the steady drummer
  Drumming like a noise in dreams.
                    A. E. HOUSMAN "Shropshire Lad"

Four years, three months, and one week after it began, the world war ended. Its political and economic effects would continue for another twenty years. As for the psychological and cultural impact it generated, there is no means of statistical or chronological measurement. "The war has ruined us for everything," woefully commented one of the characters in Remarque's *All Quiet on the Western Front*. It ruined many and much: lives, property, ambitions, ideals. "Progress," that simple word and widespread European ideal, would never again be piously proclaimed.

Yet such dismal thoughts as these filled few minds in the summer of 1914. A *frischer und fröhlicher Krieg*, a "fresh and joyous war," was what was generally expected. It was to have provided much excitement, many opportunities for heroic action; and it would leave as its rewards medals to display and acts of glory to recount before a winter fire, and over a glass of port or a stein of beer. And so German soldiers, wearing fresh flowers on their field-gray uniforms, proudly paraded before cheering Berliners; while French infantry in blue jackets and red trousers gathered at the Parisian railroad stations, where they were greeted by lilting military marches and finely dressed female admirers.

This bright moment was very short. It did not last beyond the summer.

The Schlieffen Plan nearly succeeded, but did not. Against the relentless and well-timed advance of the Germans, the French suddenly rushed reinforcements northward to keep the "swinging door" from closing on their nation. The two rival military forces now began what has been called the "rush to the sea," in reality an improvised set of actions on the part of the Germans to maneuver around the French, and an equally hasty effort on the part of the French to prevent this. Each side moved laterally until the North Sea was reached.

For the next four years the war was in fact a stalemate, an unrelieved linear war, with two forces sufficiently matched to prevent one or the other from "unlocking the front," from breaking through the enemy lines. Therefore, it is best to imagine the military scene as composed of two parallel lines, separated by a newly created wasteland, a "no man's land" dug out of French soil by artillery fire and kept starkly barren by the constant interplay of machine guns and the presence of twisted coils of barbed wire.

The parallel lines were, of course, the rows of trenches in which the soldiers stood, slept, cursed, and waited, until the signal for an attack on the other side was given. Seldom more than a few miles of territory were yielded by one force or the other in these wanton exercises. The battlelines therefore remained nearly static.

What was the result of this unanticipated military situation? The war has been described as a grand artillery duel. And it was that. The Germans concentrated 1,400 guns along an eight-mile front for the opening of the Battle of Verdun in 1916. They also stocked 2,500,000 shells for the occasion. In the following year, at the Battle of the Chemin des Dames, the Germans concentrated 2,541 artillery pieces, while the French and English concentrated 3,810. Figures such as these were repeated in the preparations for all the major battles.

The war has been described as a war of attrition, in which each side was drained economically and demographically. And it was that. By 1918 the war was costing $25 million an hour. As a result, France and England lost their positions as the world's two great creditors; they both became debtors, notably to the United States. And Germany was so badly hit financially by the war and by subsequent war costs that a postwar inflation reached the preposterous situation in October 1923, when 62 billion marks were worth only one dollar. The demographic situation was even more horrible. The war bled Europe white. In 1918 France was losing a soldier every minute. All told, some 9 million combatants were killed in the war, some 7 million permanently disabled, another 15 million seriously wounded.

The war has been described as a new and unusually grotesque social experience, one in which a "lost generation" was spawned, a multinational group of front-line soldiers who were no longer convinced of the good purposes of European civilization or of the fundamental decency of human beings. And it was that. Hundreds of accounts described conditions like the following, from Robert Graves, *Good-Bye To All That*:

> *Cuinchy-bred rats. They came up from the canal, fed on the plentiful corpses and multiplied exceedingly. While I fought there with the Welsh, a new officer joined the company and, in token of welcome, was given a dug-out containing a spring-bed. When he turned in that night, he heard a scuffling, shone his torch [flashlight] on the bed, and found two rats on his blankets tussling for the possession of a severed hand. This story circulated as a great joke.*

The Changing Military Dimensions of the War

The war began in the tangled confusion of Balkan politics. The immediate cause was the assassination on June 28, 1914, of the heir to the Austrian throne, the archduke Francis Ferdinand, at Sarajevo in Bosnia. The act had been carried out by members of "The Black Hand," a terrorist group opposed to the Austrian political presence in the Balkans and operating out of Serbia. Within a month the Austrians used this tragic occasion to force war on Serbia, which was the political focal point of Balkan nationalism, an ideology primarily directed against foreign domination. From the Austrian perspective, the assassination was an opportunity to remove the Serbian threat.

The anticipated local war by which Austria would destroy Serbia quickly expanded, for the other major powers, ensnarled in their alliances and anxious over the immense problems of national military mobilization, responded in a reckless and militant way. In a frightening example of cause and effect the European states followed one another into disaster. It all occurred within one week. On July 28, Austria declared war on Serbia; on July 30, Russia began total mobilization, this directed against Austria and in support of Serbia; on July 31, Germany, determined to stick by Austria, also mobilized. Then, in face of Russia's continued mobilization, Germany declared war on Russia on August 1, and on Russia's military partner, France, on August 3. England joined France and Russia on August 4.

The major participants and the sides of the conflict were thereby quickly determined, only to be modified by the entry of Turkey on the German side later in 1914, of Italy on the Allied side in 1915, and—most significantly—of the United States on the Allied side in 1917. Even though the war reached Africa, the Pacific, and the Near East, activities in these regions did not seriously affect the outcome. Militarily, the war was a European affair, primarily fought on French and Russian territory.

Here were located the two major "fronts" along which the opposing sides long fought. The western front is both the more famous and significant, because the outcome of the war was finally settled there. Yet the eastern front, stretching from Poland to Austria, also was the scene of intense warfare, as Germany and Austria steadily attacked tsarist Russia. By 1917, the Russians were exhausted; their losses were high, with over one million men dead or wounded in the last major offensive against Austria, which was made by General Brusilov (hence its name, "The Brusilov Offensive") between June and December of 1916. By the end of the following year, the Russians agreed to an armistice, and thus the two-front war waged by Germany at long last ended.

However, the war in the West did not alter noticeably after this change. The grinding-down process of the large artillery duels continued. Finally, in the spring of 1918, the Germans began their "Great March Offensive," which allowed them to penetrate British lines some forty miles in depth. In May, the Germans again approached the Marne River, as they had in 1914, and drove on until they were only thirty-seven miles from Paris. There, their offensive ended. The Allies, strongly supported by fresh American troops, checked the German advance and began their own offensive in the late summer. Fearing for the fate of their armies, the German military leadership, on September 29, requested the Imperial Government to start peace negotiations.

The Changing Domestic Dimensions of the War

Of greater social importance than the extent of military involvement was the war's intensity. The war penetrated into economic, social, and psychological areas, such that it became the first of this century's total wars.

Proof of this assertion can be found in one small historical fact: German beer production had to be cut 25 percent of the prewar quantity by the end of 1915. The war reached into most every aspect of civilian life, as the battlefield engagements continued without much effect. Grinding the enemy down meant more artillery, more and heavier concentrations of infantry. What was therefore required was a nearly total effort, with the civilian economy geared to the war effort and with the vast majority of the nation's population directly supporting that effort. The increasing employment of women in munitions factories in England and Germany gives some indication of this shift, as do the national campaigns for the purchase of war bonds and the ever increasing need to ration foodstuffs. The social patterns defined in the nineteenth century were disrupted.

Of even greater consequence was the new role assumed by the state. The miscalculation about the nature of the war, the anticipated brevity of it as a "summer war," led all the belligerents to the conclusion that they were both well stocked and well prepared for all eventualities. But as they quickly exhausted their supplies, they realized the need for better organization of production to meet the ever-increasing demands made by the war offices. Moreover, the economic hardships caused by commercial strategies of war—the English naval blockade of the German coast, and the German use of submarines against English merchant shipping—gravely affected prewar patterns of foreign trade. Imports to Germany, for instance, fell to two-thirds of the prewar level.

More out of necessity than by calculation, European states began to intrude into the private commercial sector, both to regulate production and to assure the necessary distribution of raw materials required by the military machine. The most impressive of such efforts was made very clearly in Germany, where a War Raw Materials Board was established both to stockpile and distribute vital materials. This increased governmental control was called by the Germans "War socialism," the attempt to regulate the economy for the sake of the state. But later in both France and England the governments also established commercial controls, these worked out through the cooperative efforts of industrialists and trade unions.

With this new "War of Economic Endurance," sacrifices were increasingly required of the population—economic deprivation at home, the intensifying loss of life at the front—and these conditions in turn required ideological justification. The role of propaganda assumed great importance. The war was made into a crusade, or a grand historical cause. For the Allies (England and France particularly), the war was directed against "The Hun," a derogatory caricature of a modern barbarian speaking German and set upon destroying civilization. When the United States entered the war, President Woodrow Wilson provided the most striking of the war's slogans: "Make the world safe for democracy." One way of political and social life was now opposed to another. On the German side, propaganda was directed primarily against England, a nation viewed as attempting to strangle Germany by the network of her fleet and finances.

What began as a "typical" European war quickly turned into a total war. Nations and cultures were cast in a life-and-death struggle for their very existence. War had become the most successful of social institutions, integrating diverse activities and interests into a single national cause.

And yet as the war dragged on the social structure started to disintegrate. The French were confronted with serious mutinies in the army in 1917; German workers increased demands for social benefits. Also, national governments, anxious to avoid domestic discontent, undertook political reforms, as evidenced in the further democratization of the voting procedures in Germany and the granting of suffrage to women in England.

Political reform was not the only result of the severely trying wartime demands. Revolution occurred farther east. The collapse of the monarchy in Russia in 1917 was of worldwide importance. Overwhelmed by war losses, mismanagement, and food shortages, the tsarist regime quickly collapsed to liberal revolution in March, and the provisional liberal government then formed was overthrown by the Communist Revolution of November 7, 1917.

The Communists advertised themselves as a peaceful regime, opposed to further continuation of the war. The war, in their ideological view of things, was a capitalist endeavor fought for economic spoils. The new Russian government, faced with superior German military power, made a separate peace and then devoted itself to organizing authority at home and urging similar revolutions in other countries. Forced to deal with a bitter civil war between the Communist regime and its opponents, Russia briefly disappeared from the central international scene, but its revolution haunted the traditional European governments and inspired radical Marxists with the thought that the Russian Revolution might be an example to follow.

In terms of ideology, therefore, the First World War caused a new and long-lasting conflict between two opposing political and social systems, neither of which had had great influence on European political practices before. From the United States, Woodrow Wilson and the American Republic offered the ideal of democratic, constitutional government based upon "self-determination of nations." From Russia, V. I. Lenin and the Soviet Union (the new name of the Communist state) offered the ideal of Communist government based upon the rule of the proletariat. As the old monarchical systems of Germany and Austria collapsed in 1918, the territory they ruled became the battleground for these contending ideologies.

Ideologically, economically, socially, the war approached the total. Never before had there been such a concerted attempt to mobilize society, not just armies, to achieve military victory.

And, ironically, this was never done. There was no final resounding military success.

The Interminable War

The English cavalry officers who waited impatiently for the final charge against the enemy were never called; there was no dramatic gesture on the battlefield. When Germany sought an armistice in October of 1918, her armies were still intact, and her population was still anticipating a military victory. After all, most of the fighting was still taking place on French soil. What the Germans finally did was surrender out of exhaustion and out of fear of impending military collapse. After the armistice, their armies marched home in regular formations.

The long war ran counter to the thinking of all the high-placed commanders. In his memoirs, the French marshal Joseph Joffre wrote: "Due to the power of modern arms and the moral effects they were certain to produce, it appeared probable that the first battles would be short and that a decision would be promptly obtained."

Why this did not occur can be explained briefly. The unique nature of the First World War is to be found in the balance initially attained and thereafter maintained by both sides. Put in opposite terms, neither side enjoyed an unusual advantage in numbers of men and equipment, or in generalship, or in the technological development of new weapons. The war was thus a vast stalemate, which an intensification of the same tactics could not resolve. More of everything proved but two things: first, the incredible ability of the European economy to generate waste; second, the equally incredible inability of the commanding generals to contrive new strategies. As Winston Churchill commented, this was an industrial war fought by generals with preindustrial mentalities.

In operation, the First World War seemed more like a medieval siege war than a modern war in which technology should have forced mobility to prevail. The most famous statement made by any general in the war was that of the Frenchman General Pétain at the Battle of Verdun: "They shall not pass." And they did not, but neither did the French nor the English in their attempt to break through the enemy lines.

The new factor that did make an appreciable difference in the following year, 1917, was the entry of the United States into the war. The economic support provided by this country, the psychological impact of the democratic giant of the New World aiding beleaguered Old Europe, and, finally, the commitment of large numbers of troops in 1918 combined to give the edge to the Allied side. This involvement of the United States in European affairs was one of the most important changes in twentieth-century European politics, and a change that would have a pronounced effect down to the present. In both world wars the power—economic, military, demographic—of the United States was needed to overcome the imbalance created by a Germany too strong to be contained by any combination of Western European states.

For the first time in its history, modern Europe had not been able to achieve a telling victory on the battlefield, or a meaningful solution at the diplomatic table, to the political problems plaguing it. The war solved nothing, because it exhausted everything. Victor and defeated alike suffered from the same effects, these in turn repeated thirty years later when the Second World War seemed to be a continuation of the first, but with greater destructive capabilities provided by even newer technology.

Conclusion

The impact of the war was such that to speak of it as shattering European civilization is no exaggeration. It was both the unexpected intensity and duration of the war that determined its historical importance. To a world imbued with liberal notions of progress and human betterment, and to a generation instructed in the purposes of the rational mind, the effect was overwhelming. Granted that the dismal and pessimistic philosophers who wrote before the war hinted at and even occasionally predicted the horror ahead, they were not widely believed. However, by 1918 the battlefields of

Europe had exceeded the grotesque fantasies imagined earlier in pulp fiction and by science-minded novelists like H. G. Wells.

At home the regular ways of civilian life were disrupted and reordered, a preparation in regimentation, according to some historians, for the totalitarian rule that the various dictatorships of the 1930s would attempt to impose. Although it is difficult to assess the wartime conditioning of the European populations that was caused by increasing state control and domination of daily life, there is no doubt that liberal democracy suffered. A form of wartime dictatorship, in which the legislative branch delegated or abdicated authority to the executive, existed on both sides. The French premier Georges Clemenceau (1841–1929) enjoyed virtual control of the French government in late 1917 and 1918, while at the same time the two most significant generals then directing the military effort in Germany, Erich von Ludendorff (1865–1937) and Paul von Hindenburg (1847–1934), held even greater authority. Censorship of the press, harsh laws on treason, food rationing, the drafting of civilian workers for war-directed industries—these were all imposed in the belligerent states, and all to the detriment of the rights of the individual.

Culturally, the war was destructive as well. It is true that few works of art actually suffered, although some major architectural sites were reduced to rubble. Yet the spirit of confidence that inspired the construction of the Eiffel Tower, or the founding of the London School of Economics, or the compilation of the eleventh edition of the *Encyclopaedia Britannica* was gone.

The Irish poet W. B. Yeats suggested the contemporary state of European civilization with these words:

Things fall apart; the centre cannot hold;
Mere anarchy is loosed upon the world.

Europe after the war was less temperate, less measured in its thought and behavior, less humane than before. Such a statement is not meant to imply that the nineteenth century was an age of unusual and widespread decency. The novels of Charles Dickens and the dedicated work of the Salvation Army stand as testaments to the misery and pain that then existed. But the organized and calculated destruction of the First World War was of new dimensions and of lasting consequence. The value of life, so highly praised by liberal philosophers, was once again cheapened. Mass slaughter was accepted with a fatalistic resignation. The masses, which in the nineteenth century were forced to produce, were consumed in the twentieth: 100 million individuals died in the two world wars.

Lastly, the war made Europeans aware of the fragility of their civilization and the basic physicality of their earthly existence. Not only was the comfort of bourgeois urban existence shown to be rather decorative like ivory elephants on a mantelpiece, but also the fundamental principle upon which the nineteenth-century world view was positioned was shown to be a lie. Descartes's statement, "I think therefore I am," was a gross deception; the world was anything but rational. What emerges from all the literature of the war is the physical brutality, the forced primitiveness of life on the battlefield. To have the cunning to stay alive, was the major concern. Existence (the moment-to-moment concern with survival), not abstraction (the leisurely interest in systems and long-range purposes) defined the new generation, the "lost generation."

World War I was the "war to end all wars," according to President Woodrow Wilson. In fact, it was the first of the large-scale, industrially generated wars in which success was determined by the amount of destruction caused. War was no longer, if it ever had been, the "sport of noblemen." It was an organized effort at annihilation.

Engraving of the Forecourt at Versailles, 1682, by Israel Silvestre.

The Power of Architecture

The modern era, as no other period since the Roman Empire, has been characterized by the grandiose and the monumental in civic architecture. Since the early nineteenth century, public buildings have been designed to express the new sense of power and order found within Europe's expanding, industrial society.

Engraving of The Etoile circa 1865 by J. Provost.

The political symbolism provided by grand architectural scale had been initially designed in the royal residences of Europe's absolute kings. Louis XIV's palace at Versailles is both the most famous and most pretentious example.

Then, almost as if a convenient symbol marking the transition from the older royal order to the new industrial one, appeared the Arch of Triumph in Paris. This structure is the largest of its kind in the world and was intended to commemorate Napoleon's military victories. In style it is imitative of the Roman triumphal arches, an interesting allusion to imperial grandeur. Begun in 1806, the Napoleonic arch was not completed until 1836.

(Above): The Crystal Palace—Western Entrance, 1851; and (Below): The Transept Looking South, Crystal Palace, 1851. Courtesy of The Illustrated London News.

Western side of London terminus for the Southeastern Railway, 1866.
Courtesy of The Illustrated London News.

By that latter date, however, industrial power was already altering the proportions of the European cultural landscape. No more dazzling architectural example of the new age could be found than Joseph Paxton's Crystal Palace.

A light and quickly constructed shell of wrought iron and glass, the Crystal Palace housed London's Great Exhibition of 1851, the first fair of its kind and the occasion for the celebration of Europe's new industrial age. Not only was the Crystal Palace the first building to be sheathed in glass, but also it was of imposing dimensions. The entirety covered over eighteen acres of land, generously housed an old elm tree that was originally on the building site, and accommodated as many as one hundred thousand visitors in one day.

The Crystal Palace set the new style for the industrial shell, the glass-covered frame, of which the railroad station was to become the most widely used form throughout Europe.

*The Eiffel Tower,
1889. Reproduced by
Permission of the His-
torical Pictures Serv-
ice, Chicago.*

However, no building more captured the imagination—or more quickly aroused the disgust of artistic critics—than did the Eiffel Tower. An engineering feat which anticipated modern concepts of aerodynamics, the Eiffel Tower was the realization of a century-old European dream: the construction of a thousand-foot-high tower. (Actually, the Eiffel Tower was originally 984 feet tall.) The centerpiece of the Parisian Centennial Exhibition of 1889, the tower marked more than the anniversary of the French Revolution. It stood as a tribute to European engineering skill; and it expressed a new sense of verticality that would be later repeated in the modern skyscraper.

André Perret's plan for a series of apartment towers in Paris, 1922. Courtesy of Illustration *(Paris).*

By the 1920s, New York's skyline was pierced by several tall, steel structures, such as the Woolworth and Chrysler buildings. European architects saw these skyscrapers as monuments to a new urban scheme of things. On paper, many technologically advanced communities were laid out and proclaimed to be cities of tomorrow. One of the earliest, a French design of 1922, offered an awesome, if repetitious solution to the Parisian housing shortage. No such plan was anywhere realized in interwar Europe, but the thought that architecture and urban planning could define a new and "efficient" social order figured into the narrative of utopian novels, science fiction, and even futuristic movies made at the time.

(Above): *Zeppelinfeld, Nürnberg. Photograph by Albert Speer. Courtesy of The Library of Congress.*
(Below): *100,000 storm troopers hear Hitler, 1936. Reproduced by Permission of Wide World Photos.*

Moscow State University Building in Lenin Hills. Reproduced by Permission of Tass from Sovfoto.

Moreover, the dictatorial regimes which sought their own "new order"—whether that be inclined to the Left or to the Right—attempted to define it in reinforced concrete. Hitler, an amateur architect of conventional style and outsized dreams, took a personal interest in the design of the Nazi Party stands at the Zeppelinwiese, Nuremberg. As monotonous in order as the party rallies it was built to accommodate, the Zeppelinwiese coldly captured the Nazi spirit of regimentation. Moreover, the setting was complemented by the hundreds of thousands of soldiers and party members who annually gathered to provide an imposing display of the modern concept of "masses."

During the Stalinist era after World War II, the Soviet Union pursued the architecture of power in the skyscraper mode. As early as the 1930s, the Russians had planned a building taller than the Empire State Building in New York, but nothing came of this project. However, a series of smaller variations appeared after the war, such as the Palace of Culture and Science, constructed in Warsaw, Poland, and the main building of Moscow University. Critics see both of these buildings as tired copies of the flamboyant skyscraper style of the 1920s, as evidenced in Perret's plans, shown on page 113.

London Post Office Tower. Courtesy of the British Tourist Authority.

For modernity, however, no building broke more dramatically with old patterns than did the Post Office Tower, opened in London in 1966. Designed to assist rapid telecommunications by means of microwave transmission, the 580-foot glass and steel structure shimmers above a more Victorian setting.

In 1977 the most recent and unusual of the grand European public buildings was opened in Paris. The Georges Pompidou National Art

The Georges Pompidou Cultural Center. Courtesy of the French Embassy Press and Information Division.

and Cultural Center blatantly displays the building's support systems on the exterior, and in bright colors. Air-conditioning ducts, electrical conduits, even escalator tubes are out in the open so that the enclosed space can be temporarily arranged to suit the needs of exhibitions and performances. As a modern shell, the Pompidou Center continues the tradition established by the Crystal Palace over a century ago.

PART THREE

Reconstruction and New Order:
1918–1945

*J*n his most significant novel, The Trial, published posthumously in 1925, the Czech novelist Franz Kafka has a descriptive scene in which the victim of a meaningless judicial system peeks into the law books at court and finds that they contain pornographic pictures. In the bizarre realm of his imagination, Kafka was suggesting that European values and institutions were turned upside down and distorted beyond recognition. This was a world gone mad.

Kafka's vision was certainly to approach reality in Nazi Germany, Fascist Italy, and Stalinist Russia, to name the most important of the repressive regimes existing in Europe of the 1930s. But in 1919, when the treaties ending the war were being drawn up, there were many people who hoped that a new peaceful order might be established. "Mankind is once more on the move," remarked an important politician of the time.

That move was imagined to be toward international conciliation and harmony. A number of organizations appeared, all dedicated to the common goal. The League of Nations, designed to resolve international disputes by parliamentary procedures, was at the head of the list, and further down was the P.E.N. Club, made up—as its initials suggested—of poets, essayists, and novelists, who assumed that international understanding could be achieved by those writers who were "men of goodwill."

For a moment their aspirations seemed to be approaching reality; democracy was on the rise. The new nation of Czechoslovakia was provided with a constitution modeled on that of the United States; Austria and Poland became democratic republics with elected chiefs of state; Germany under the Weimar Republic (named after the city in which it was established) was given the most politically sensitive constitution yet devised by Europe, and this instrument was seen as a triumph of democracy. Even Turkey was made over into a constitutional republic.

However, the most telling activity of the time was that seen on the big boards of the international stock exchanges. After an immediate postwar inflation and slump, the world market righted itself and stock sales and values began to climb, until 1929 when "The Crash" occurred. The Depression was a belated result of the First World War, its most significant and far-reaching delayed-fuse bomb. From Vienna to New York, it brought the capitalist edifice down. And with the crash went the remaining hope in the idea of nineteenth-century progress; there was now grave unemployment, not great expectations. Little Man, What Now? was the title of a popular German novel published in 1932. It was also a question asked by many individuals who found themselves without work and money as did the main character of the novel, a department store clerk. The Nazis promised guns and butter; the Russian Communists promised electricity and workers' councils. Many individuals turned ideologically and personally to these movements that pretended to provide a new order.

Socially, the 1930s introduced the age of totalitarianism, the attempt by the state to regulate the lives of its citizens, to subsume all politics under the will of a self-appointed leader and a single party. This also was the decade of despair in Europe, and many who turned to communism or fascism did so out of resignation, not new hope. "Two cheers for democracy," exclaimed the English author E. M. Forster at the outbreak of World War II. Three cheers he would reserve for the kingdom of the blessed, and Europe was far from that realm.

And then there was another world war, this one "worthy" of its name. Europe once again was the central theater of operations, although well rivaled by the Pacific as the war progressed. After nearly six years of collective destruction, Europe emerged from this war in 1945 as a fire-gutted continent, a shell of its former self, its population without home and immediate hope.

Thus, the social history of the interwar period ended in despair as it had begun with disorder. Yet at the outset there was some hope that "normalcy"—to use President Harding's term for stability—could again be attained, this through sustained industrial production and economic well-being. This hope was not realized in Europe. Promises were turned into problems—and worse.

One bit of detail from that age now has the quality of a parable. It was Adolf Hitler who gave his support to Dr. Ferdinand Porsche, an engineer who in the early 1930s designed a small automobile that he hoped could be cheaply produced so that the German population might enjoy the freedom of the open road. Hitler liked the car and endorsed its development. Only the prototype of the Volkswagen, the "people's car," was completed before the war approached. The Volkswagen plant thereupon turned its efforts to production of a military scout car, a variant of the original model. As for Porsche, he turned his attention to the design of heavy tanks. And as for the new highways along which the Volkswagens were to roll, they carried motorized troop convoys and, in the last days of the war, they were made to serve as runways for jet fighter aircraft.

Kafka's view of his world ultimately proved not to be badly distorted. Out of the new order, all that was left in 1945 was rubble—and a major question: How could Europe rebuild?

9

Disorder: Europe in the 1920s

To *the faithful, toil-burdened masses the victory was so complete that no further effort seemed required. . . . A vast fatigue dominated collective action.*
WINSTON CHURCHILL
The Aftermath, 1929

No figure after the war captured the popular imagination and represented the condition of the masses of society better than did Charlie Chaplin. He was called by an English publication "Everyman on the Screen," the allusion being, of course, to the character in the medieval morality play who stood for the human condition. Chaplin's film roles were constant: the gentle, little tramp, simple of mind and purpose, who was in search of happiness but was continually frustrated by authority (in the form of the policeman) and modernity (in the form of the gadgets and activities of the industrial age). That Chaplin's success—unlike the tramp's—was international can in part be explained by the fact that films were then silent, the style of acting therefore bordering on exaggerated pantomine within easy reach of all viewers. More important, however, was the identification of the Chaplin tramp with the pathetic humor of the time, the hollow laughing of people uncertain of the future and not reassured by the past.

For millions of war veterans readjustment to civilian life was an immense problem. The search for jobs, the attempt to repair marriages disrupted by years away from home, the bitterness over reports of war profiteering, and the disappointment over the shortages of housing were personal difficulties quickly dampening the enthusiasm for the long sought-after peace.

Psychologically, the leaders of Europe looked backward. The very word used to describe the early postwar mood was "reconstruction," an attempt to reorder what had been. Western European politics tended to be conservative, and so did the business outlook. But drastic changes had taken place that made such an attitude unrealistic.

The readjustment to a peacetime economy was never made successfully in the interwar period. True, prewar production figures would be reached and surpassed in most industries by the middle 1920s. And the newer industries, like the automotive, radio, and the film, were providing highly exportable products. However, in face of these rising production figures stood the much more impressive world output of the United States and, somewhat later, of an industrialized Japan. The sum of the matter is this: While European production recovered and exceeded postwar records, the percentage of the growing world market held by Europe declined. Relatively speaking, therefore, European economic vitality had slipped.

More significant, however, was a general condition of instability that was widely felt and recognized. And it was a condition with its own hard facts.

First, Europe was no longer the world's banker. The capital reserves of the major nations were badly depleted: England had lost one-fourth of its foreign investment; France, one-half; Germany was deprived of most of its foreign investments. Added to this fiscal difficulty was the indebtedness of the Allied Powers of France and England to the United States for war loans. The result was a severe weakening of European currency. Some idea of the problem can be grasped from the fact that the French premier, Raymond Poincaré, who stabilized the franc in the mid-twenties, was given the title "saviour of the franc." Only once before in French history had "saviour" been popularly employed—and that was for Joan of Arc.

Second, industrial needs drastically shifted. Certain heavy industries like steel and shipbuilding were no longer required to meet the grotesque demands of the military. They therefore cut back in production, hence in manpower as well. And other industries, like aircraft and munitions manufacturing, collapsed with the advent of peace. Finally, the increased production of certain resources like copper, phosphates and wheat, all essential to wartime needs, now meant overproduction—a glut which sent prices reeling.

Third, the rearrangement of the European political map disturbed the economy. The increase of protective tariffs among the newly created nations slowed down the flow of goods on the continental level. Nowhere was this more evident than in the lands of the former Austrian Empire now divided, as a result of the peace settlement, into separate nation-states that had once existed as a large customs union but now were burdened with national trade barriers. Moreover, as the new nations took form, populations suddenly found themselves with a new political allegiance. Thus, problems in manpower availability and distribution within national economic units occurred as large

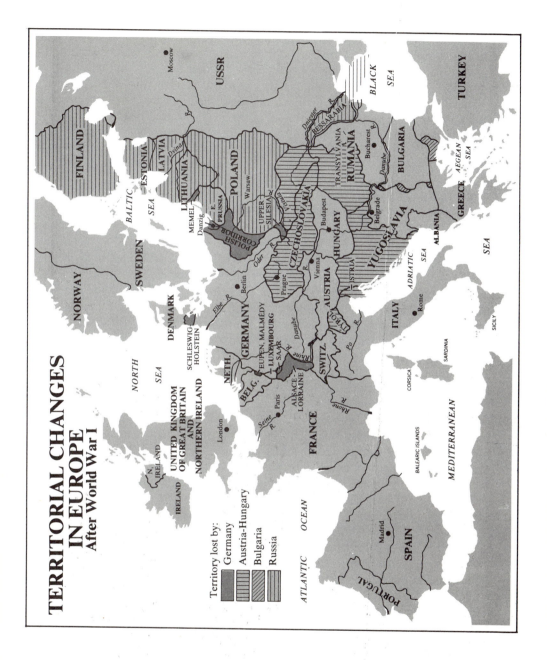

TERRITORIAL CHANGES IN EUROPE
After World War I

Territory lost by:
- Germany
- Austria-Hungary
- Bulgaria
- Russia

FINLAND

USSR

Moscow

ESTONIA

LATVIA

LITHUANIA

MEMEL

Danzig

E. PRUSSIA

POLAND

Warsaw

UPPER SILESIA

POLISH CORRIDOR

BALTIC SEA

SWEDEN

NORWAY

DENMARK

SCHLESWIG-HOLSTEIN

Vistula R.

Oder R.

Elbe R.

Berlin

Prague

CZECHOSLOVAKIA

GERMANY

EUPEN MALMÉDY

LUXEMBOURG

SAAR

ALSACE-LORRAINE

NETH.

BELG.

Seine R.

Paris

London

N. IRELAND

IRELAND

UNITED KINGDOM OF GREAT BRITAIN AND NORTHERN IRELAND

NORTH SEA

ATLANTIC OCEAN

FRANCE

Rhône R.

SWITZ.

Danube R.

Rhine R.

Vienna

AUSTRIA

TYROL

ISTRIA

HUNGARY

Budapest

Po R.

ITALY

Rome

SARDINIA

CORSICA

BALEARIC ISLANDS

MEDITERRANEAN

SPAIN

Madrid

PORTUGAL

SICILY

ADRIATIC SEA

YUGOSLAVIA

Belgrade

ALBANIA

GREECE

AEGEAN SEA

SEA

TURKEY

BLACK SEA

BULGARIA

RUMANIA

Bucharest

Danube R.

TRANSYLVANIA

BESSARABIA

Dniester R.

Dvina R.

numbers of people were added or subtracted politically. The German demographic situation was one of the most telling. By 1925 some 705,000 Germans had left territories incorporated into the new state of Poland, while 132,000 Germans left Alsace-Lorraine, once again part of France. ·

Fourth, the war reparations program, whereby Germany had to assume financial responsibility for civilian war damages, had unanticipated effects. The German treasury was soon emptied of precious metals, a condition that caused German money to become all but worthless, hence a grave matter for all those Germans who had bank accounts and stocks and bonds. Because of Germany's precarious position, international trade with neighboring states was adversely affected. And those countries to which the reparations payments were made felt the impact of imported German industrial goods, now that the new German republic tried to pay in kind because it could no longer pay in cash.

Under these conditions, the fact that labor unrest was a major problem in the postwar era is easily understood. Workers feared for their positions in an economy that was undergoing conversion from wartime to peacetime needs and in an economy that was out of equilibrium. Returning servicemen sought employment, and in so doing displaced many of the women who had been given job opportunities for the first time during the war. Finally, the depletion of capital inhibited the modernization of older industries and the creation of new ones so that job opportunities were not expanding significantly in new directions.

A sign of the times was the increase in the number and frequency of strikes, particularly in the years immediately after the war. In Italy and France a series of strikes in major industries caused national alarm in 1919 and 1920. Then in England in 1926 a most impressive general strike occurred with 2½ million workers participating. Begun in the coal industry, it ran through other heavy industries, but was conducted with little violence and some goodwill. All such strikes were manifestations of a grave economic situation and of the government's seeming inability to arrive at a plan for meaningful economic recovery.

The plight of the industrial laborer was converted into a fear among many middle-class entrepreneurs. The British Socialist Harold Laski, one of the most influential thinkers of the interwar era, looked back at the postwar condition and wrote: "Capitalism's conception of what was reasonable was limited by two factors—the economic crisis on the one hand, and the profound fears engendered by the Russian Revolution on the other." His assertion was not much exaggerated.

If the economic situation was chaotic to the laboring masses, it was precarious to the entrepreneurial classes. The popular myth of the "Bolshevik" quickly grew: a fear of conspiratorial activity between citizens who were Communists and the newly established Soviet Union, committed to International revolution and the overthrow of capitalism. The establishment of the Third International, the Communist International—or Comintern, for short

—in 1919 lent credence to this fear, because the newly emerging Communist parties in Western Europe joined the Comintern. In 1920, for instance, the French Socialist party split in two over the question of adherence to the Comintern. The emergent French Communist party had, by 1921, some 140,000 members, while the residual Socialist party only had 30,000.

Communism added a new but ill-defined dimension to many aspects of European life in the interwar period. Governments were concerned about subversive activities because of the control Moscow maintained over the Western European parties; much of the upper middle class saw communism as a threat to private property; yet some intellectuals assumed that the Soviet Union heralded the advent of a new social order soon to redress the worst evils of modern industrial society.

As the French Revolution before it, the Russian Revolution of 1917 introduced a political and social system that stood in opposition to the established European order. But the first two decades of Soviet rule were chaotic, repressive, and brutal. With the ascendency of Joseph Stalin to power in 1927, the regime took on the characteristics of a police state, one far removed from the earlier Marxist proclamation that under communism the "state would wither away." Prison camps in Siberia for enemies of the regime, severe regimentation of labor in order to develop the economy according to state planning, the creation of a secret police organization used primarily as a weapon of terror—all were characteristics of interwar Russia and the features which led later critics to compare Stalinist rule with that of Hitlerian Germany.

If the enthusiasm some European intellectuals had initially felt for the Communist experiment now declined, fear of the new Soviet regime as a potentially disturbing force both in domestic and international politics continued. "The Red Menace" and "the Bolshevik Threat" were popular terms suggesting that Marx's introductory statement to the *Manifesto* had belatedly come true: "A specter is haunting Europe—the specter of communism." And it was a specter all the more ominous because of the instability of the postwar economic order.

Not everyone despaired of the economic situation, however. A newly emerging managerial elite, professionals concerned with the social implications of modern technology, addressed the perplexing question of how to assure industrial development. They had behind them a wartime experience in industrial management, brought about by the accelerated growth in productive capacity, the amassing of labor for new tasks in the factory, and the distribution of scarce raw materials. "War socialism" created conditions of state intervention and rudimentary governmental planning that ran counter to older free-trade and competitive-market concepts. Moreover, enthusiasm for the American industrial system, so recently distinguished by the mass-assembly techniques developed by Henry Ford, was generated as a result of the steady flow of wartime supplies from the other side of the Atlantic.

In the peacetime environment, this new group of technocrats, the professional managers and planners, turned their attention to the reordering of society so as to make it more productive, but by means of techniques that stressed "social engineering." Here the ideas of Frederick W. Taylor, an American engineer who had tried to regularize labor with machinelike precision, were persuasive because they suggested the route to greater efficiency. But the resulting efficiency in production was seen by many of the European technocrats as a means to social as well as to economic betterment. Through "social engineering," worker, manager, and machine would be harmoniously integrated into something approaching an economic community. Output would increase; social tension would decrease. And thus the older utopian dream of a society based on cooperative and well-integrated economic activity, not on political factionalism and dispute, would be realized.

The translation of these managerial ideas into the working of the postwar factory system was not made to any great degree, however. The widespread interest in "rationalization" suggested that the European economic order was in need of renovation. While the era did witness new corporate growth and integration, this was primarily made in the form of mergers and international consolidation: Unilever, the great English soap combine, and Royal Dutch Shell, the oil refining company, are two notable examples. Planning, even though tried in the Soviet Union with considerable success but at an enormous cost in human life, remained excluded from European economic considerations until World War II.

Modifications in Social Structure

Against the general background of economic instability and managerial concern, there occurred some important modifications in the social order. While at no time in the modern age was European society firmly fixed, class structure did have a certain consistency before the war. It was said of France, but it might as well have been said of most of Europe, that an ambitious individual could move upward from one social stratum to another, but no one could not expect the strata themselves to be altered. Yet the war changed this general condition also.

First, because it was most visible, there was a political decline of the aristocracy. With the collapse of the Russian, Austrian, and German Empires, the social order in which were maintained the greatest privileges of this class disappeared. Moreover, the poor performance of the English aristocracy as leaders on the war front—notably the senior officers who badly bungled many of the charges—caused a considerable diminution in the general respect which this group had been accorded earlier. The political authority that the aristocrats had been able to maintain as a class even in the age of European democratization declined. Throughout the nineteenth century, men of noble title had occupied positions of great importance in the various foreign offices. Some critics have argued that such individuals had a particular European vision, unimpaired by domestic party strife, that therefore allowed them to perform more wisely than would have individuals from other classes. True or not, the aristocrats lost their hold in this domain. Moreover, the mediating functions they had also performed in domestic politics narrowed in significance.

Finally, the social image and the cultural model they projected disappeared. The notion of the "country life" that seemed so appealing from afar and supposedly conferred on European life a certain gentility dissipated along with the clouds of war. The vast estates and the legions of domestic servants, which had been directed leisurely by this duke and that count, now entered history. Few lamented the departure of the aristocracy from the center of European affairs, but it was a historical occurrence of great importance.

Yet the most important change in class arrangements occurred at the lower end of that large and amorphous group, the middle classes. There, there was a quantitative change in the "white-collar" workers whose position, if not aspiration, was similar to that of the blue-collar worker in the factory. The white-collar workers gained in numerical significance primarily through the bureaucratization of the state during the war. Although the peacetime situation saw the retrenchment of state activities, government had become a major employer and would continue to be so henceforth in European history. But it was not only in the public sector that the white collar was the distinguishing feature of the new middle-class uniform. The growing administrative aspects of commerce brought the salaried individual into view as bank teller, department store clerk, and office secretary.

Here was the modern "Everyman," whom Charlie Chaplin treated with kind humor. He was the person seedily but neatly dressed, his costume complete with that final touch of upward-bound elegance, a flower in his lapel. It was this white-collar contingent, precariously placed on the lower-edge of the middle-class world, that was the first to know the dire effects of the economic depression and, consequently, among the first to listen seriously to Hitler.

Most unusual of all and most disturbing was the appearance of one more social element, peculiar to the interwar period in its influence. More a "cohort group" than a social class, those war veterans who generally expressed a right-wing political attitude joined together in organizations through which they could express either a common spirit of nostalgia for the war days or of discontent with the dull confusion and lack of national direction that they found in the new era of peace. Although their displays of camaraderie, as when they met in pub or beer hall to drink and reminisce, were socially acceptable enough, they also formed into political pressure groups which disturbed governmental officials. The *Stahlhelm* (Steel Helmet) in Germany and the *Croix de Feu* (Cross of Fire) in France worried republicans and radicals alike as the possible source of a coup d'état.

More threatening, however, were the markedly paramilitary organizations that sprang up immediately after the war and that did disturb the domestic peace. These were private forces, organized and armed as if for battle, and led by former officers who were directly challenging governmental policy. In Germany in 1920 an attempted overthrow of the government took place. The event, known as the Kapp *Putsch*, consisted of a march on Berlin by a discontented free-booting brigade, under the command of a Prussian official named Kapp, that hoped to dislodge the new government. The army, not wishing to fight its former brothers-in-arms, did nothing. It was only a hastily organized general strike that brought the Kapp *Putsch* to a speedy failure.

Another such military escapade had been successfully maneuvered by Gabriele d'Annunzio (1863–1898), an Italian romantic who wrote passionate poetry, sported a monocle, wore a black shirt, and found in Mussolini an ardent admirer. D'Annunzio and his "forces"—a small band of dedicated followers wearing black shirts and giving the old Roman salute, soon to be the Fascist salute—seized the Adriatic city of Fiume, which they wanted Italy to have as part of the spoils of war to be obtained from the former Austrian Empire. There they established a short-lived dictatorship in 1919.

Such new forms of collective protest and violence made no sense either in terms of liberal political ideology or in the considered thoughts of Karl Marx. Neither a social class nor a group directly motivated by dissatisfaction with the industrial system, the paramilitary group was further indication of a decline in civic spirit and civilian law.

There were few signs in the domestic scene of the major European countries that could be read as hopeful. Peace had been achieved, but still the effects of the war worked their way through many aspects of European life. Economic and social existence was precarious; unemployment and inflation persisted in the 1920s, even after the decline in the value of European currency had been arrested and European production figures had exceeded the prewar level.

Instability had become the norm of modern Europe, a situation that few people failed to notice.

A New Mood

The unpleasant conditions that were so evident in the immediate postwar years at the national level seemed to be contradicted by the developments in popular culture. Here there was a sense of exuberance and freedom unmatched by any attitude previously generated, certainly since the French Revolution. The social upheaval of the world war had produced a revolution in public behavior. The destruction of authoritarian government in Germany and Austria, the readjustment of sexual mores and general ethical standards brought about by the fact that the majority of young men were fighting at the front, and the large-scale employment of women in wartime industry were important factors in the collapse of what has been called "Victorian morality."

Perhaps there is no term like the "Roaring Twenties" that can be applied to all of Europe at the time. The French did call their epoch *les années folles*, the wild years. Indeed, there was a lot of frenzied activity. One contemporary critic noted that Europe seemed to be moving merrily along the road to hell.

Speed took on a new form of social significance. Someone who lived "fast" lived well—and incautiously. Moreover, speed also implied elegance. Luxury liners raced across the Atlantic to win the "blue ribbon" for the shortest time in transit. And, starting in 1926, the German dirigible *Graf Zeppelin* flew regularly to Argentina, thereby offering new comforts aloft. Airplane races became the rage. Railroad travel was not left behind. It was at this time that the Orient Express gained its exotic reputation for polished service and swift connections. (Agatha Christie made this international train the setting for one of her most famous detective stories.) Finally, fast-moving Rolls-Royces, Alfa-Romeos, and Hotchkisses conveyed a smart social set from London to Brighton or Paris to Nice. The well-known dancer Isadora Duncan died in an unusual automobile accident, when her long, flowing scarf got caught in the spokes of the wheel of her chauffeur-driven convertible, causing her to choke to death. This example of youthful death was to become a symbol of modern futility, commented upon down to the death of the American movie star James Dean in 1955.

Such physical movement was also matched by a new social openness, the occasion for people to act themselves or act outlandishly. For the first time women smoked in public. The cabarets of Berlin became notorious gathering places for the *demi-monde*, those "twilight people" given to pleasures and pursuits that would have been unthought of in Victorian drawing rooms. And Paris held its own as the city of lights, complete with brighter and evermore provocative music hall productions. When the American singer and dancer Josephine Baker appeared on stage at the *Follies Bergère*, attired in little more than a few bananas, she created a sensation—and a name for herself.

Any such review of Europe, like that of the United States for the same period, is kaleidoscopic, presenting in gaudy and ever-changing patterns, a world without the form of the prewar era. What was here represented was that not unusual burst of libertarianism following upon the hardships and severity of an extended war. As the popular English social commentator and science fiction writer H. G. Wells (1866–1946) wrote: "The world is at present drifting into an era of humor, an era of fun. . . . The world is now sick of wars and tumults and is looking for lighter entertainment in order to forget the Inferno it has just passed through." But Wells was prophetic, and so he added the following comment: "Between now and 1940 or 1960, when the nations will be tested by their next bloody tragedy, they will chiefly look for fun."

Even in its early years—Wells wrote in 1923—postwar Europe seemed to some observers not to be headed to a new era of peace and progress but only fixed in a brief space between catastrophes. However, the anticipated crisis was not always imagined to be another traditionally organized and executed war. For the first time numbers of social critics considered the grave implications of a technologically organized social order. In contrast to the technocrats they argued that if there was to be a stainless steel and glass utopia, it would not house a harmonious society of cooperative citizens, but a mechanically functioning world devoid of basic humanity. Novelists like the English Aldous Huxley in *Chrome Yellow* (1921), playwrights like the Czech Karl Kapek in *R.U.R.* ("Rostow's Universal Robots," 1922), and film directors like the German Fritz Lang in *Metropolis* (1926) all described the routinized inhumanity of a social order given over to production, to efficiency without human purpose. This theme was realized in its most popular and lasting form in Huxley's *Brave New World*, in which the author satirically showed that the modern way to salvation was the conveyor belt.

The criticisms contained in popular commentaries such as these suggested that, with the advent of modernity, it was form and process, not substance and purpose that counted. The horrors of the First World War were transfigured, to appear now as the destruction of the soul and heart of Western civilization. What was left was a world of "hollow men," to take out of context the title of a T. S. Eliot poem of the time. This sense of hollowness, found also in the purposeless existence led by so many of the heroes of postwar novels—and perhaps even in the person of one of the most famous of these novelists, F. Scott Fitzgerald—extended to institutions. What was left of European liberalism resembled a hollow shell, incapable of supporting the heavy burdens the war and its effects had imposed, the heaviest of which would be felt in a few years when worldwide depression struck.

But this is hindsight, evident to anyone who looked back after 1933. For a few years, between 1925 and 1929, the European state and social systems seemed to have righted themselves. The League of Nations was functioning well; Germany, France, and Great Britain, in the persons of their foreign ministers, were displaying an outward appearance of friendly understanding. And the intellectual community, the world of Sigmund Freud (the Viennese psychiatrist), Albert Einstein (the German mathematician), Igor Stravinsky (the Russian refugee composer resident in Paris), and Thomas Mann (the German novelist) was briskly at work. It promised and produced new theories, thoughts, and works that clearly indicated the continuing vitality of European civilization.

Yet what will remain striking to all historians viewing the interwar period is the very brevity of the period of "normalcy" that so many people sought and expected.

Conclusion

The destructive effects of World War I were not only restricted to the battlefield; they were noticeable throughout the interwar period, marking it with uncertainty. Even the efforts at adjustment, undertaken with great hope in the 1920s and initially offering promise, were soon frustrated. Except for the so-called "halcyon years," the period between 1925 and 1929 when stability and peace were briefly secured, the 1920s and 1930s careened along both socially and financially.

This was a time without much clear direction, either philosophical or political. The older bourgeois ideal of material and social progress in an atmosphere of international peace had been shattered by the war and was not again successfully restructured because of the continuing economic and financial dislocation that war had caused. Particularly, the law of the marketplace —the long-held assumption that supply and demand would tend toward balance and hence to self-regulation—was shown to be badly inoperative, first in the immediate postwar period when inflation caused the rapid depreciation of European currency, and economic conversion from a war-time to peacetime economy brought problems of unemployment. Thus, within government and among businessmen there was a growing concern that the liberal "laissez-faire" state could not be restored. Put otherwise, the Wilsonian call to "make the world safe for democracy" needed to be extended to the economic as well as to the political order of things. Economic well-being would be the most important concern and the least successfully approached problem of the interwar period for the democratic states.

Furthermore, the precariousness of the results of postwar "reconstruction" was demonstrably expressed in the social attitudes of the 1920s. The new social openness of the time was an indication that the customs and institutions which had, at least outwardly, bound nineteenth-century bourgeois and "Victorian" Europe had collapsed. And the new epidemic of fads in clothing, music, art, and social manners also suggested the underlying instability of the postwar social structure, for now superficial change substituted for needed reform.

Yet none of these comments would have been seriously received in the few years before 1929. Then the general European outlook was hopeful, if not serene. "The Crash" was much more than a figure of speech.

10

An Era of Despair

The temptation of our day is to accept the intolerable, for fear of still worse to come.   HERMANN RAUSCHNING
1939

The decade that ran from the stock market crash in October of 1929 to the outbreak of war in September of 1939 was the most dismal recorded in the peacetime of modern European history. Unemployment and political disintegration in the democratic West, political persecution and the establishment of concentration camps in Nazi Germany and the Soviet Union, and mounting international tension across the Continent are the major features of these years. Thus the words of Rauschning, quoted above, hardly exaggerated the sentiments of millions of individuals who endured hardship and lived in fear. The sense of despair that had dampened the minds of the "front generation" some fifteen years before was now universalized: to vast numbers of the population, the older purposes of European civilization appeared to be hopelessly lost.

In this time of social disintegration, new institutional forms were hastily contrived. At the center of the European continent, both geographically and politically, rose a new order, that of Nazi Germany. The stark reality of Hitler and Nazism were confirmation that European notions of progress and humanism had been debased, made part of the debris still scattered by the previous war. Hitler's regime grew out of economic confusion and governmental helplessness. It thus can be considered one of the results of the mal-functioning, liberal, capitalist system.

The last widespread belief in self-generating progress toward greater material well-being collapsed in 1929.

The Depression

"Black Thursday," October 24, 1929, was the dramatic moment when the decade of the 1930s opened. On that day and the next, the sale of stocks on the New York stock exchange reached enormous and unimagined proportions, as investors clamored to get their money. The great banking house of J. Pierpont Morgan used its incomparable financial resources to balance the market, but sales only temporarily wavered before they again plunged precipitously downward. Even "Jupiter" Morgan did not have the gravitational pull to change the tide.

What occurred in that dark moment in American financial history would soon be repeated less dramatically but equally disastrously throughout the Western world. Because the world economy was now American-based, what happened on Wall Street was international news.

As early as the middle of the nineteenth century, European critics anticipated the day when the growing economy of the American nation would be the dominant force in international commerce. By the beginning of the twentieth century the United States had shifted, as noticed in the amount of exports, from an agrarian to an industrial nation. During the "War of Endurance," this trend intensified, as did European dependency on American products. Moreover, the accelerating costs of the war caused European nations to borrow from the United States. Finally, the increase of American wheat-growing to accommodate the wartime needs of Europe brought more wealth to this land and would unbalance the European grain market after the war.

By the end of the war the United States stood as the center of a new world economic order, with New York City as its capital. For a few giddy years New York was universally admired for its high finance and its high-rise buildings, both suggestive of economic exuberance. The construction of the Chrysler Building in 1929 served as an appropriate symbol. The first skyscraper to reach above 1,000 feet (it is actually 1,046 feet tall), it was built on American industry: Walter Chrysler became a millionaire as an automobile manufacturer.

Like the Chrysler Building, the growth of the American economy, after a brief agricultural depression in the immediate postwar era, was spectacular. But the Chrysler Building went up in the same year the economy came down. Overspeculation on the stock market and overexpansion of production were the major causes of the Depression.

Although New York was the focal point of "The Crash," the Western world was its setting. The Depression was an unexpected outcome of the unsettling conditions brought on by the world war.

After 1918, an unusual and ultimately disastrous flow of currency characterized the international monetary market. Germany was the tidal basin out of which and into which the money went. German bullion was quickly drained because of the need for the nation to pay the heavy reparations required by the Allied Powers. In order to maintain a semblance of financial stability, the German Republic borrowed heavily on the international money market with American bankers and investors purchasing bonds and buying into German industry. (Henry Ford was one such prominent investor.) Even though British and Swiss financiers also participated in this activity, the American effort was by far the greatest in sums lent and invested. In turn, the money Germany borrowed provided one means by which the reparations payments could be partially met. In a sense, therefore, American capital flowed into Germany, only to have much of it flow out again to France and England in the form of war payments. Yet, ironically, Germany borrowed more money in the 1920s than it paid out in reparations.

As for France and England, they had incurred a considerable debt to the United States for "offshore" wartime production provided by American industry, and for the capital loaned to help with the war effort. "They borrowed it, didn't they?" replied President Coolidge to the question of whether the European states could afford to repay the debt.

Part of the problem was the nature of American national economics. The American system of protective tariffs meant that the European nations found the repayment of American loans difficult because the importation of European goods into the United States was hindered by these very tariffs. Moreover, the gold that did come from Europe was stored underground at Fort Knox, Kentucky, by which action it was removed from the money market and thereby inhibited European capital reconstruction.

Clearly, then, this circular flow of capital neither generated much new European wealth in the form of capitalization—new industrial development and, hence, employment opportunities—nor did it auger well for international stability. The precariousness of the world financial situation was recognized by the European nations which did, through a series of international conferences, attempt to adjust the enormous debt payments to the United States and to seek some arrangement for Germany that did not involve astronomical figures for reparations. (No sum could originally be agreed upon for Germany, but in 1921 the figure was rounded out at some $40 billion—still beyond the bounds of financial reason.) Only in 1931 with a moratorium proposed by President Herbert Hoover did the problem cease. The Hoover moratorium called for a cancellation of all intergovernmental debts for one year. In effect, the decision became a permanent one; few state debts were paid after this date.

That Europe had become so clearly an economic dependency of the

United States explains why the October 24, 1929 "crash" would have such quick repercussions abroad. Short-term loans were quickly recalled to cover the falling stock value and the rush on bank deposits at home. In a matter of months the international golden web was broken, and the economy it supported fell through. The capitalism of the "free market" was finished; henceforth governmental intervention of some sort in the economic workings of private enterprise would be a characteristic of the economy of the Western world. But this economic interventionist role of the state was haphazard and ill-defined at the beginning. Indeed, no European democratic state moved as effectively as did the American government. And as for the dictatorships, state control was such that the labor market was manipulated—with rearmament employing many workers and the army taking many more away from the market.

Within most European states the governmental response was that of confusion and desperation. National budgets were cut and balanced; governmental salaries were reduced; and variants of the British "dole," state payment of modest sums to unemployed and underemployed workers, was made. There were some efforts at governmental subsidy of industry—as in England, where the construction of the two superliners, *Queen Mary* and *Queen Elizabeth*, was done as much to help the badly depressed ship-building industry as to provide luxurious travel for the few who could still afford it. Yet the most strenuous measure was also the most unfortunate. Countries, in an effort to protect home industries, introduced high protective tariffs which blocked the flow of foreign goods. The international economy was thus segmented, chopped up into national parcels that were not self-sufficient.

In Europe, as in the United States, the most glaring effect of the Depression was unemployment. In Germany, one-half of the labor force was ultimately without sufficient employment; in Great Britain, the figure approximated one-quarter. Only France among the major Western European nations had a low figure, this because the French economy was more domestically than internationally oriented and because a high percentage of the population was still engaged in small-scale agriculture.

Social despair grew out of economic depression. The world of the self-adjusting marketplace, which had been the center of European domestic existence for a good century, no longer made any sense. One observer in Vienna in the 1930s recounted the curious argument used by a Nazi street orator trying to win over a small group of poorly dressed listeners. "We don't want high bread prices," the orator remarked. "We don't want low bread prices. We want National Socialist bread prices!" He was cheered, a small indication of the deep economic confusion of the day.

Both economic security and the belief in material progress were shattered by the Depression. And the liberal principles of politics, based on individualism as was the economic system, were also badly affected. As hope in the old order declined, opportunities for the political parties on the "Right," those usually grouped generically under the name "fascism," rose. These parties were characterized by their activism and antiparliamentary stance. Their membership was outfitted and used as if soldiers: they took to the streets to march and often to attack their opposition in gang fights; they looked to a strong leader who usually promised a new order as a substitute for democracy, which was denounced as the government of the weak.

For many individuals who turned to these new authoritarian parties, personal freedom seemed a burden; democratic processes seemed inept and ineffective. A new desire for relief from personal anxiety led to a search for social order.

To many people a strong government with powerful leadership was now necessary. The British *Journal of the National Union of Manufacturers* struck this tone in an editorial of 1934:

> We cannot help wondering, rather wistfully, whether a British Mussolini would not play the excellent cards we hold in our hands a great deal better than our popular form of government does . . . whether a democratic form of government is really capable of directing the destinies of the Empire in these difficult times.

Here was a call for a new order in the most democratic of European nations. On the Continent itself, fascism and Nazism were responses to the confusion of the day.

Fascism and Nazism

Behind the military pageant and public festival that made up the official image of the new regimes in Italy and Germany was to be found the decomposition of nineteenth-century liberalism. The "new orders" established a different set of values and purposes. Ideologically, the state, not the individual, counted. Politically, dictatorship from above, not consent from below, was imposed. Institutionally, repression of the rights of the citizen, not respect for them, was practiced.

Both Benito Mussolini (1883–1945), *duce* (leader) of Italy, and Adolf Hitler (1889–1945), *führer* (leader) of Germany, boasted that they would provide strength where weakness had before prevailed. The anti-democratic thought of the prewar, discontented, intellectual elite now became part of a popular ideology of brute force. Mussolini offered this definition: "The Fascist state is will to power and domination." A thought like this suggested how far European political considerations had declined from eighteenth-century liberal principles. The sacrifice of civil liberties for the communal promises of the mid-twentieth-century dictators was made without a whimper by large segments of the new masses and by equally impressive numbers of the old middle classes.

This development, a contradiction of nineteenth-century social trends and popular ideology, has provoked an impressive array of historical interpretations. Yet the major factors or conditions which explain the new phenomenon of dictatorship can be briefly assembled.

Public attitudes were affected by the seemingly oppressive problem of personal responsibility and individual freedom in a world of economic insecurity. The Enlightenment ideal of the self-sufficient man, capable of determining his own destiny, now seemed fraudulent, at complete variance with contemporary social and economic conditions. Liberty was seen to result in meaningless struggle, not self-improvement. Moreover, the individual seemed to be a victim of the many adversities created by a mass-production economy within a social order made up of masses of population. Like Charlie Chaplin's tramp, the individual seemed incapable of understanding or controlling the world in which he lived. The one obvious way out was to reject individual responsibility, hence the freedom of choice, in favor of having decisions made by others, by the "leaders" willing to assume political authority. "What this collectivist age wants, allows, and approves," wrote the German novelist Thomas Mann in 1935, "is the perpetual holiday from the self."

Economically, there was the "purse string" argument. Fascism and Nazism are here seen to have gained popularity as defenders against an imposing Communist menace. With the successful advent of communism to power in Russia, and with the loudly made argument that the abolition of private property would sweep away class differences and create an equitable economy, much of European middle-classdom worked up a fear of the "Bolshevik menace," the possibility of the forceful overthrow or the subversion of the existing social and political order. Both Mussolini and Hitler made opposition to communism a major element of their ideologies. For Hitler, communism and Nazism were competing world systems, locked in mortal combat. As he stated in his closing speech to the Nazi party rally at Nuremberg in September 1936: "Bolshevism has attacked the foundations of our whole human order, alike in State and society; the foundations of our concept of civilization, of our faith and of our morals—all alike are at stake."

To many intelligent observers, even those of a traditionally liberal persuasion, Mussolini seemed to have provided in the 1920s a sound political compromise between an uncontrolled capitalism on one side and an uncontrollable communism on the other. Thus Fascist Italy was described as the middle term between two untenable social conditions. It supposedly provided the necessary amount of order and state control without severe interference with the old economic system. In sum, the dictators of Italy and Germany promoted their systems as the means to reconcile the profound problems existing between labor and management so that capitalism would not be destroyed.

Historically, the two dictators also posed as upholders of glorious tradition and followers of national destiny. Mussolini stood as the colossus of the New Rome, and Hitler donned the armor of a Teutonic knight. Both men had popular appeal as they promised both new national hope and glory.

In the interwar period, it was fashionable to speak of Italy and Germany as "have-not" nations, those without sufficient national resources or territory to enjoy the privileged position of France, England, or the United States. This notion was one that the dictators of these two states were most willing to foster. They frequently blamed their supposed national containment on the diplomatic intrigue of the "have" nations. To break out of encirclement or to once again seek an important place in the sun (the Nazi hymn, the *Horst Wessel Lied*, contains the words, "Europe Today, Tomorrow the World") became ideological objectives. The Nazis even encouraged the development of a theory of geopolitics, in which Germany was considered to be the heartland of a great "world island" (the Eurasian land mass) and therefore destined to be its ruler. To the south, Mussolini harped on the splendor of Imperial Rome and demanded that once again the Mediterranean become *mare nostrum*, "our sea."

From this brief review, the major elements of appeal that were gathered around the swastika or the fasces can be seen. As guarantors of order and economic security, as defenders against the threat of an impending bolshevism, as upholders of sacred national purpose, Fascist Italy and Nazi Germany offered an alternative to the supposed indecision and immediate ineffectiveness of parliamentary democracy. That the alternative would prove to be both false and horrendous was not anticipated by many of those who followed the flags of these new systems.

The New Social Order

Visitors to Italy after 1922, when the Fascists came to power, were often shown the swamps that Mussolini had had drained and the public buildings he had ordered constructed. Visitors to Germany after 1933, when the Nazis had come to power, frequently commented on the cleanliness of the city streets. These New Orders outwardly appeared to be efficient systems where, as one critic commented, "The trains run on time." If there were all too many people parading around in black and brown shirts, and if the profile of the jutting-jawed *Duce* of Italy or the moustached *Führer* of Germany appeared in tasteless photographic profusion, these were matters of no major consequence. Even Winston Churchill remarked in the mid-1920s that, had he been an Italian, he would have been a Fascist.

Initially, then, there was a popularly entertained thought that the dictators would get their countries back on an even keel, and the national communities would therefore be all the better for their brief rule. Even the soon apparent nastiness of the servants of the New Orders was frequently discounted as a temporary inconvenience.

The truth was soon learned, however: the dictatorships were not very orderly, and they were extremely oppressive. Political opposition was exterminated or imprisoned; censorship was rigidly imposed, and earnest effort was made at thought control by strict supervision of the education of the young and by the elevation of propaganda into a new popular art form. Lastly, police forces were used, not for the maintenance of public order, but for its destruction.

If these general characteristics appeared in varying degrees of intensity in all countries that were dictatorially ordered in the 1920s and 1930s, they were most pronounced in Italy and Germany. And yet there were obvious distinctions between the two national societies that qualify any simply historical comparison that might be made.

Italian Fascism produced a less effective, less repressive, and, hence less socially destructive "new order" than did Nazism. At the most inconsequential level, the Fascists tolerated jokes about the regime which the Nazis did not. In Italy, the Catholic Church played an institutional role which forced some accommodation by the new regime. More important, the Italians never generated a spirit of racism such as that which was profoundly important in the ideology and practices of Nazi Germany. Finally, the Italian army never enjoyed the unique position nor gained the reputation for efficiency that the German army had in modern history. Add to these social differences the industrial capacity of the German state, the effectiveness of its bureaucracy, and the sense of national frustration over defeat in the world war, and the differences in the real power and the public attitudes existing in both countries are discernible.

Yet Hitler had stated that Mussolini was his model, his early political idol. Mussolini enjoyed this dubious honor because he was the first individual to make dictatorship successful in a modern, large-scale European state. Taking advantage of the parliamentary crises that had disturbed Italy in the immediate postwar era, crises brought on by disappointment over the Italian war effort, and by labor strikes, war scandals, and a multiparty system that could find no clear majority by which to govern effectively, Mussolini "marched on Rome" in 1922. (He actually took a night sleeper from Milan.) The Fascists, organized as a political party but active in street fighting, now threatened to overthrow the regime by force. Rather than risk this, the political leadership in Rome gave in; the king, Victor Emmanuel II, invited Mussolini to be prime minister and to form his own government.

The changes the Fascists proposed were never fully realized; the New Order existed on paper far more than in reality. What changes did occur came as much in response to intensifying economic difficulties as to well thought-out plans. The Fascists did acquire international appeal by their theory of a "corporate state," one in which labor and management would act together, or "corporately," in nationally organized labor cycles, bringing together all of the factors of production, from acquisition of raw materials to distribution of finished products. Thus, potential class conflict was to be removed by governmentally sponsored institutions forcing labor and management to work in unison. Most critics of the regime like to point out that only in the movie industry was anything of this sort seriously tried. In fact, the Fascist regime remained inefficient and disorganized.

Nazism in Germany was of quite a different order. The regime was ruthless, the effects of its activities inhumanly destructive. In his remarkable novella *On the Marble Cliffs*, published in 1938, the German author Ernst Junger, captured the grotesque spirit of the regime in a medieval allusion: "Such are the dungeons above which rise the proud castles of the tyrants. . . . They are terrible noisome pits in which a God-forsaken crew revels to all eternity in the degradation of human dignity and human freedom."

This degradation was awesomely horrible. Political opponents, whatever their religious or ethnic background, were tortured and exterminated. Terror was institutionalized, given dreadful public expression in the infamous "Crystal Night" (November 1938), when Jewish synagogues and shops were attacked by the Nazis, who broke windows and store fronts (hence the name of the event.) Culture was barbarically despised, with books burned and censorship ruthlessly imposed. More significant was the creation of racist doctrine and policy. The official ideology of the regime assumed the existence of an "Aryan race," destined to rule the world. There was also the *Judenfrage*, the "Jewish question," as it was coldly called. The Nuremberg Laws of 1935 denied the Jews citizenship and forbade "intermarriage" with them. Finally, 6 million Jews died during the history of this regime—and by calculated state policy. They were forced into concentration camps, like Dachau and Auschwitz, where they were worked and beaten to death—or exterminated in gas chambers, with their remains cremated in mass-production ovens.

These matters must be remembered and understood in order to achieve a meaningful appraisal of the basic inhumanity of Hitlerian Germany. But to further appreciate the social significance of the Nazi regime, the contemporary observer must look at Nazism as an expression of discontent with modernity. In its semi-religious pageantry, its mystical concern with nature, and its ideological fabrication of a medieval spirit of guild and community, Nazism was culturally backward looking. It deprecated the secular and material spirit of modern urbanism—and renounced the Jew for supposedly representing that spirit. Confused, superficial, and most frequently tawdry in expression (as in the official pageants), this anti-modern attitude suggests that Nazism was in part a reaction against the new industrial system.

And yet, it was this very industrialism that made the Nazi regime successful. The radio, the machine gun, the armored car were among those technologically created devices which assured the oppressiveness of the new police state. And so, for the first time in history, the potential of dictatorship and despotism was realized. The agencies of the state could reach into all matters of private life with the intention of regulating them by force or by control. In this sense, the state became totalitarian. Most distinctions between the private and the public sectors of human activity were ideologically removed, and so they frequently were in actual practice. The individual was now significant only insofar as he or she was integrated into the total system, political and social, and made to serve it.

Although the totalitarian effects of Nazism were not so pervasive as the regime and its early critics suggested, Hitler's followers did succeed in destroying a variety of intermediary public institutions, such as labor unions, rival political parties, and professional organizations, that stood between the individual and the state.

Only the monolithic party stood beside the monolithic state. If imagined as a large, vertically posed column (hence the use of the term "monolithic") that paralleled the state in its activities, the monolithic party is seen as distinct from its nineteenth-century parliamentary predecessors. Indeed, the most unique political institution of the totalitarian state, whether Fascist, Nazi, or Stalinist, was the single, legal party that alone accounted for organized political activity.

To succeed in this new system one needed to be a member of the "party," much in the way one needed to be a member of the aristocracy in the eighteenth and preceding centuries. Unlike the democratic political party, which was a voluntary association open to anyone who wished to inscribe and to support its purposes, the party in the "one-party" state was entered by special admission only, and for younger people, such entrance was often preceded by initiation through a party-sponsored youth group (like the *Hitler Jugend*). The single party thus served both a social and political purpose, filtering members of the society and determining who would serve the state.

The totalitarian state stood as the antithesis of the liberal state. Whereas the latter upheld the importance of the autonomous individual who was to enjoy a maximum of personal freedom guaranteed by the state's benign maintenance of domestic order, the former denied all personal freedom and demanded complete political submission. In sum, the liberal state depended on the principle of parliamentary compromise, while the fascist state depended on force and terror.

But such categorization of purposes and functions was not crisply clear to those people in Europe who turned to the Nazi or Fascist parties out of sheer desperation. These parties represented for many the last hope, the only apparent alternative between economic chaos and communism. And as each party used a vocabulary replete with socialistic terms (after all, "Nazi" was an acronym for "National Socialist German Workers' Party"), many adherents initially assumed that they would find social justice as well as national purpose and full employment in this new order of things.

Although the late nineteenth century was no doubt the "seedbed of fascism," in that it was the time when ideologies protesting democracy, emphasizing race, and extolling elites were disseminated, it was the conditions caused by the First World War that generated the climate in which fascism and Nazism were to thrive.

No European country—the Soviet Union obviously excepted—was without a form of fascist party, its members bedecked in uniforms, its "leader" promising strong-handed rule. Outside of Germany and Italy, the most successful of these fascist regimes was that introduced by Francisco Franco in Spain. Waging a long and bitter civil war against the legitimate republican government, between 1936 and 1939, Franco promised national regeneration and defense against communism, but he was personally without much ideology, other than a disposition to traditionalism. What he gave Spain was a military dictatorship, the one that endured the longest in Europe, dying only with him in 1976.

Even the democratic states witnessed the rise of fascist groups within their midst. More nuisances than threats, these organizations nonetheless demonstrated the yearning felt by many citizens for authoritarian government. In Great Britain there was the "British Union of Fascists"; in the United States there was a Long Island-based group calling themselves the "Silver Shirts." And in 1936 Lawrence Dennis wrote a book entitled *The Coming American Fascism*, which many readers thought was prophetic. Even in South Africa, a group of "Black Shirts," directly modeled on the Nazis, added to the growing racist condition of that state.

All of these dictatorial parties and regimes were primarily expressions of political discontent with economic conditions, but they were also responses to the confusing complexity of modern existence. The democratic industrial order had become intricate and convoluted: international finance, the world marketing system, parliamentary debate, and political party factionalism— these were aspects of an elaborate system which few understood well and which many saw as a conspiracy against the "little man." Hitler sensed this and admitted his responsive tactic in an interview of 1936: "I . . . simplified the problems and reduced them to the simplest terms. The masses realized this and followed me."

They followed as well because they sought strong leadership. Democracy appeared to many critics to be inefficient, cumbersome, and therefore unsuited to the pressing problems of the times. The liberal historian Benedetto Croce stated in the 1920s that perhaps a few years of Mussolini were necessary to get Italian affairs in shape. And the industrialists of the Rhineland, who financially cooperated with and supported Hitler just before he assumed power, thought likewise. They intended to get rid of Hitler once economic and political order was assured. That the political fortunes of the Nazi party, as determined by the number of votes acquired, increased as German unemployment increased is a statistical correlation that says much.

Conclusion

In many analyses of Europe in the 1930s contemporaries employed two metaphors, "cancer" and "twilight", to describe the state of European civilization. "Cancer" was used in reference to totalitarianism. Fascism and Nazism were seen as malignant outgrowths of modern society, slowly consuming it. The metaphor "twilight", most frequently applied to the state of affairs in France, suggested the end of an era. The high noon of liberal democracy was past, and now Europe was basking in the last light of a glorious day before the night of fascism would fall.

Neither metaphor was new nor particularly subtle in nuance. But each clearly conveyed the sense of despair, of tragic conclusion that so many observers foresaw for the European civilization that had been part of their prewar youth.

The Depression of the 1930s was, therefore, not just economic but also psychological. European society had lost its confidence.

11

The Precarious Peace

It must be a peace without victory. Only a peace between equals can last.
WOODROW WILSON
1917

The domestic situation of confusion and despair that characterized the two generations after the First World War had international parallels. Even as the war ended, there were many observers—including the French commander Marshall Foch—who looked ahead with a sense of foreboding. They already feared a future war, generated by a newly risen Germany. And, indeed, it could be and was argued that even in defeat Germany was potentially stronger than France in victory. The continuing peace of Europe therefore depended essentially on the reconciliation of differences between these two major military powers and, moreover, on the establishment of a spirit of cordiality and respect among their leaders and populations.

Viewed from the Western continental perspective, therefore, the interwar period was one in which a war-wearied France confronted a defeated and chagrined Germany. The diplomatic problems that had plagued European statesmen from the middle of the nineteenth century on were still present. And, in truth, many statesmen well knew that the "German problem," like the "French problem" of the Revolutionary and Napoleonic Eras, was one that only concerted effort could solve. The condition was that no single nation bordering Germany was strong enough to keep it contained.

The starkness of this political reality was all the more evident with the withdrawal of the two powers whose geographical situation in Western Europe was, at best, peripheral. Neither the United States nor Russia continued the "balancing" role each had performed in the world war.

After the peace negotiations, largely directed by the United States delegation, the United States failed to ratify the treaty because of strong senatorial opposition to the League of Nations. The interwar period was to be characterized as the era of American isolation from European affairs. "Isolationism" as a concept applied only to diplomatic activities, and not always there. The United States increased its economic activity in Europe, participated in a number of international organizations, and even co-authored a famous peace resolution, the Kellogg-Briand Pact of 1928. But no treaty obligations were incurred and, for the most part, the attitude of the American government after the presidency of Woodrow Wilson, was that of a studied noninvolvement in the international affairs of the European continent.

The condition of the new Soviet Union was another matter. Fear of international communism drove the Western European nations to construct a *cordon sanitaire*, a sort of diplomatic wall of immunity against Russia. The intention was to isolate the country. Where and when the Soviet Union did participate in diplomatic activities, its motives were suspect. Only after 1934, when the Soviet government entered the League of Nations and the threat of Hitler intensified, did Soviet foreign policy move toward cooperation with the Western democracies, and did they, in turn, look upon Russia with less concern.

The consequent triangulation of European affairs, with Great Britain, France, and Germany related as the major powers, seemed geometrically satisfactory during the 1920s when an outward effort at reconciliation was maintained by their governments. Many Europeans then thought that President Wilson's "war to end all wars" had probably achieved its purpose.

However, with Hitler's rise to power in 1933, the precariousness of European peace was once again sharply illuminated. Hitler assumed a strident and demanding tone from the outset. His rhetoric was bombastically militant in tone, his armies soon prominently displayed, and his diplomatic actions suggestive of a man impatient to claim what he considered his nation's right. Hitler's diplomatic stance was, therefore, at severe variance with the general diplomatic attitude that had publicly characterized European affairs before then.

The Spirit of International Conciliation

The most striking institutional change in European diplomatic behavior of the 1920s was the extension of the liberal, parliamentary practice to international relations. Liberalism had fostered the idea that political compromise arrived at by open discussion was the best means to assure both political stability and peaceful change. This notion of conciliation, or of accommodation of different interests, was now structured in the League of Nations and infused in the spirit of diplomatic cooperation that marked the many international conferences of the 1920s.

The League of Nations does not appear in bright colors in most historical analyses. Its seat, the city of Geneva, Switzerland, is often considered the site of international failure, hence a city to be avoided in present-day international negotiations. Yet, if the League was an overblown, even naive scheme for settling international differences, and if its purposes were interpreted differently by the statesmen of Europe, it was an idea that had a certain nobility about it—and a certain chance of realization.

The rub in international affairs has been and remains the concept and practice of national sovereignty, best summed up as the right of a nation to conduct itself as it deems fit and necessary in international relations. This pursuit of national self-interest was looked upon as a major cause of international disorder and its severe outcome, war. If national self-interest could be moderated by a countervailing spirit of international conciliation, then perhaps the nation-state system, like the national political one, could function peacefully. This was the hope and the idea in the minds of those statesmen who thought the League of Nations would be useful.

Proposed in various forms by several statesmen and political writers in the early twentieth century, the League was actually the brainchild of Woodrow Wilson, and its form was evidence of its liberal heritage. A bicameral legislative body, in which member states acted as political equals in the lower house—the General Assembly—and in which the "Great Powers" acted as an elite senate in the upper house—the Council—the League was given the authority to consider and legislate on all international matters submitted by its member states.

Without describing the various pieces of machinery by which the entire system was to work, let it be said that two major questions existed from the outset: (1) where were the fine-line distinctions between domestic and international issues (was a colonial problem a domestic or an international problem, for instance?); and (2), far more important, how was a League decision to be imposed: where were the "teeth," to use a then contemporary phrase. Throughout its brief history, the League contended with these problems and found that its collective will could only be imposed easily where small states were involved in the issue under consideration, or where the national interests of large states were not seriously involved.

The most ingenious device by which a League decision could be imposed was that of economic sanctions: a sort of internationally imposed blockade against the offending nation, by which League members would neither trade with nor supply the offender, hence economically paralyzing the state in question. In principle commendable, in practice ineffective, the economic sanction approach was tried against Mussolini's Italy when that state invaded Ethiopia in 1935. Mussolini's military effort suffered more from incompetency and Ethiopian resistance than it did from economic sanctions.

The League was not a political success. And, in truth, it could not have been, for its membership never included all the great powers of the world. The United States, its sponsor in the form of Woodrow Wilson, did not join, for the American Senate refused ratification of the treaty in which the League idea was contained. Germany was refused entry into the League until 1926; Russia did not join until 1934, by which time both Germany (1933) and Japan (1931) had withdrawn. Only partially representative, the League was essentially a European affair, and one in which the European states had declining enthusiasm.

Yet the League is historically important, for it does represent an unusual, if short-lived, mood of cooperation; this, in turn, generated by a deeper fear of war. The French foreign minister Aristide Briand (1862–1932) announced at this time, "Peace at any price." The phrase had a certain ring about it, of course, the sound of despair. Briand spoke not for himself, but for a particular generation of Europeans who had no desire to endure another war. As foreign minister, Briand knew full well that France had been "bled white," that his nation could never tolerate another war of such grotesque human proportions.

This anti-war attitude was reflected in the popular press, in the theater, and in the myriad of war novels, most of which spoke of the horrors of war and to the need for peace. There was, therefore, a popular mood directed toward peace. Diplomatically, a long series of disarmament conferences was held in order to prevent the escalation of weapon production and to effect a balanced limitation of numbers of weapons and size of armies so that aggressive warfare would be nearly impossible. The most striking example of this new attitude is that which is known in history as the "Locarno Spirit."

In the Italian lakeside resort city of Locarno in December of 1925, the major powers of Western Europe reached an agreement that supposedly assured the peaceful maintenance of the Franco-German borders and the integration of Germany into the new European political order. With England and Italy acting as guarantors of the maintenance of the border between these two continental rivals, and with both Germany and France accepting the principle that any future alterations would be achieved only by diplomatic negotiations, there was widespread feeling throughout Europe that a major cause—perhaps the major cause—of European war had been averted. Germany and France had, in effect, agreed to settle any future major grievances by negotiation.

Locarno is the pivotal point in interwar diplomacy, the moment when the spirit of goodwill and international conciliation was at its highest, after which negotiations declined to competitive confusion and impending conflict in the 1930s. Historians, looking behind the scenes at Locarno, have found insincerity on the part of one of the participants. The German foreign minister, Gustave Stresemann (1878–1929), has been seen as entering into the agreement out of convenience, not with conviction, while the German army was already secretly planning for another war, about which the foreign minister was aware.

Whatever the dismal results of later diplomacy, Locarno and the League are expressive of the spirit of reconstruction that characterized so much of the general activity of Europe in the 1920s. However, like the reconstructed economies, the diplomacy of the period was not well founded. If the Depression tragically demonstrated the weaknesses of the liberal, capitalist economic system, the international activities of Adolf Hitler equally tragically demonstrated the weakness of a European political order in which the "German problem" was not effectively resolved.

War, Peace, and Germany

The causes of the Second World War are to be found in the peace terms of the First World War, it has been frequently stated. One point is certain: the peace was not, as Woodrow Wilson advertised it should be in 1917, a peace without victors and without recriminations. On the contrary, the main feature of the peace treaties insofar as they concerned European affairs was their attempt to assure the submission of Germany.

By Article 231 of the Treaty of Versailles Germany was declared responsible for aggression. This clause has been termed the "war guilt" clause, and was the one the Germans tried to avoid and were soon to denounce bitterly. The peacemakers of 1919, like the historians who have since followed them, were determined to establish a causal pattern that would explain why the war had occurred. Germany's defeat was the immediate reason why that nation was selected as the guilty party, but the ideological nature of the war had already conditioned the populations of France, England, and the United States to acceptance of the idea. Moreover, subsequent historical investigation has yielded considerable proof that the Germans acted both recklessly and aggressively. Yet the issue, quite simply, is still not resolved. Article 231 satisfied the victors, however, and on the basis of it they fixed the requirement of reparations to be financially assumed by Germany. This new diplomatic term—"reparations"—replaced the older concept of "indemnities," or war spoils. The reparations scheme was designed to pay for damages caused by German aggression to Allied civilian property, but also ingeniously covered the expense of veterans pensions.

Germany was not only thus financially burdened; it was also politically constrained. The treaty makers, assuming Germany's war guilt, were determined to deprive that nation of the means of making war again. The German army was, therefore, restricted to a professional force of one hundred thousand; the navy was severely reduced in size and scope (the battleship was denied to the Germans, for instance); and the newer weapons in the arsenal of war—tanks and aircraft—were also forbidden.

One traditional condition of defeat was also introduced to hold Germany in place: territorial reapportionment. Germany's colonies were taken away and placed under the control of the victors and under the supervision of the League of Nations; some of the national territory was dismantled, given to Poland, Czechoslovakia, and France (notably the return of Alsace-Lorraine). Most unusual of all these territorial arrangements was the creation of a "demilitarized zone" along the west bank of the Rhine River, in some points of which Allied forces were temporarily stationed, but in all of which German troops could not be placed. The intention of this territorial adjustment was to assure France of what was considered to be a very necessary buffer against possible future German attack.

As this brief review of the peace terms should suggest, Germany was purposely disadvantaged, primarily because of French insistence, but with the concurrence of the other victorious states. What was widely feared was German industrial and military potential. If not contained or boxed in, ran the argument, Germany would rise and expand aggressively again. The German population perceived the peace to be a *Diktat*, an unjust, dictated peace, forced on the entire nation. And, in truth, this was the case: the German delegation had not been invited to participate in the discussions. And it had been peremptorily required to sign the concluded treaties, and this in the presence of the haughtily silent Allied representatives who gathered in the Hall of Mirrors at the palace of Versailles.

The new German Republic began its political career already weighted down by the heavy burden of Versailles. The Nazis and others opposed to the republic would call its leadership the "November Traitors," those who had signed the armistice and endured the peace terms. Seldom before in history had a new government been so diplomatically isolated (the Soviet Union was, however, another contemporary example); never before had a sense of national chagrin and anger been so susceptible to political use by those who opposed the new regime.

No single political issue worked more advantageously to the Nazi cause than did the Versailles settlement. Hitler promised the German people that he would regain and embellish the national honor so badly sullied by the conditions of peace. And once in power, Hitler used the repressive features of the Treaty of Versailles as the basis for a series of demands for diplomatic change.

The peace treaties, then, can be considered self-contradictory: establishing international conciliation in the form of the League of Nations, and severely repressing Germany, making it a pariah, or an outcast among nations.

Peace and Appeasement

After the "spirit of Locarno" in 1925, the prospects for peaceful resolution of European political problems were never again so bright. In that year, the combination of economic recovery and political cooperation—clearly manifested in the personal goodwill among the English, French, and German foreign ministers—suggested a Europe on the way to recovery in several domains. But the soon-following economic depression and its related political feature, the rise of the Nazis to power, altered the general European situation. One of the major reasons for German economic recovery was rearmament: the marketplace became the parade field.

Hitler's political triumph and the inauguration of an era of diplomatic tension came in 1933. Nazi Germany lost no time in denouncing the *Diktat* and in demanding change in the European order of things. But Hitler did not always bother to wait for conferences around the traditionally green-covered rectangular table. He daringly took matters in his own hands, beginning what was to be a series of "Saturday surprises," so-called because they occurred on Saturdays when foreign offices were not regularly staffed. In 1933, he walked out of the League of Nations; in 1935, he announced that Germany was rearming in defiance of the peace treaty stipulations. In 1936, he marched his troops into the demilitarized Rhineland. Along with these dramatic and successful acts went a seemingly ever-revised list of territorial changes and adjustments that he wished.

The audacity with which Hitler waged his paper war on several fronts cannot be denied. Yet what stands out as more striking was the passiveness the lack of resistance displayed by England and France to these expansionist activities. Hitler's diplomatic activities were certainly against their interests, it would seem. Why, therefore, was he allowed to proceed as he did?

The answer to this historical question is found in the concept of "appeasement." Today the term is used as synonymous with defeatism, or "selling out." In the 1930s those politicians who fostered the policy did not see it as such; indeed, they thought it was the means, perhaps the only means, to continued peace. To effect compromise with Hitler, to come to an accommodation with him, to appease him would prevent him from reverting to war. Such was the thinking behind the policy; it was consistent with a widespread mood of the time.

The desire for peace was very strong within the Western democracies. One world war had been enough to convince many that another would mean the destruction of European civilization. The "peace at any price" principle of Aristide Briand was thus a very persuasive one. Indeed, a "peace ballot" floated in England in 1934 and 1935 was signed by over eleven and one-half million Englishmen, all of whom stated that they endorsed the League and the quest for peace. In the same year, the French government was building its famous Maginot Line, an intricate system of permanent defenses, made of reinforced concrete pillboxes and deeply buried subterranean garrisons, behind which the French nation hoped to defend itself economically—in terms of manpower—against any possible German attack. As was obvious, once the line appeared, this armed wall of concrete announced France's intentions to fight a defensive war, one that automatically provided the Germans with the initiative.

Standing as a complement to this anti-war spirit was the revisionist thought of some statesmen of the middle 1930s that Germany had been badly treated at the peace table and should now be accorded political readjustment. As later critics have stated, what should have been given the Weimar Republic was finally given Hitler. Yet even if this argument touched their own thinking, statesmen of the time assumed that Hitler's demands could be met. What they found outrageous were not the changes desired, but the voice in which they were uttered. Even then, many assumed Hitler's public stance was struck to win the support of the German people, not to threaten the integrity of European peace.

Appeasement was, in simple terms, predicated upon the need for peace and upon the possibility of politically satisfying Hitler. As a policy, appeasement was first practiced by the new English prime minister, Neville Chamberlain (1869–1940), who came to office in 1937. Son of the famous manufacturer and politician Joseph Chamberlain, Neville Chamberlain approached foreign affairs with something of a businessman's attitude: the belief that differences could be negotiated or settled, much as a ledger could be balanced. Chamberlain was a sincere man, and one deeply dedicated to peace; he genuinely strove to preserve "peace in our time," and he did, until quite late in his negotiations, assume that Hitler was a reasonable man whose political demands were limited.

Chamberlain's policy was not uniquely English, however. The French followed in his wake. Indeed, one of the striking diplomatic developments of the 1930s was the French abdication of leadership in foreign affairs. That nation followed English policy more than it initiated its own—another indication of the profound sense of fatigue that lay heavily over all French affairs. Thus, both England and France responded to the diplomatic initiatives and the unilateral political actions taken by Hitler with the assumption that the New Germany might be fit into the traditional European scheme of things.

The diplomatic history of the 1930s may be summarized as Anglo-French adjustment to the aggressive acts of the continental dictatorships, but chiefly to the policies and practices noisily imposed by Hitler's Germany. The language of peace that the democratic leaders spoke was met by the sound of the machinery of war. Both Mussolini and Hitler beat the drum and forced their peoples to march 4/4 time. German rearmament was particularly blatantly displayed. As the new air force, the *Luftwaffe,* provided an impressive fly-over

MAJOR ACTS OF AGGRESSION IN THE 1930s

October 3, 1935

Mussolini began his war of colonial conquest against Ethiopia, an east African country long coveted by the Italians. After strong Ethiopian resistance was checked, primarily by aerial strafing, the capital fell on May 5, 1936, and Ethiopia was made part of Mussolini's new "Roman Empire."

July 18, 1936

Civil war broke out in Spain with the Loyalists (supporters of the established Spanish Republican government) engaged in a struggle against the Insurgents (supporters of Francisco Franco, a conservative, authoritarian military figure.) The war took on an international character as the Soviets offered aid to the Loyalists, while Germany and Italy provided massive support for Franco. The war ended in victory for the Insurgents on March 28, 1939, after which Franco and his Falange party ruled dictatorially.

March 12, 1938

The German army marched into Austria and thereby an *Anschluss* (political union) was forcefully effected between Germany and Austria. Although there had been popular Austrian sentiment in the 1920s for such a union, it was now achieved through threats by the Nazis and fearful capitulation of the Austrian government.

---

for a visiting Charles Lindbergh in 1939, Lindbergh referred to it as "invincible."

The low point in European diplomacy of the time was the high point of success in Hitler's foreign policy: Munich, September 1938. The issue being diplomatically discussed was the fate of Czechoslovakia; the provocation was Hitler's demand that the heavily German-populated Sudetenland of that country be made part of his Greater Germany. Initial resistance by England and France to the dismemberment of this little nation, wedged between Germany and Russia, and representing the outstanding example of Wilsonian liberal democracy, was greeted by Hitler's dramatic fulminations. Put starkly, he would have it his own way, or he would give the order to unleash his military forces. To prevent war, therefore, the despairing prime ministers of England and France allowed Hitler to slice away what he wanted politically. In all of this, neither the interests of Czechoslovakia were considered nor were its leaders consulted. The Munich decision was greeted with joy in London and Paris, but this sentiment was short-lived as people realized that Munich was the tragic end of appeasement.

Hitler did not stop with a piece of Czechoslovakia. In early 1939 he proceeded to dismember further and to control totally the remainder of Czechoslovakia. Chamberlain felt that he had been deceived, and the French leadership felt a numbness of despair from which it did not recover.

Now, in one final diplomatic coup, Hitler managed to sign a "Non-Aggression Pact" with the Soviet Union in August 1939. This was done out of necessity, not out of a change of heart upon the part of the violently anti-Communist Nazis. Hitler wanted his eastern front secure, as he prepared to invade Poland; Russia, therefore, had to be considered. Once a satisfactory division of future spoils had been worked out between these two dictatorships, the Nazis turned against Poland. However, the English and French boldly announced their intention to defend that state, and, indeed, the English had already signed a pact of mutual assistance with the Polish government, to be operative should the Nazis strike. When Hitler's war machine, the *Wehrmacht*, invaded Poland on September 1, 1939, both England and France responded; they declared war on September 3.

Conclusion

In diplomacy, as in domestic politics and economics, the interwar period was one of failure. The old "balances" that had seemed self-regulatory in the nineteenth century were impossibly out of alignment after 1918. The market system collapsed quickly and dramatically in 1929; the democratic system of government wobbled in England and France, and was viciously destroyed in Germany and Italy. In the phrase of Anne Morrow Lindbergh, authoress wife of the aviator, the dictatorships seemed to be the "wave of the future." She did not, however, anticipate the fullness of her metaphor. Like a wave, they did indeed surge upward, crash on the beach, but only to wash quickly away, leaving behind flotsam and debris, the wreckage of Europe.

The hopes for international conciliation were dashed in the 1930s by the mighty wave of Nazi Germany. Nothing seemed to prevail against it, until the two major European democracies declared war with a sense of fatal resignation. Winston Churchill remarked in the introduction to his war memoirs that it was his purpose to "show how easily the tragedy of the Second World War could have been prevented."

Easily, yes, but only if there had been a strong will to treat Germany without recrimination in 1918 and an equally strong will to resist that state twenty years later when Hitler was making unwarranted demands. If the modern historian wrote Greek tragedy, he might state that the drama of interwar Europe was found in the loss of "moral fiber," of those ideological convictions that steady courage. The liberal ideal—the notion of progress based on rational assessments made by the autonomous individual—had faltered. Quite simply, people had lost faith.

The powerlessness of the individual and the omnipotence of the forces of the modern industrial state characterized the condition of the interwar era, as many people then and since have pointed out.

The Fascist-ringing lines of the South African poet Roy Campbell, published in 1939 in a work omniously entitled "The Flowering Rifle," suggest much, by announcing:

> *The tidings that Democracy is dead*
> *And that where'er he strives with the New Man*
> *The Charlie still must be an Also Ran.*

The New Man marched ramrod erect in the parades staged by the dictators, while Charlie Chaplin, as Everyman, only shuffled along, each foot inclined in a different direction. The power and order of dictatorships, and of Nazi Germany in particular, extended to diplomatic thought as well. In face of their strength and determination, appeasement seemed a proper course to many people in the democracies.

But this was all ended on September 3, 1939. Once again, as before in 1914, the Parisian railroad stations were filled with soldiers preparing to go to the western front. However, those that were there put on no display of colorful heroics. The mood was somber, as it was elsewhere in Europe. The English were dutifully digging bomb shelters and distributing gas masks to schoolchildren. The German commanding general of infantry in Poland telegraphed Hitler that the morale of his troops was much lower than that evident in 1914.

People feared this war, as no war had been feared before. Yet they had no intimation of the range and degree of destruction it would finally attain.

12

Another World War

Almost all of us leaders of the National Socialist movement were actual combatants. I have yet to meet the combatant who desires a renewal of the horrors of those four and a half years. ADOLF HITLER
October 19, 1933

When Germany invaded Poland in 1939, the Nazi propaganda minister, Josef Goebbels, ordered that no newspaper use the term "war" to describe what was happening. In a few days this rhetorical effort at avoidance of a new reality was abandoned. Great Britain and France were once again Germany's military foes. The term "war" would henceforth dominate not only Germany's but also the world's news until 1945.

The Second World War was in reality the first world war, with battle fronts on several continents. First, there was the European military scene in which the Nazi *Wehrmacht* initially met with spectacular success. After the defeat of Poland in September, the Germans invaded Norway and Denmark in March of 1940, and then only did they turn their attention to the West. There, after nine months of inactivity often described as the "phony war," the German forces moved suddenly and quickly. The attack began on May 10, 1940, with Belgium and Holland overrun and a deeply invaded France suing for peace on June 16, 1940. In six weeks Hitler had mastered the Continent. Only Great Britain still stood apart. Although Hitler spoke of peace terms, the British prime minister, Winston Churchill, echoed his countrymen's sentiments when he stated that the war would go on. And so it did, but now away from Western Europe.

Following a military excursion into the Balkans to extricate Italian forces bogged down in a campaign against Greece, the Nazis seemed to set upon a geographical course previously prescribed by Napoleon. In February 1941 they landed light forces in North Africa, again to assist the Italians. The desert war which ensued for the next year and a half turned out to be a series of dramatic tank battles between Field Marshal Erwin Rommel and Field Marshal Bernard Montgomery. Rommel, the one outstanding Nazi general who did not behave in the traditional Prussian manner, was selected by Goebbels to be a hero. He was so treated in the German press, and even Winston Churchill respected his military genius and dash. Had Hitler poured more men and equipment into the intensifying North African campaign, Rommel might have been able to conquer Egypt, as had Napoleon before him. But Montgomery gained the initiative in the summer of 1942, and the Germans were routed. The fact was Hitler's major military effort was found elsewhere.

Again, in Napoleonic fashion, Hitler unleashed a mammoth invasion against Russia on June 22, 1941. The largest army the world had yet known was amassed for this gargantuan enterprise. Some 3 million German troops moved across the spatial immensity of Russia by operating on a two thousand-mile-long front. Again the *Wehrmacht* met with initial success. In the autumn of 1942, General Friedrich Paulus, commander of the German Sixth Army that was moving against Stalingrad in the East, informed Hitler that the city would fall by the tenth of November. A few months later this same German army was being ground down, a distance of feet from its objective.

The Battle of Stalingrad was the decisive turning point in the war in Europe. It reached its dreadful conclusion on February 2, 1943, when Paulus, who had been promoted to Field Marshal only a few days before, was taken prisoner along with his army. The extended Nazi supply lines, the ancient Russian ally, "General Winter," and the incredible determination of the Russian people held the Nazis at bay and then pushed them back.

Never again was the *Wehrmacht* able to regain the offensive in any enduring manner. The war had turned against Germany. For the remaining two years, the formerly expansive Third Reich was being converted into *Festung Europa* (Fortress Europe) which Hitler could only defend. As the Russians relentlessly pushed westward against the German armies, the Allied forces, chiefly made up of British and American troops, invaded Italy on July 10, 1943. (French North Africa had been previously invaded by an Anglo-American force in November 1942.) And then, in the most daring and extensive naval landing in history, the Allies attacked Western Europe in Normandy, France, on D-Day, June 6, 1944.

Many high German officials despaired of a successful outcome of the war after the Battle of Stalingrad. However, by the autumn of 1944, all hope was lost, and the German nation had taken on a siege mentality, its population suffering severe deprivations, enduring constantly increasing air raids, and awaiting inevitable defeat.

With the new year, 1945, the New Order was in a final state of chaos. On April 21, Soviet tank forces reached the outskirts of Berlin, unwelcome news that caused Hitler to rant violently in the rooms of his bunker, located underground next to the Reich Chancellery. But his words were no longer of avail. There were few people who could hear him. On April 29, 1945, as the Russians were occupying the heart of Berlin, Hitler put a pistol in his mouth and committed suicide. The Third Reich ended as sordidly as it had begun.

A "More Total War"

Even a brief résumé of the military facts of the war suggests its enormity in numbers of soldiers involved and in geographical area covered. But such figures do not tell much about the social implications of the war. This, indeed, was a total war, sparing no class, no age group, and few nations in Europe. The devastation exceeded anything previously imaginable.

The raw statistics are deplorable. The Soviet Union estimated a loss of some 20 million people. Some 6 million Jews were exterminated by the Nazis. More than 30 million Europeans were moved from their established residences as the result of Nazi policy or of war exigencies. The air raids, adding a new apocalyptic dimension to war, indiscriminately destroyed the civilian world centered in the cities. The Germans destroyed Rotterdam and Coventry in the early days of the war. And later the Allies effected similar results on a large number of German cities. The fire-bombing of Hamburg, undertaken by the British on December 1, 1943, was described by that city's police-president in dire terms:

> The scenes of terror which took place in the firestorm are indescribable. Children were torn away from their parents' hands by the force of the hurricane and whirled into the fire. People who thought they had escaped fell down, overcome by the devouring force of the heat and died in an instant.

The war was fought ferociously on both sides. It was truly a total war. But it had not begun as such.

In 1939 neither the Germans nor their enemies, the British and the French, had organized their nations for the sort of warfare that came to characterize World War I. In part the German attitude derived from military planning: the waging of *Blitzkrieg*, or lightning warfare, that would be quickly won by combined air and land operations. The mobility of the tank gave to strategy a quick and offensive authority. In part, the English and French attitudes derived from peacetime thinking and a "Depression mentality" that still calculated in terms of balanced budgets and controlled expenditures. Both sides were once again unprepared for a war of endurance.

Although the war itself enlarged enormously as a military undertaking, its striking configurations were of an economic order. Eventually, every nation was geared to a wartime economy. More than World War I, this one became a grand industrial duel, in which organizational techniques, scientific developments, and mobilization of resources made the state all powerful. England soon had a special Minister of Economic Warfare, and by early 1942 the Germans assigned wartime production to the Ministry of Armaments and Production, thus subsuming much military planning under a civilian ministry.

Furthermore, for a span of three years—from the defeat of France in June of 1940 until the invasion of Italy in July of 1943—the war in the West was of a new complexion: an aerial attack on the domestic front. When Hitler found he could not negotiate a peace with the English, he allowed Herman Göring, head of the Luftwaffe, to begin his "Eagle Attack" on the British homeland. Thus began the Battle of Britain, a battle which nightly provided a scene of German bombers unleashing death from the sky and which daily offered a scene of determined Britons cleaning up rubble and adjusting to wartime hardships. Between these two activities the Royal Air Force undertook the defense of English skies, a task done with skill, heroism, and success. The R.A.F.'s role in the Battle of Britain marked the heroic moment of Britain's "Darkest Hour"—to borrow Winston Churchill's phrase.

After 1940 the zone of aerial combat shifted to the Continent. Germany's European war in a way now became a two-front war: the military activity in Russia waged in a rather traditional, continental manner; the war of the air, now a defensive operation, the chief objective of which was to minimize the damage done by British and American bombing runs.

In the late spring of 1942 the British Bomber Command began its "saturation" bombing of Germany. The strategic philosophy that now came to prevail is summed up in a joint statement of the Chiefs of Staff on American-British Strategy, written on December 31, 1942:

> *The aim of the bomber offensive is the progressive destruction and dislocation of the enemy's war industrial and economic system, and the undermining of his morale to a point where his capacity for armed resistance is fatally weakened.*

And yet, despite the ever-increasing and destructive bombing, the Germans fought on.

That Germany was able to maintain the industrial capacity for continuing the war is largely attributable to the advent of a managerial phase in the operation of the war. After the disastrous Battle of Stalingrad, the nation was organized on a total war basis, with the Ministry of Armaments and Production assuming a dominant position in wartime industrial management. As incredible as it may seem, this was a major deviation from earlier policy. With the initial success of his war efforts in Russia in the summer and autumn of 1941, Hitler anticipated victory and therefore cut back armament production, while Berlin briefly took on the appearance of a peacetime city, with restaurants and luxury shops doing a bustling business. But Stalingrad created a new national mood. Goebbels made a major speech on February

18, 1943, that signaled the change. "Stalingrad is the voice of Fate sounding the alarm," he cried. And then he offered a brief list of rhetorical questions, the most important of which was this: "Do you want war, if need be, even more total and more radical than any we can imagine today?"

Although the crowd cheered him, the German people were in fact forced to accept "more total war." The destruction of their homeland was to become the most obvious and awesome aspect of that form of warfare, but the management of the nation's industrial system was another aspect. Under the leadership of Albert Speer, now minister of armaments and production, German industrial output was rationalized and reworked. Bombed factories were reassembled, with efficiency of effort as important an objective as any. Both bomber and fighter plane production rose as Allied bombs fell. When the war ended, the Germans had a more impressive air fleet than when the war began: 6,638 planes in 1945 as against 4,161 in 1939. What they lacked were the men and the fuel to make the planes fly.

To understand the German war effort, one must remember that it was European-wide in scope and influence. Slave labor from the East, notably from Poland, and forced labor from the West, particularly from France, helped compensate for the manpower shortage caused by the millions of troops fighting on the several fronts. During the brief era of German domination of Europe, one of the most striking demographic developments was that of population displacement. Millions of foreign workers were forced to serve the Germans; millions of Jews were herded into concentration camps where they were exterminated with a dispassionate cruelty that starkly illuminated the inhumanity of the Nazi regime. And, of course, the massive bombing caused the forced relocation of many millions of Germans. In April 1944, over one million citizens left Berlin as it became the object of intensive air raids.

The situation in the civilian sector of the two major Western Allies, Great Britain and the United States, was striking by contrast. After a slow beginning, Great Britain organized its society for total war with greater efficiency and intensity than any other nation—save the Soviet Union. Most significantly, scientific personnel joined the generals in war planning. Indeed, it was Churchill's scientific adviser, Lord Cherwell, a physicist, who was the most forceful proponent of strategic bombing. Moreover, the wartime leadership, unlike the Nazi, genuinely encouraged scientific development. The British breakthrough with radar was a major achievement in turning the Battle of Britain to British favor. The now familiar "blips" appearing on the radar screens in 1940 alerted the R.A.F. to approaching German bombers. Finally, British technology gained mastery of the air. The production of Hurricane and Spitfire aircraft provided the R.A.F. with large numbers of two of the finest military aircraft then developed, an industrial outcome soon matched in bomber production.

If the Island Kingdom thus proved that it still had sufficient Cromwellian spirit to produce another "New Army," the major industrial impact on the war came from across the Atlantic.

Franklin D. Roosevelt announced that the United States was the "Arsenal of Democracy." He did not exaggerate. American wartime production was phenomenal, beyond the belief of many Europeans. When, for instance, Goebbels was informed of the American aircraft production figures for 1943, he dismissed them as sheer fantasy.

American industry was not, however, geared to wartime production until this nation's entry into the war after the Japanese bombing of Pearl Harbor on December 7, 1941. Thereafter, American factories won a continuous victory in the battle of statistics. American military equipment and industrial equipment (such as heavy machine tools) went to Great Britain and to Russia. Despite the fact that the Americans found themselves fighting a two-front war—a naval war in the Pacific against the Japanese; and a land war, first in North Africa and then in Europe against the Germans—there were no major shortages in manpower or equipment.

The combination of military forces and equipment that the Soviet Union, Great Britain, and the United States brought to bear on *Festung Europa* was overwhelming. Hopelessly looking for miracles in the last days of the war, Hitler was briefly cheered by the news of Franklin D. Roosevelt's death on April 12, 1945. The bearer of these tidings was Josef Goebbels, who personally telephoned the declining *Führer*. Then Goebbels ordered champagne for his own staff to rejoice in the thought that "this is like the death of Tzarina Elizabeth." In this statement, Goebbels referred to the dark days when Frederick the Great was badly embattled in the Seven Years War (1756–1763). Suddenly, the Tzarina's successor, Peter III, withdrew from the war. What Goebbels did was make a false historical comparison, for he now assumed that the death of Roosevelt might cause the United States to withdraw from the war. Not only did Goebbels' jubilation demonstrate how far Nazi war leadership was then removed from harsh reality, but also it proved the major role that the United States had come to play in European affairs.

Hitler was no Frederick the Great; and the outcome of this war, unlike that of the Seven Years War, sealed Germany's military fate. German militarism, so important in modern European history, was no longer to be a constant condition in European affairs. Nevertheless, "Hitler's War" was a major formative factor in the redesign of contemporary Europe.

The Effects of the War

Beyond the monumental devastation and the incomprehensible waste of human life, World War II brutally altered European social life.

The most important new activity in German-occupied Europe was the appearance of organized civilian resistance. At first, there were only individual acts of defiance, like that of the Dutch film projectionist who ran a newsreel of advancing Germans backward, to the brief delight of his audience. But the resistance movements took shape in every country and grew to become a major problem in policing for the Germans as the war turned against the Nazi regime. "Silent republics," the resistance organizations ruled by stealth and at night what the Germans still forcefully dominated by day.

The resistance movements destroyed military installations and attacked Germany's war economy by blowing up power plants, railroads, and other vital elements in the system. In retaliation, the Nazis increased the severity of the military occupation, imprisoned and executed hostages. Thus a shadow form of civil war intensified as the regular war front crumbled before the Germans.

Civilian life was plagued by shortages of food, fuel, medicine. "Ersatz," or artificial substitutes, were devised, the most important being the German discovery of the means of producing artificial gasoline. But the most pressing problem was housing, and this most drastic in Germany. Consider only the following single statistical unit: On August 24, 1944, the German city of Koenigsberg was attacked by 175 British bombers. The estimated damage of the raid was one hundred and thirty-four thousand people made homeless, and sixty-one thousand people forced to live in badly damaged houses. After the war, new cities had to be built—Coventry, Rotterdam, and Berlin being examples—and they were technocratically planned.

With an irony that once again underlined the fact that history is a human affair, the destruction of the war brought about considerable reorganization. Even before the war, the Soviet leadership began the relocation of Russian industry in and beyond the Ural Mountains so that it would not be susceptible to immediate ground attack from the West. During the war the Germans decentralized industrial production by dispersing aircraft factories around the country in order to protect them against concentrated bombing attack. And under the German occupation, the puppet government of France, known as the Vichy Regime from the city in which its capital was located, sought economic reorganization and began the foundations of what would be postwar planning under Jean Bichelonne, an engineering professor who was Minister of Production and Transport. Even more unusual, and with effects not easily measurable, was the intellectual migration the war produced. In the 1930s eminent scientists like Albert Einstein had left Nazi Germany, but immediately after the war, both the United States and Russia undertook a rushed treasure hunt as they sought to find and then utilize German scientists, notably those involved in rocket research. Werner von Braun, guiding genius of German war rocketry, came to the United States, eventually became an American citizen, and is today recognized as the technocratic father of American space efforts.

Thus, the war destroyed and forced the rearrangement of much of the old social and economic structure of Europe, just as it rearranged the political map. The truth is the European world we now know was born in debris.

The War in a Global Setting

No balanced historical analysis can afford to treat the European war as disunified from the global war. Among the major continents, only Latin America was spared serious involvement. Even Australia, traditionally known as "down under," feared Japanese invasion. And American blimps patrolled the Atlantic coast of this formerly "isolated" nation in search of preying submarines.

For once in military engagement, the world was viewed from above. While it is certainly true that the infantry soldier struggled and sacrificed to defeat the enemy, and ultimate victory was his, the war of the air was all important. The fighter defense of Great Britain and the bomber offensive against Germany after 1942 altered the proportions of the war. In a tone of despair, the British prime minister, Stanley Baldwin, had said in 1932, "The bombers will always get through." They did not, but they did frequently enough to make the cities of Europe the new "no man's land." Yet for all of this technological havoc, the bomber did not win the war, nor did it affect the enemy's war capacity anywhere as severely as had been anticipated. Across the world, the Pacific naval war was essentially an aerial war, with aircraft carriers serving as seaborne take-off points. The dramatic sinking of the magnificent and brand-new British battleship the *Prince of Wales* by Japanese torpedo bombers on December 10, 1941, can be taken as the symbolic end of the age of battleships. Thus, the first major naval warfare since the Napoleonic era also announced the end of traditional naval warfare. Again the war of the air triumphed.

As if adding to the symbolism of a closing age, the Japanese military activities in the Far East resulted in the fall of Singapore. That bastion of British imperial might, its fortress grimly confronting the sea and its heavy guns prepared to ward off an enemy navy, was taken in February 1942 by Japanese troops who descended overland through the seemingly impenetrable jungles that lie behind the city. The Japanese conquest of Singapore marked the beginning of the end of European colonial empire, the most obvious expression of Europe's domination of the world. Within two decades after Singapore's fall, the European worldwide colonial structure had collapsed beside it.

The dramatic point is this: World War II ended German domination of Europe and European domination of the world. It might be said that European history ended in 1945, and global history then began.

Conclusion

There are those critics, mostly European themselves, who have suggested that the two world wars were a new "Thirty Years War," separated by an extended interlude of uneasy peace. The analogy is tempting, and necessarily false—as are all analogies. But it does illuminate several persistent problems and conditions.

Surely the most obvious is the preponderance of Germany in European affairs of the first half of the twentieth century. This nation was the major industrial power in that period (and so remains in Western Europe today) and potentially the major military threat. Germany's defeat in World War I did not result in the annihilation of its military power, but rather only in its brief check. Indeed, the Allies in World War II introduced the concept of "unconditional surrender" to assure that Germany would be completely under their control, hence prevented from rising again as a military problem.

Furthermore, the suggestion of a "Thirty Years War" implies a continuity in the play of external European political and economic forces. Once again Russia and the United States added their national efforts to World War II as they had to World War I. What was perceived by many at the end of the first war as a shift in the locus of European power from the center to the rim—from France, Germany, and Great Britain to Russia and the United States—was a fixed reality after World War II. Europe had been denied its position as the focal point of a world system; it was now one of the areas of contention in a series of global maneuvers by the two "superpowers," the Soviet Union and the United States.

From the perspective of diplomat and academic scholar alike, the older balance-of-power system had been replaced by a bipolar one: Communist Russia and democratic America were the two centers of ideological and political attraction. What had begun in 1917, when the United States entered the war and Russia had undergone revolution, was now politically consummated. And just as the United States and Russia had played the major roles in the defeat of Nazi Germany, so they played the major roles in the division of postwar Europe.

Winston Churchill would speak of an "Iron Curtain" descending on Europe. What he observed was a division of Europe into two camps, one dominated by Russia, the other by the United States. The line of demarcation was the Elbe River in Germany. Germany, no longer master of Europe, was now the border country divided between two competing world political systems.

But the so-called Second Thirty Years War can be forced no more in this historical analysis. There were decided differences that marked the war of 1914–1918 and that of 1939–1945. Perhaps the most obvious is the shattering psychological effects of World War I. At the risk of the use of simple metaphor, let it be said that World War I took the spirit out of Western civilization. The sense of despair, of fatigue, of emptiness that was so frequently commented on was not repeated after World War II. This difference can be discerned in one easy way, by a glance at the literature of both periods. No large numbers of significant "war novels" appeared after World War II as they had after World War I. There was little that had not already been said. In other terms, World War I was the last war in which the myth of the heroism and glory of war had been maintained. In World War II the most popular war song was a haunting German melody entitled *Lilli Marlene*. Its lyrics spoke of love and loneliness, not of martial ardor and patriotism.

(Left) Portrait of Louis XIV by H. Rigaud, from the Louvre. Reproduced by permission of Cliché des Musées Nationaux, Paris.

(Right) Napoléon blessé à Ratisbonne (1809). Reproduced by permission of the Musée Carnavalet, Paris.

Visions of Authority

The art of modern political leadership has included posing. Every important European head of state has projected a public image that the artist and photographer have been called upon to help define and enhance. Earlier, notably in the seventeenth and eighteenth centuries, royal portraiture served as an emblem of absolute monarchy.

The political uses of such images has gained in importance during the last 150 years, when the printing press allowed for pictorial representation in great quantity and when personal popularity became a major political factor because of the extension of the suffrage. Through the widespread distribution of lithographs and photographs, chiefly through the press, political figures could be recognized and identified, a first step in that media development by which television today makes

Napoléon Bonaparte franchissant les Alpes au Mont-Saint-Bernard, by Langlois. Courtesy of the Musée National du Château de Versailles.

politics immediate and direct.

It was during the Napoleonic era that pictorial propaganda was elevated into a modern art form. Cartoons, already familiar in eighteenth-century France, centered on Napoleon's military attainments; and famous painters reworked events to assure that Napoleon was cast as a romantic hero, a man of destiny.

Queen Victoria with members of the Royal Family (c. 1875). Reproduced by permission of the Radio Times Hulton Picture Library.

Alongside this sort of romantic view of the modern ruler, the pictorialists placed another, one conforming more to middle-class standards of conventionality. Royalty acquired a stiff, familial image, as the reading public took a new interest in the daily affairs of their rulers.

Nevertheless, the official ceremony of monarchy took on new meaning in this age of nationalism. State visits were regularly recorded by newspaper artists and photographers. And the coronation, an event of medieval pageantry, was an occasion for national celebration and a resplendent reminder of historical continuity.

King Edward in Berlin—February 9, 1909. Reproduced by permission of the Radio Times Hulton Picture Library.

The Coronation of Edward VII (1902). Courtesy of The Illustrated London News.

Benito Mussolini. Photograph by Trampus. Reproduced by permission of the Historical Pictures Service, Chicago.

Portrait of Adolf Hitler by B. Jacobs (1933). Reproduced by permission of the Historical Pictures Service, Chicago.

With the rise of modern dictatorship, the idealized portrait of the new "leader" was made a regular feature of propaganda. Both Mussolini and Hitler, who had been political outsiders before their rise to power, now stood as the embodiment of the will of their nations.

The new Soviet regime of the 1920s created its own iconography, that of stylized, realistic portraits depicting Lenin as the counselor, if not the father, of the Russian people.

(Above) *Lenin with friends in Kiev, by B. A. Petyakhov; and* (Below)
*Lenin in the Polish Highlands, by B. Pudshikovsky, from the Lenin
Museum. Courtesy of Agentstvo Pecati "Novosti," Moscow.*

(Left) General Charles de Gaulle, President of the French Republic (1959–1969), in full dress. Courtesy of the French Embassy Press and Information Division.

(Above Right) Edward Heath (Prime Minister of England 1969–1974) conducts the Annual Carol Concert at Broadstairs. Reproduced by permission of Alan Band Associates, Farnham (England).

Although official portraiture continues to exist, and continues to reinforce the symbolic importance of the state, the contemporary era has witnessed a flood of candid and casual photographs, reflective of the familiarity with the world's leaders that modern communications media have assured to the public.

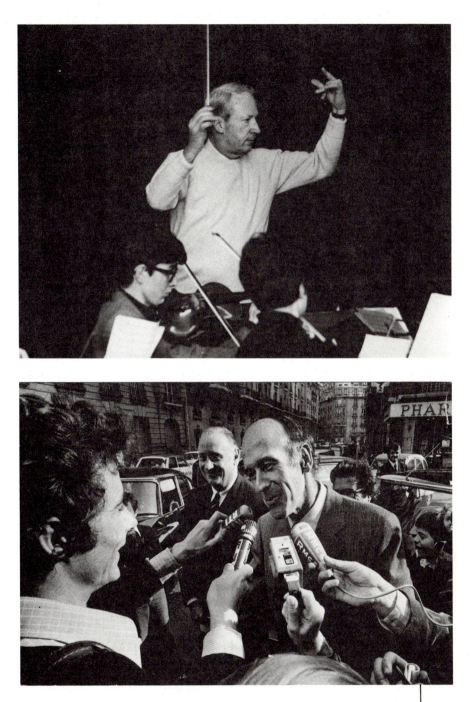

*Valery Giscard d'Estaing (President of the French Republic)
campaigning in 1974. Photograph by Alain Nogues. Reproduced
by permission of SYGMA, Paris.*

PART FOUR

Europe in the Contemporary World

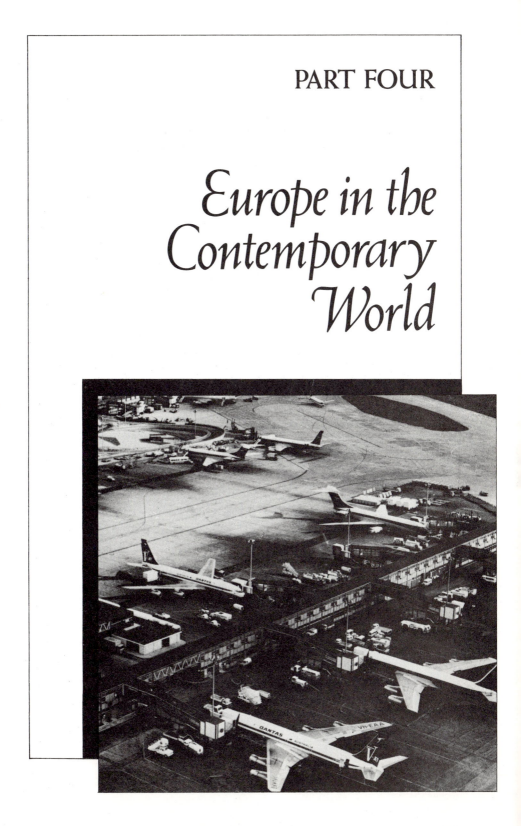

$\mathcal{T}$o celebrate the first anniversary of the end of the war, the city of Paris sponsored a grand ball at the Opera House. Despite the fine quality of the Parisian night and the elegance of the participants, this was no real occasion for rejoicing, either in Paris or in any other capital of Europe.

The first year of the postwar era was a very bleak one, characterized by a bad harvest, a very cold winter, a shortage of capital funds, and a still barren urban landscape of demolished buildings. The term "recovery," already widely used as descriptive of the first order of business, seemed a mockery. In 1946 peace was only the absence of war.

Yet within two decades Europe would be transformed, endowed with one of the world's most impressive industrial establishments, enjoying one of the highest standards of living, and cleansed of the worst wounds of the war. By the 1970s German schoolchildren no longer knew who Hitler was, and the name of Porsche, formerly associated with the design of Royal Tiger tanks, was now affixed to one of the world's most popular sports cars.

The economic development of the postwar era has been called a "miracle," not because it happened mysteriously, but because it happened with unanticipated rapidity. And the economic "miracle" was the basis for a number of other quite remarkable changes, often described as the "Americanization" of Europe, or, in more sedate and prophetic economic terminology, the "post-industrial" era.

Alongside economic progress traveled an unusual social development in general demography. European populations grew in number so that the Old Continent became youthful in terms of its median-age population. Youth culture was as much a European as an American phenomenon, as witness three of England's most important exports of the 1960s: the miniskirt, the Beatles, and the hard rock of Mick Jagger and the Rolling Stones. More recently, youth gangs and youth revolutionary groups have added a deeply disturbing element to contemporary European social life, but still more pronounced in the last decade has been the youth-defined notion of fun: skiing, sunning, dancing have all altered the tertiary sector of the economy. The discotheque replaced the bistro; blue jeans have replaced the blue serge suit; the transistor radio has replaced the briefcase as hand baggage.

New economic wealth has meant the end of old class distinctions. Today the Marxist social structure of modern industrial society is as much a museum piece as is each of the estates on which the aristocrats used to live. The variety of economic activities, the redistribution of wealth, and the greater social mobility characteristic of contemporary Europe have altered both the conditions and the perceptions of social structure. It used to be said that the difference between an American worker and a French worker was this: when the American worker saw an expensive automobile, he longed for the day when he would be driving a similar one; however, the French worker longed for the day when he could pull the driver out of the car. Today French roads are crowded with worker-owned automobiles.

Europe has left its past behind. It has entered a global political system and a global economy. What more simple symbol of the passing of the old order can be found at random than a Bic pen. This French writing instrument, mass-produced, world-marketed, comes from a nation whose literary tradition is only matched, perhaps exceeded, by its military tradition. Now the French have learned that the "pen is mightier than the sword." France, like every other state of Western Europe, is decidedly modern.

13

The Decade
of European Recovery

In our task of reviving the glories and happiness of Europe, her culture and her prosperity, it can be said that we start at the bottom of her fortunes.

WINSTON CHURCHILL
May 14, 1947

In the summer of 1945, with the citizens of Munich filing by the human remains laid out in front of Dachau's crematoria, and with American troops already returning home to the possibility of ownership of a 1946 Chevrolet, the postwar era began. The summer suggested new directions, but that season was stretched out over a setting of rubble and ruin.

Once again statistics simply tell a story of horrible magnitude. Twenty-five million Russians were homeless. All major German cities had about 80 percent of their prewar housing destroyed. Half of France's and Italy's railroad equipment was destroyed. England had used up one-quarter of its foreign investments to finance the war. Nine and one-half million Germans from other regions were resettled in Germany. Four million Poles and Soviet citizens moved into the new areas of Poland acquired from Germany. One million Russians migrated within the Soviet Union.

In every sense of the word European life was unsettled. But, retrospectively, one can see that the most significant of the unsettling effects came not from recovery, but from reconstruction. The ill effects of the war were quickly overcome as a new Europe took shape.

Economic Reorganization

All critics agree that the European economy had not been demolished by the war; rather, it was only severely impeded by it. That England had already returned to a prewar rate of production by the end of 1946 was proof of industrial resiliency; and by 1947 almost all of the European countries were approaching their prewar capacity, except Germany.

The crucial problem was not industrial know-how or raw materials. Nor was it basic plant—even though the war had devastated so much. What Europe needed most was capital, and this came in unusual quantity from a new source: the American government. After a series of emergency loans in 1946, the United States embarked on a different financial venture. In June of 1947, General George Marshall, then secretary of state, offered an unusual address to Harvard undergraduates. Instead of speaking about "pie-in-the-sky-by-and-by," the stock theme of recipients of honorary degrees, Marshall used the occasion to outline a new program of foreign aid for war-ravaged Europe. Authorized by the United States Congress in 1948, the Marshall Plan, which granted credit to individual European states, poured some $12 billion worth of aid into Europe in the first four-year period, the most crucial time and the span for which the Marshall Plan was officially to run.

As a result of this great financial infusion, the European economies made remarkable recoveries. Moreover, the plan was economically important for other reasons as well. It helped stimulate multilateral trade, which had so badly declined in the Depression period, and it brought the United States into the European economy as a major financial factor. Dollar reserves were rapidly built up; and the dollar became the basis for all currency negotiation. (The term "Eurodollar" became a popular one.) Although slowly and reluctantly at first, American investments grew by the second decade of recovery. By that time, also, European products started to find a major market in the United States: typewriters, automobiles (in the forefront, the VW Beetle), aircraft (the first medium-range jet prop in extensive use was British; the first medium-range jet in use was French), sewing machines—all such industrial products that might be called traditionally American in manufacture now also came from overseas.

Nonetheless, Europe developed its own distinctive economic organization as well. No doubt the most striking feature was the double-faceted one of state planning and nationalization of industries. The tendency toward state intervention had already begun in a marked way during the war. Now, in the immediate postwar era, pressing demands for economic rehabilitation, frequently joined with the confiscation of property, brought the state into the realm of entrepreneurship. For instance, two major European automobile manufacturing companies now came directly under state control. In France the Renault Company was taken over because of its wartime collaboration with the Nazis. The company was converted into a semi-public corporation, with a government-appointed board of directors. In Germany, the Volkswagen Company went through a comparable readjustment. During the first years of military occupation, Volkswagen was held "in trust" by the German federal government, but in 1960, its ownership was split three ways: the federal government held 20 percent of the stock; the state government of Lower Saxony (in which the company is located) held another 20 percent; and the public was allowed to buy the remaining 60 percent of company shares.

The nationalization of key energy and transportation industries was one of the most important measures taken in both France and Great Britain. Railroads, banking (both the Bank of England and the Bank of France), forms of domestic energy (coal in England, electricity in France) were all nationalized and placed under the jurisdiction of semi-public directorships, responsible to the government but also responsible for the efficient and economically profitable operation of these activities. In France, nationalization was accompanied by state planning. The Monnet Plan, named after its originator, Jean Monnet, who was one of France's most important technocrats, appeared in 1947, and was the first of a series of four-year plans designed to improve the nation's productivity. With a certain linguistic boldness, not hitherto characteristic of them, the French introduced the word *planification* into their governmental vocabulary, in order to properly term this new process of state planning.

Although France and England were in the forefront of Western European state intervention in the social realm—Sweden was the most advanced of such countries—most of the European nations now introduced health programs and engaged in the construction of badly needed public housing. Furthermore, by revision of the laws for both income and inheritance, they forced the redistribution of wealth so that the gross inequities of the prewar era were toned down.

Thus the "welfare state" replaced the laissez-faire state. If there was a prevailing political philosophy behind such alterations, it was socialism, not liberalism. Bentham's older notion of "utilitarianism" acquired a new social connotation. "From the womb to the tomb" was the way one English politician explained the range of new health services in his country. Even though this sloganlike phrase was quickly dropped because it disturbed English sensibilities of the era, it clearly defined the new governmental norm. The state had become responsible for the citizen, not the citizen responsible for the state.

Yet the nation was no longer seen as being a self-sufficient economic unit.

New Economic Dimensions

Even before World War II there were some outspoken Europeans who urged a "United States of Europe." Immediately after the war, some eminent statesmen, "Eurocrats" of sorts, thought that the future of the Continent lay not in nation-state organization, but in political federation. Two world wars had weakened the enthusiasm for nineteenth-century nationalism, and now economic recovery clearly exceeded the abilities of individual states. The technocrats and the visionaries imagined at least an economically integrated Europe.

Several steps were taken immediately after the war for the purpose of consultation and cooperation. Indeed, the Marshall Plan in 1948 spawned the Organization for European Economic Cooperation (OEEC), which sought ways to enhance commercial cooperation as well as the most efficient means to utilize American aid. However, the major step forward came in 1950 with the announcement of the European Coal and Steel Community, initially formed by France and Germany, but later joined by several other continental states.

The Coal and Steel Community was an administrative device created to assure a free or common market within participating states for these basic commodities. Efficiency of development and distribution was the key concept, and the result was success. Moreover, this success was measured in the extent of interstate cooperation as well as in financial statistics. The guiding genius of the Coal and Steel Community was Jean Monnet, who was sufficiently convinced of its results to urge a large sort of economic community.

Approved by the Treaty of Rome in 1957, the European Economic Community—better known now under the title "The Common Market"—extended the scope of economic integration. Within the boundaries of the participating states (soon to be called "The Inner Six") there was to be a common market, with no restrictions on the flow of goods. Conversely, the Common Market would establish an external tariff with respect to all goods entering its trade area. The evolution of this program took place over a ten-year period and was, as might be imagined, one of demanding, close negotiation. Vested interests in each country, but particularly agriculture, did not wish to be placed at a disadvantage.

The defining noun of the official title, "community," also acquired a real significance. As the Common Market developed, other restrictions relating to economic activities were removed. There was a free flow of labor from one region to another. This, in turn, caused the removal of passport restrictions and reduced the policing of state frontiers. Medical facilities approached continental scope as foreigners were allowed to use the services of the country in which they were living. Even such a minor but daily problem in the industrial world as traffic citations were now handled on an international basis. Finally, there was a hope—but one not realized—that a common European currency would be introduced by 1976.

Raymond Aron, one of the most renowned of contemporary French social commentators, coined the phrase "continental monolith" to describe the superpowers of the postwar era. He contended that the United States and the Soviet Union were the two principal states that had the resources, the market, the tax base, and the productive capacity to succeed handsomely in what has now come to be called the "Second Industrial Revolution." Jet aircraft production, atomic research, and computer technology all require enormous sums for development and large markets for viable production. This second Industrial Revolution, that of electronics and nuclear physics, seemed most likely to occur in Europe if the Continent were organized as a productive and trade unit.

Behind the plans for such economic integration, therefore, was the thought that Europe could be a third industrial force, rivaling both the United States and the Soviet Union. The Common Market acquired a political and cultural objective: the assurance of Europe's place in an altered world. And that world was characterized in the 1950s as bipolar: nations and international affairs gravitating around Washington or Moscow.

The Cold War and Bipolarization

As much as Winston Churchill had hoped and diplomatically maneuvered to guarantee that Great Britain would be worthy of its qualifying adjective in the postwar era, that grand old nation slipped from the forefront of world powers, as did every other European state. Within two years of the end of World War II, the British were retreating from the areas of the world in which they had long enjoyed dominance. Big power politics was now beyond the strength of the British economy to play.

Dramatically, the world split in two. This condition was nowhere more evident than in Germany, where interallied disputes over that country's fate led the initial zones of military occupation to become political lines of division. West Germany (formerly the zone occupied by the United States, Great Britain, and France) and East Germany (formerly the zone occupied by the Soviet Union) emerged as two separate states. This obvious political split was soon extended to global proportions, aggravated by the opposing ideologies of the United States and the Soviet Union and by the intensifying suspicions harbored by the leadership of each nation. The Cold War began.

The truth is that the United States and the Soviet Union had a different vision of the postwar world. While the war raged, projections of what the post-Hitlerian era would be like were vague, ill-focused. Even at the two major conferences held by the Big Three (Great Britain, the Soviet Union, and the United States) at Yalta in February of 1945 and at Potsdam in July of the same year, little happened to regulate the peace.

The war was decisively won; the peace was indecisively prepared. Two views of the European world were gained, one from the East and the other from the West. Russia, heavily invaded and almost defeated by the Germans, had developed a tremendous fear of that nation and was determined to protect itself, primarily by buffer states, from any future outbreak of German militarism. Moreover, the Russians wanted a severe peace, one that would provide large reparations to compensate for the destruction wrought by the Germans. The United States was more Wilsonian in its attitude, now pushing for the establishment of a United Nations Organization as a strong successor to the League of Nations and for a reconstructed Europe in which democratic principles, defined within reconstructed nation-states, would be assured.

The difference of objectives, compounded by a strong difference in ideology—the ghosts of Wilson and Lenin had returned to haunt the world—explains the new mood of tension.

In sum, Russian fear and American suspicion lay behind the antagonism of the Cold War. But Russian fear of Germany was also matched in intensity by Stalin's desire to expand Russia's sphere of influence for more persistent political reasons. What had proved impossible immediately after World War I now seemed ripe for success immediately after World War II. "World revolution," not "socialism in one country," was the dusted-off watch-word. The Cominform, the Communist Information Bureau, officially designated to be the coordinating agency of Communist party policies in the various European nations, was established in 1946 and soon seemed to be serving in much the same way as had the Comintern before it.

From the Western perspective, therefore, the Soviets were back to their old historical tricks. A rash of new facts offered confirmation of this contention. In 1946 the Soviets attempted to establish a Communist-dominated state in Iran's northern province, but were forced by American pressure to stop. In 1946–1947, Communist guerrilla warfare in Northern Greece threatened to bring that country down. In February of 1948, a Communist coup d'état in Czechoslovakia placed that nation under Communist rule. And in 1948–1949, the Soviet occupying forces blocked off West Berlin, then under French, English, and American jurisdiction, so that the city was isolated. A massive airlift, now known as the Berlin Airlift, supplied the besieged population, and in the spring of 1949 the Soviets again opened roads to the city.

Thus, within a span of four years, the wartime allies had become the peacetime antagonists. In reply to these Soviet advances, the West, under the direction of the United States, evolved a policy of "containment." The Soviet Union was to be held back, contained by both military and economic means. On March 12, 1947, President Harry S Truman announced his plan for military assistance to Greece, and the plan was broadly defined to include military and economic aid to any nation struggling to maintain its freedom. The Truman Doctrine was soon joined by the Marshall Plan. Although the latter originally began for economic purposes, and Eastern European countries were invited to participate, it now clearly became part of American Cold War strategy. American aid was no longer singularly directed to reconstruction, but was given for military purposes as well. By 1953, some $15.7 billion had been given to Europe as economic aid, as against $7.7 billion for military aid. Moreover, in 1949, again under American direction, the North Atlantic

Treaty Organization (NATO) was established. This defensive alliance, the first European one in peacetime in which the American government was involved, boldly proclaimed that an attack against any one of its members would be provocation for war on the part of all others. The alliance was directed against Russia and the Communist states in eastern Europe, and was one of the most forceful actions taken during the Cold War.

Of course, the Soviet Union responded. From the Soviet perspective, the United States was ringing Russia with military bases and diplomatic negotiations. The Warsaw Pact of 1955, generally seen as Russia's answer to NATO, organized the defense of Eastern Europe under the Soviet military and allowed for the stationing of Soviet troops in the satellite states.

The Cold War in Europe thus came to mean rival military alliances, rival economic aid, intensifying political propaganda and mutual suspicion. When Soviet forces invaded Hungary in 1956 to put down a rebellion against the Soviet-dominated regime there, the already tarnished image of Soviet communism was further darkened in the West.

Even though the postwar recovery of Europe was thus marked by intensifying rivalry between the two superpowers, the domestic political situation did not long reflect such anxiety.

Politics and Classes

In an interesting reverse ratio, as international politics became more ideological, domestic European politics became less so. After a series of general strikes, precipitated by the Communist parties in 1946 and 1947, the democratic order seemed to become a re-creation of the prewar one. There were notable exceptions, however. The Communist party remained an important political force, even if it did enter into the governments of most of the Western European states. The new political strength was that of the Christian Democrats in Italy, the Christian Democrats in Germany, and the Popular Republican Movement (MRP) in France. All of these large left-of-center parties were made up primarily of Catholic constituents now committed to programs of social action. In France, Italy, and Germany, they were the major governmental parties, and it was their leadership that directed the destinies of the democracies in the first two decades of peace.

Yet the appearance of new political forces did not represent the appearance of new ideological concerns or the intensification of older ones. The French spoke of *depolitisation*, meaning less the end of politics and more the transformation of their purposes.

The universal, or all-embracing ideologies of the late nineteenth century declined in appeal in European domestic politics.

To many critics writing on the subject in the 1950s, ideology had first emerged historically as a function of economic imbalance, the protest of the oppressed and the dissatisfied. In a Europe of the economic "miracle," such distinctions were blurred by the glare of automobile headlights or unnoticed on food-laden tables. Industrial technology, state planning, and the increase of workers' benefits, like paid vacations and participation in management decisions, removed the earlier harsh conditions that suggested a class-divided, hence conflicting, society.

Equally important, there was a new social spatialization. Worker and place of work were separated as never before. The traditional workers' districts, like the famous "red belt" that ran around the outskirts of Paris, were greatly altered. Residential distinctions were no longer as sharp as they had been. Moreover, continuity in family employment, so evident in nineteenth-century European working families, declined. The working-class son might even go to the university and become a professional, or he might escape his working-class origins by entering new forms of employment—as did "The Beatles" in both an unusual and dramatic manner. The working-family ethic, described by Charles Dickens and Emile Zola, was lost in the modern rush forward and upward.

The social and economic fragmentation of families was proof that social mobility increased as the European economy improved. If class lines were ever a stark reality, they were in the days of Karl Marx. But that aspect of the mid-Victorian world was now as anachronistic as the stove-pipe hat. The expansion of the economy meant the diffusion of class distinctions. Social conflict was not removed; it was mitigated and altered. The older "social question"—what to do about proletarian unrest—need then no longer be asked.

However, the truth is the European economy recovered more quickly than did the European mind.

The Reshaping of the European Mind

The war had numbed all intellectual enthusiasm. In 1946 there was no expression of hope or any outburst of rage. A sense of bleak resignation settled into the thinking of postwar intellectuals who came to accept evil as a permanent element of existence and absurdity as the fundamental human condition.

In the most significant play of the 1950s, Samuel Beckett's *Waiting for Godot,* the two main characters wait at a road's edge for the arrival of someone they have never seen, for reasons they are not sure of. This is the meaning of life—or life as imagined by many who then reflected on their times.

Beckett's play was a statement about existentialism, and existentialism was the most popular stance taken by Europeans in the first decade after the war. Philosophers, journalists, café conversationalists, students—and even students in the United States—all discussed it.

The absurdity of life, its fundamental meaninglessness because nothing existed outside one's self—these were the dreadful realities that the existentialist saw and accepted. But to overcome these realities, or, at least, to defy them, the individual had to act, to act totally, to be "committed." It was in acting that being was found. Albert Camus, the most widely read of the existentialist novelists, stated in *The Rebel* (1951) that he had to act against reality: "I proclaim that I believe in nothing and that everything is absurd, but I cannot doubt the validity of my proclamation, and I must at least believe in my protest." It is defiance of life's absurdity by searching for an order that does not exist which gives life purpose. Again, to quote Camus: "Man is the only creature who refuses to be what he is."

Some critics have argued that existentialism was an ad hoc philosophy, an interim statement by Europeans worn out from war, despairing of the future, and deeply suspicious of all ideologies. Although the intellectual roots of the movement reach across the subsurface of twentieth-century European thought, existentialism gained in definition and resonance among those Europeans, and particularly Frenchmen, who had served in the Resistance, who had fought against the evil of Nazism, and yet had witnessed its pervasiveness.

Now many of the same individuals were witnessing the betrayal of communism. George Orwell's *1984* was satirically concerned with mind manipulation, ideological gamesmanship, and managerial control that modern totalitarianism, in the name of some doctrine, might engender—and with Big Brother watching malevolently over all of us. The basic deception of ideology was put most pungently by the Romanian-born, French playwright Eugene Ionesco in 1958: "If there is something that needs to be demystified, it is those ideologies which offer ready-made solutions (and which are the provisional alibis of parties taking over power)."

As Ionesco suggested, the process of intellectual disengagement from ideologies in the postwar era was demystification. The world was observed coldly, harshly, in light of the wartime experience and of postwar Stalinist Russia. The Enlightenment was now indeed centuries away. The universe as reasonable, history as progress, ideas as moral guides—each and all were seen as false. As *Life* magazine told its readers in the June 17, 1946, issue, existentialism meant that "what man does with his life depends on his own stoical reaction to his environment."

In 1959 Federico Fellini, one of Italy's and the world's greatest film directors, finished his *La Dolce Vita* (The Sweet Life). The film dealt with contemporary moral decadence, with middle-class, urban life brocaded in wealth and sensuality. The film was Fellini's personal vision of the state of postwar European culture. If *La Dolce Vita* did not suggest that life was endowed with more meaning than did the thought of the existentialists some ten years before, it did demonstrate that extending materialism might mean growing decadence, not a morally improving world.

Historians, philosophers, and film makers all wondered whether European culture would recover. The new environment of economic prosperity was not yet matched by new philosophical purpose.

Conclusion

"Where the elite meet" announced the statement on the checks that were handed to customers at the fashionable "Aux Deux Maggots" café on the Left Bank of Paris. Here the existentialist leaders, Sorbonne students, and American tourists still gathered in the early 1950s. That the slogan was printed in English says much; that a French café even bothered to employ an advertising slogan of this sort says much more.

The war was far removed, as were many aspects of prewar European culture by the early 1950s. The first decade of recovery was spectacular. Rotterdam was rebuilt, now displaying one of the most fashionable shopping centers in Europe. West Berlin presented an American skyline. The French were doing research on one of the world's finest color television systems. And London, so long depicted as the capital of financial sobriety, was known as a "swinging city."

Scholars, particularly in the United States, studied the Nazi regime with continuing intensity. But the "Thousand Year Reich" that had lasted but thirteen years was now only publicly displayed through its regalia offered for sale at flea markets.

Perhaps the most pronounced change in this new Europe was its consumer-directed economy. Both the generation of new wealth through increased industrialization and the redistribution of much of the old wealth through taxes meant more people had more money to spend. In England alone the number of registered automobiles jumped from less than 2 million in 1940 to 10,816,100 in 1968.

True, Europe was no longer the center of the universe, whether it be defined politically, culturally, or economically. The Continent itself was divided ideologically between the two superpowers. And the colonial empires that Europe had extended around the world were beginning to disintegrate. Yet for all that, Europe was rebuilding and reasserting itself. The Old Continent would remain an important part of the new global community.

14

The Retreat from Empire

For this much the whole world knows, that the right of a people to rule themselves does not depend on the generosity of the overlords, nor does it depend on the preparedness of the people. The truth is . . . that any man has the right to break crockery in his own house. If he bungles, he will soon learn how to set up things right.

LEWIS NKOSI
A Black African Journalist, 1961

After 1945 members of the British royal family found unanticipated employment as ceremonial representatives on those many occasions when political power was transferred from Great Britain to its former colonies. The quick retreat from empire, generally labeled "decolonization," was one of the major characteristics of postwar world politics and stands as striking proof that the older Eurocentric state of global affairs now only has a place in the history books.

However, few were the prophets who had imagined the end of the empire would occur so quickly and completely. During the interwar years theorists estimated that colonies would remain part of political reality for perhaps another century. Even in the early 1950s, more than one experienced observer assumed that European rule in Black Africa could possibly continue until the year 2000. Such predictions were all grossly wrong. Within two decades empire was over in Africa too.

Despite the rapidity of the transaction, there had been some signs that the old order could no longer be maintained. Two events in the interwar period occurred which altered the landscape of the colonial world. The first was Mussolini's invasion of Ethiopia in 1935; the second was the growth of "passive resistance" in India.

When Mussolini boastfully spoke of creating a new Rome, he certainly had empire in mind. A series of petty border disputes between the Italian colony of Somalia and the state of Ethiopia gave Mussolini an excuse for invading Ethiopia on October 3, 1935. The ensuing military campaign, waged by the Italians with tanks, aircraft, and poison gas against the Ethiopians who were heroically fighting with nineteenth-century equipment, was condemned by most of Western Europe. The Ethiopians held the Italians off for half a year, an embarrassing development for the belligerent Mussolini and a magnificent defense to the credit of the Ethiopians. The Ethiopian emperor, Haile Selassie, appeared before the League of Nations to plead his country's case, and in so doing, he emphasized the brutality of the power politics and the rapacious imperialism pursued by Mussolini. If the Italian campaign was the last act of militant overseas imperialism on the part of a European state, it was also seen as one of the most vile. It had the historic effect of announcing that the older form of imperialism was no longer defensible, whatever rhetorical statements about "civilizing missions" might be conjured up.

More telling of the altering composition of empire were the developments in India. Under the direction of Mohandas Gandhi, leader of the large and powerful Congress Party, anticolonialism became a popular cause. There is no doubt that Gandhi was one of the most influential leaders of his day—and one of the most respected.

This small and fragile man, clad in a loincloth and carrying a walking staff, was a figure of striking contrast to the chest-thumping, bemedaled Mussolini. His policies were equally at variance. Gandhi made "passive resistance" a workable political instrument. He personally went on hunger strikes which threatened his life and greatly annoyed the British who feared his death would provoke civil disturbances. Although Gandhi did not enjoin his followers to engage in the same practice, he did encourage them to avoid cooperation with the British and yet also to avert conflict with them. This neither-nor policy, perhaps most closely resembling a boycott, was designed to impede British rule. For the British the policy was singularly disturbing. First, it removed the political support they had earlier received from the Congress Party; and, second, it ran counter to the violent type of political resistance they had already learned to deal with elsewhere. Passive resistance forced the British into a "no-win" position: the resisters tolerated arrest and imprisonment, thereby making the British appear as the aggressors; and they disrupted colonial rule by "standing in the way," by not assisting in the everyday operation of a colonial system that so heavily depended upon "native" labor.

In an era when public opinion was becoming a new force, by way of movie newsreels, the radio, and illustrated magazines, Gandhi found a marvelously confounding formula that made him the most important decolonizing force of the age. What Gandhi proved possible in the 1930s, other leaders, by differing means, would prove possible after the next world war.

Italian aggression and Indian passive resistance, at opposite ends of the political power spectrum, were nonetheless both factors in dissuading Europe from a continuation of the colonial rule defined in the late nineteenth century. Then came World War II, devastating in its effects on Europeon global policy and thereby accelerating colonial change so that plans for reform soon gave way to demands for independence.

India gained its independence in 1947, but in the process split into two rival nations: India and Pakistan. One decade later, in 1957, the first black African colony gained independence as the state of Ghana, formerly the British Gold Coast. And in the next two decades the rest of empire disappeared so that today only a few remnants of the once global imperial system remain.

The two terminal decades of decolonization in the middle twentieth century and the two initial decades of imperial conquest in the late nineteenth century were both characterized by rapidity of change in the political order. That such a grand-scaled affair as European empire was so quickly constructed and then so quickly dismantled suggests that it was a rather flimsy undertaking. But if it was Disneylike in its façade and even in its mock-heroic activities, colonial empire did have enduring effects. Therefore, the transitory nature of the political edifice must be contrasted with the persistence of the social system.

The End of Empire

Some sixty nations emerged from the five major colonial empires in about twenty years. That is an arresting sum in modern political arithmetic. It also adds up to an interesting problem in historical causation, which provokes two questions: Did the colonized peoples gain their own independence? Or, did the European nations grant it? Once again historical reality allows for an affirmative answer to each of the opposing questions.

Immediately after World War II, the major colonial powers formulated grand schemes for reform. Empire was then going from an administrative phase to one of economic development or modernization. State planning, which had become an element in contemporary European life, was now transferred to colonial endeavors. Ports were enlarged, airports were constructed, new roadways developed, medical and educational facilities increased. The universal symbol of modernization, the high-rise building, made its appearance in just about every colonial city, so that Singapore in the Far East, Nairobi in East Africa, and Casablanca in North Africa, all looked rather like variations of Los Angeles from the air.

The technician now replaced the colonial officer. Bare-headed (the colonial pith helmet was no longer worn), with shirt sleeves rolled up, he pored over charts and diagrams. "Development" was the key word, and it suggested a new effort to reorder the "native world" so that it would be set on the way of Westernization. In a few years, when the United States became an influential force in the former colonial world, this process of change would be derisively known as the "Coca-Colazation" of the world.

Nevertheless, these economic efforts were far from being of universal benefit. Rapid urbanization created a colonial proletariat, with Africans and Asians crowding cities that could not support them, but which they regarded as the setting for economic opportunity. The further incorporation of colonial economics into the global market system placed each such local economy at the mercy of vacillating world prices. And this situation soon proved very disadvantageous because industrial goods rose in value while agrarian products remained rather static. As importers of industrial goods, the colonial regions would find a severe imbalance of payments after independence.

In the final years of the colonial era, European planners sought to diversify the local economies. Then they began to stress the commercial and industrial sectors as much as the agrarian, a stress to be continued after independence by the new national leadership. A major outcome, however, was denial of anything approaching agricultural self-sufficiency. Along with industrial imports, food imports increased.

The unintended result of these efforts at modernization was a precarious dependency which often conflicted badly with contemporary social aspirations of the decolonizing peoples. The "revolution of expectations," the assumption that with independence a better life would be achieved, was not to be realized. The former colonial world lies in a general condition of economic desperation nearly as bad as it had ever been before.

Significantly, it was in this changing and unbalanced economic environment that the politics of independence expanded. Economic hopes and economic difficulties created a new political consciousness. Urbanization, as has frequently been asserted, is an important factor in stimulating nationalism. Labor unions, newspapers, universities, and political clubs were generally urban in location. Modernization was thus an important element in popularizing the independence movements.

Until after World War II, the colonial political situation had been broadly characterized by the confrontation of two political minorities: colonial administrators and a colonized elite. The mass of the population was generally indifferent to the activities of both. Indeed, the colonial elite shared more in common with the administrators than it did with the general population from which it had emerged. Speaking the same European language, using the same political philosophy—essentially, liberalism—and often trained in the European professions, the colonial elite established a symbiotic relationship with the colonial administration. Therefore, until the last decade of colonial rule, the relationship between these two leadership groups was one of cooperation as frequently as it was one of confrontation.

Immediately after the war, widespread contemplation of independence was not yet evident. Retrospectively, however, we can see—or impose—a pattern of decolonization. In crescentlike fashion, nationalist protest grew and succeeded in Southeast Asia, then swept westward to North Africa, across to the Caribbean, then back to West Africa and over the continent to East Africa. Much as geographical proximity was a cause for further annexation of colonies in the late nineteenth century, now it was a cause for decolonization. Power abhors a vacuum, reads the old European political argument. And the new power of national independence swept in where European colonial rule was declining.

The decline of colonial rule was, of course, a function of the decline of European power in general. It should be again stated that World War II was itself a major factor. No European colonial power, except Great Britain, emerged from the war victorious—and Great Britain was badly weakened. The others had been defeated, an outcome that starkly proved the myth of European invincibility. Moreover, the temporary success of the Japanese military effort in Southeast Asia helped stimulate a sense of national awareness. Later, as the Japanese retreated, they turned power over to local nationalist groups. Thus, when the Europeans returned to Southeast Asia after the war, they found an entirely different—and hostile—political climate.

Of equal importance was the role once again played by the colonies in a war not of their own making. African and Asian troops served in the European armies in a war that was being waged against dictatorship and a form of military imperialism: the empire of Hitler in Europe; and the empire of Japan in Asia. The war became a school of indoctrination for many colonial troops who witnessed the discrepancy between European colonial practices and European principles. In Ghana, for instance, the military veterans were an important element in urging independence.

Last but not least was the impact of the United States and the Soviet Union as anticolonial powers. Both were officially opposed to overseas empire, and each stood as representative of a different political alternative. The United States had been the first group of colonies to revolt in the name of "self-determination." And the Soviet Union offered communism as the solution to colonial, capitalist exploitation. In the United Nations, which served as a world forum for the colonial peoples, the two superpowers lent support to the arguments for decolonization.

But the United States and the Soviet Union would soon be involved in a world power play for client states in the colonial world. In the 1950s the European Cold War was globalized, when North Korea invaded South Korea and the Truman administration committed American troops in what was now seen as a world struggle against communism. At the same time, the

French, who were frantically fighting to hold on to Indochina, took on a new political appearance in American eyes. Heretofore denounced as colonialists, they were soon praised as being engaged in a defense against militant communism.

This global turmoil and competition, in which Europe was no longer the center, worked to the disadvantage of empire. It was the combination of new world problems and new colonial dissatisfaction that caused overseas empire to collapse.

Decolonization

The singular fact of decolonization was the outward political ease with which most of it was accomplished. With few exceptions, negotiation and peaceful retreat, not bitter resistance, was the pattern. True, Europeans perceived what lay ahead if they did not negotiate, but for the most part the transferral of power was made without severe animosity, such that the ceremonies attended by members of the British royal family were decorous enough to appear in the Sunday pictorial supplements at home.

After the war the politics of the colonial world were altered by the appearance of mass-supported parliamentary parties, whose objective was to play the role of loyal opposition. In some regions, notably South Asia, politics had already been further advanced. Gandhi's efforts should be recalled, and parallel in time with them was the growth of a Communist party in Indochina under Ho Chi Minh. In North Africa there were also important political factions demanding an end to colonial rule. Yet by and large, the mass-supported party was a postwar phenomenon, and one born in a promising environment of political change. The major colonial powers, Great Britain and France, were already restructuring their colonial administration and their principles of rule.

Just the alterations in the official names by which these two great empires were called is an indication of the new mood of the times. The British Empire had become the British Commonwealth of Nations in the interwar period, but after 1945, it reappeared as the Commonwealth of Nations. The removal of the qualifying adjective suggested an official equality of the participating units. The French Empire was reclassified as the French Union in 1945, and then was redesignated "The Community" when General Charles de Gaulle returned to political power in 1958.

It is true that the French still hoped for a unified and integrated colonial community, while the British moved more toward autonomy and self-government. But both nations recognized that political change was necessary. By allowing colonial affairs to move from administration by Europeans to political participation by local populations, the home governments encouraged the move toward local government. The colonial councils, primarily appointed and consultative bodies in the prewar system, now became elective and responsible agents of government. It was in this changed environment that the parliamentary parties of the colonized peoples appeared.

By the 1950s, within a decade after their formation, these parties were transformed from a parliamentary to a nationalist status. Their leaders no longer saw the future as one in which they ought to work within the context of colonial government, but rather one in which they would direct the destinies of new nation-states.

As the political intentions of the colonial elites changed, the response of the colonial governments altered also. One after the other, the colonies were granted independence. Where a colonial administrative unit had stood one day, an independent nation stood the next. The vast majority of colonies in Black Africa, the Caribbean, and Oceania received independence in this peaceful manner.

However, there were two instances of severe colonial warfare, both of which proved the dire effects European resistance could precipitate.

In both Indochina and Algeria the French were determined to maintain their political status. In both colonial regions the outcome was extended warfare of a bitter sort. Between 1947 and 1954 the French in Indochina fought against the guerrilla armies of Ho Chi Minh. The war was an effort made by the French to prevent the collapse of empire immediately after World War II, and it was an effort on the part of Ho Chi Minh to make the provisional republic he had declared in 1945 a political reality. Finally, the French found themselves in a military debacle at Dien Bien Phu in the winter and spring of 1954. The Vietnamese forces had surrounded the French garrison there and soon were demolishing it. This French failure on the battlefield led to negotiation at the diplomatic table. In July of 1954, at Geneva, the French government recognized the existence of the People's Republic of North Vietnam. Ho Chi Minh had triumphed, but the war in Indochina would continue again in 1956, this time with the Americans replacing the French.

Beginning in November of 1954, and in part as a consequence of Ho Chi Minh's success, a National Liberation Front in Algeria engaged the French in guerrilla warfare. Determined not to allow a repetition of Indochina, and anxious to provide support for the large white settler population in the area, the French government eventually mounted a major military effort against the Algerian nationalists. Fighting continued until 1962 when the government of General de Gaulle finally negotiated a peace that assured an independent Algeria.

The struggle in both Indochina and Algeria proved that guerrilla warfare was an effective means of wearing down the enemy. The excessive cost in lives and money of retaining colonial domination was one that sapped French national strength. Gaining the support of the local population, engaging in hit-and-run operations that disrupted military supply lines and frightened the local French populations, the guerrillas forced the French to increase the

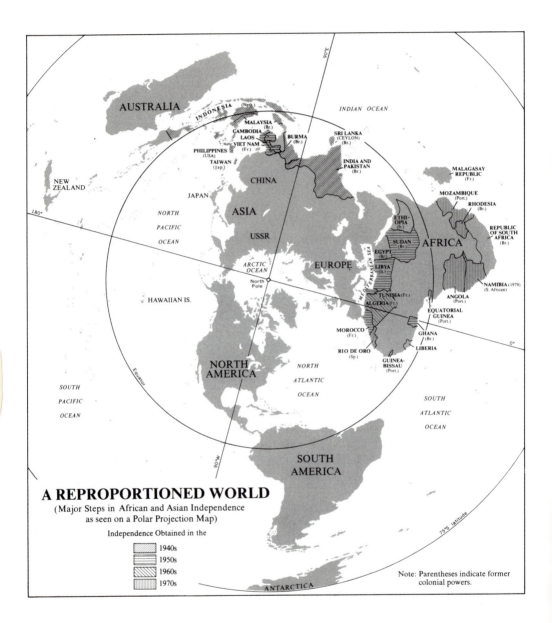

A REPROPORTIONED WORLD

(Major Steps in African and Asian Independence
as seen on a Polar Projection Map)

Independence Obtained in the

	1940s
	1950s
	1960s
	1970s

Note: Parentheses indicate former
colonial powers.

number of troops needed for policing activities. It was calculated that one guerrilla could hold down ten to twenty regular troops.

Guerrilla warfare—or its threat—was therefore a most useful, because a most dreadful, tactic available to the colonized peoples. It disrupted any semblance of colonial order, and it effected an isolation of the colonial authorities from the masses of the people.

Whether by force or through negotiation, the European retreat from empire was as quick as it was total. But the effects of the imperial age continued.

The Significance of Colonialism

Prime Minister Jawaharlal Nehru (1889–1964) of India once wrote that the "shock value" of European imperialism was all important. He meant that European culture, with its scientific and technological base, aroused other cultures from their centuries-old complacency or traditionalism.

The dichotomy between the "traditional" and the "modern," to which Nehru was alluding, has no doubt been exaggerated. Old and new were not always in opposition and, quite obviously, no culture has ever remained fixed. But the European colonial world, centered in the Eurafrican and Eurasian cities, did suggest a different pace and way of life.

Perhaps it would be more accurate to say that the colonial world was one of two cultures. The introduction of a wage-based economy, of a modern transportation system, of new techniques in medicine and—equally important—of a value system based on the principles of change and material progress, altered the old order. The North African driving a donkey cart equipped with pneumatic tires is one example of such change, as is the Hindu peasant listening to his transistor radio. These daily scenes of the incongruous should not lead to the conclusion that the two cultures were consciously blended.

What occurred in the colonial setting was juxtaposition, not intermixture. Few of the benefits of European culture and fewer of the most important positions in colonial society were open to the African and Asian populations. Except for the small elites previously discussed, and except for an emerging commercial bourgeoisie most noticeable in the port cities of Southeast Asia, North and West Africa, access to the European side of the colonial world was highly restricted. In his remarkable colonial novel, *A Passage to India* (1924), the English author E. M. Forster depicts a lawn party held by some Indians for some British. He refers to it as a "bridge party," the irony being that there was a great gap between the two peoples, even though they were assembled on the same lawn.

If not a multiracial society, the Europeans provided a model for political and economic development that served as a major legacy of the imperial age. The very fact that the colonies emerged as nation-states, structured on European principles of national sovereignty and republicanism, and functioning with administrative bureaucracies, is an indication of the effects of alien rule. Moreover, in developing a counter-ideology with which to combat imperialism and the cultural smugness it implied, the indigenous leaders of Africa and Asia sought to adapt their own past to contemporary uses. The reformulation of local, precolonial history was often along the romantic nationalist lines that characterized similar European development a century before. Finally, a European trained military element, one of the most "modernized" segments of society, became a major political force. Many of the contemporary rulers in Africa in particular acquired their first public service in the European colonial armed forces.

Whether the term "modernization" or "Westernization" is used to describe the many social and economic alterations which made the world take on a common appearance, the fact remains that a primary agent in the process of change was European imperialism. Recently, critics have asked if similar change would not have occurred without colonial imperialism. The question is an interesting hypothetical one. But it in part contains its own answer. Only in the last two decades of European empire, in the period since World War II, were the most striking alterations in indigenous societies effected. It was at the time when colonial empire moved from political domination and administration to technological improvement that the "one world" of jet aircraft, television, industrial pollution, and four-lane highways appeared.

Concomitant with this Westernization, there was a new form of colonization taking place in Europe itself. For the first time since the era of the Viking invasions in the ninth century, Western Europe was the setting for a significant immigration of peoples whose homes were outside of the Continent. By the middle 1960s, over five hundred thousand Algerian workers were in France, and another one hundred thousand were found in Belgium and Germany. At the same time residents of the Commonwealth holding British passports appeared in large number in Great Britain. Indians from East Africa, blacks from Jamaica and Barbados, Pakistanis from the Indian subcontinent, resettled in the former seat of empire where they hoped to find economic opportunity. Finally, in the Netherlands there was a small but significant community of Moluccans who fled their native islands when the territory was turned over to the Indonesian government at the time of Dutch decolonization.

The presence in Europe of around 2 million émigrés from the various colonial empires is explained chiefly by economic reasons. Crowding populations and limited opportunities in the decolonizing regions made Europe appear to be a continent of opportunity. Moreover, the economic surge— "the European miracle"—of the 1960s created a temporary labor scarcity on farms, in mines, and in factories. The colonial émigrés formed something of an itinerant, alien proletariat, primarily interested in earning enough money to send to destitute families at home. However, the presence of such a significant new racial component led to social tensions and in England to an outbreak of racial violence. Moreover, as industrial unemployment increased in Europe in the 1970s many working-class Europeans saw the colonial proletariat as an immediate economic threat. Racism, formerly considered by Europeans to be a unique national condition of the United States, appeared in all of its ugliness in Europe.

The problem of temporarily displaced populations is in part a measure of the failure of the "revolution of expectations" in the former colonial world. Decolonization turned out to be a false promise for many Asians and Africans who realized that the economic order of the world was not dramatically changed as a result of the departure of the colonial administration.

After Imperialism

In the 1950s the French coined the expression "The Third World" to distinguish that vast portion of the globe that was removed from the West (Europe and the United States) and the Soviet Union. Originally, the term applied primarily to those newly emerging states which had no desire to affiliate with either of the two major world power blocs. It was at Bandung, in Indonesia, that the first sense of Third World solidarity was expressed in 1955. There, some twenty-nine nations from Africa and Asia convened in conference to condemn colonialism. Chou En Lai, foreign minister of the People's Republic of China, stated the purpose of the conference clearly: "The epoch when the Western powers controlled our destinies is over. The peoples of Asia and Africa must now guide their own destinies."

Since Bandung, the Third World nations have become as wary of Soviet intentions as they have of American. Both "superpowers" seem to be peddling influence, and on occasion both have found their technical assistance staffs sent packing by suspicious governments. In 1973 the Egyptians forced the Russians to leave, and in 1977 the Ethiopians forced the Americans to leave.

Such suspicions of the technologically advanced, militarily powerful, and economically rich nations have, in one form, been structured into an ideology of "neo-colonialism." According to this theory, Western influence remains as strong as it was before in the colonial regions, even though European flags and the personnel who served under them have left. Neo-colonialism suggests that economic exploitation continues, now primarily maintained by the multinational corporation and international aid rather than by the colonial administration.

The great amounts of military aid and capital investment made by the former colonial powers and the United States, notably in Africa, was the factual basis for neo-colonialism. It has been argued that such money and equipment could be manipulated to control the policies of the new sovereign states. And with the resources of large international conglomerates like International Telephone and Telegraph (ITT) and Unilever, domestic policy could be turned to the advantage of the foreign investor. Arguments such as these engendered new concerns. The first president of Ghana, Kwame Nkrumah, warned of a "new scramble for Africa, under the guise of aid."

Neo-colonialism is another form of ideological protest against the economic disparity in the contemporary world. The Third World is the world of poverty, of hunger, of exceedingly low per capita income. It remains dependent upon, hence sensitive to, the wealthy part of the world, which the West primarily occupies.

Conclusion

Like the battleship, empire was made obsolete by the Second World War. A creation of nineteenth-century power politics, such empire depended on a set of cultural values in which paternalism was a pivotal concept. The relationship of colonial ruler to colonized people was frequently symbolized in the statuary found in colonial city squares: the figure representing Europe was a sturdy adult; the figure representing the local population was a dependent child.

Different concepts of authority issued forth after 1945. In a belated way, the Wilsonian principle of "self-determination of nations" was realized on a worldwide scale. Hitlerian imperialism, the most horrendous form yet imposed, cast a gloomy shadow across all forms of empire. The United Nations stood for a new spirit of parity, of equality among nations. It is true that the long-vaunted principles of Western liberalism, particularly the notion of self-sufficient individuals deciding their own political fate, were seldom translated into the daily life of citizens living in the new nations. Military dictatorship and one-party rule were far more common than the English "Westminster Model" of parliamentary rule with a loyal opposition. Nonetheless, decolonization meant a world of quite different political proportions.

Europe is no longer the center of a political network cast over the Tropics. Now European chiefs of state make official visits to African and Asian capitals as frequently as leaders of the nations of the Third World come to Europe. Ours is an age of many lines of international diplomatic traffic. All roads do not lead to Rome—nor to Paris or London.

15

An Era of Booming Success

It is an international cliché that deeds are more important than words —but action does not have to be political. It can be commercial. International trade, not international talk, will assure genuine communication among nations.
HEINZ NORDHOFF
President, Volkswagenwerke
October 26, 1962

      In the middle of the period of Europe's impressive economic success, the United States sank into deep mourning. No state funeral, since that held for King Edward VII in 1910, was so solemnly majestic and international in its ceremony as that of President John F. Kennedy in Washington, D.C., on November 25, 1963. Victim of an assassin's bullet, the president was honored in death by some two dozen heads of state, including the presidents of France, Ireland, and West Germany, the king of Belgium, and the consorts to the queens of England and Holland.
      To view that group of leaders walking together, one would have thought that world unity had become a reality. Of course, it had not. However, the international congregation on that sad day was an expression of the growing interdependency of the regions of the world. It particularly expressed American dominance in Western Europe.
      It was during the second decade of Europe's recovery from World War II that the "Americanization" of the Old Continent intensified. The American language made incredible inroads, with terms like "okay," "pipeline," "jet," "jeans," and "parking" becoming part of several European vocabularies.

As if this were not enough, branches of American fast-food and hotel chains soon located in the major capitals of Europe and added a pungent and colorful quality to the cultural invasion.

"Americanization" is a rather loose term, descriptive of the contemporary consumer-oriented economy and mechanically structured daily life. It furthermore implies an accelerated pace of living—with ulcers becoming the modern European equivalent of eighteenth-century gout. And, as in the United States, European magazines soon carried advertisements for a variety of labor-saving devices, which could now be widely afforded. For the bourgeoisie, the maid went out as the electric dishwasher came in.

The period of recent European history which roughly straddled the years 1958–1969, the time when General Charles de Gaulle was president of France and near-arbiter of European affairs, was the extended moment of Europe's greatest economic development, the period when the benefits of industrial society were for once widely spread throughout European society. As in the previous decade, economics again dominated European history.

The Economics of Plenty

The success of the Common Market seemed one indication of an era of domestic peace and comfort. All European countries, even those outside of the Common Market, fared quite well. Between 1957 and 1961, for instance, the per capita income in Western Europe rose about 20 percent. One easy measure of modernization was the purchase of television sets. In 1957, Italians owned 647,000 sets; in 1967, they owned 7,669,000. The French numbers grew equally spectacularly: from 683,000 in 1957 to 8,316,000 in 1967.

The growth in family income allowing for such purchases was matched by its redistribution within family budgets. Europeans, particularly in France and England, were now spending less on food and more on rent and leisure-time activities. Vacation travel increased, as the automobile and better train service made a vacation in the mountains or at the beach as fashionable as it was attractive. Traditional patterns of purchasing also altered. The local market and the small shop declined in commerce, as large concerns replaced them. The supermarket became a part of European culture, such that self-service, hitherto an alien practice, was made an aspect of daily domestic routine.

Such changes resulted from many factors, of course, but none was more significant than the new economy of scale. European companies grew in size, output, and range of market. But more important was the intrusion of American firms into the European market. Between 1958 and 1961, some 843 American firms established subsidiaries on the Continent. By 1966, American investment had reached the staggering figure of $16.2 billion. European reaction was mixed, but a sense of concern over Europe's future independence was widely asserted. As one French politician remarked, the colonization of Europe by America appeared to be under way.

Behind all of this activity loomed a new corporate form: the multinationals. These companies, operating in a global market, established their own branches or subsidiaries abroad and thereby operated on a truly international scale. In 1967, for example, the largest of the lot, General Motors, had $20 billion in world sales and owned production facilities in some twenty-four countries. Chrysler, with $6.2 billion in sales, and facilities in eighteen countries, had already bought out the French automobile firm Simca and also owned the British company Rootes. In some instances, these large concerns engaged in what has been called "third-nation exchange." The Ford Motor Company manufactured parts in both Belgium and West Germany. Trade in these parts between both countries was a major element in Belgian foreign commerce. In other instances, these concerns amalgamated with European firms by buying into them. The French computer company Machines Bull, the largest independent European manufacturer, found that it had to accept financial support from General Electric because of severe IBM competition. In this manner, GE gained entry into the European computer market. Most impressive of all was the staggering statistic that 80 percent of European electronics production was owned by American firms.

There were several disturbing aspects about this new economic development noticeable at the national level. In the first place, it marked a departure from established American trading practices. Before, American goods had been primarily exported; now they were both manufactured and sold abroad. Thus, while American investment figures increased, American foreign trade declined, to the point that the United States found itself with a $10.6 billion trade deficit in 1970. As seen from the perspective of European politicians and technocrats, the multinationals were a direct threat. Although the United States did not control a majority share in any one European national economy, American firms definitely controlled those new key industries that counted in the age of the Second Industrial Revolution. It was the field of electronics and communications that American corporations dominated.

What was not lost on Europeans was the hard fact that research and development were funded far more lavishly in the United States than in Europe. It consequently seemed as if Europe was relatively underdeveloped technologically, despite the great advances it had made in the education of scientists and the establishment of research centers. For instance, France, with one-fourth of the population of the United States, spent only one-tenth of the amount that the United States invested in research.

To compound the problem, Europe endured an unexpected form of intellectual emigration. The "brain drain," as it was called, further weakened European technological progress. The expanding American economy, with its higher wages and more attractive standard of living, was an inducement to trained technocrats to leave Europe. About fifteen hundred scientists and engineers left Europe each year for America in the period 1956 to 1961.

Underlying this curious dual development of European well-being and American economic domination was the problem of capital. Despite the rapid increase in gross national product and per capita income, no European nation was able to match the enormous sums of money generated in the United States.

Whether the multinational corporation was a threat or a boon—a self-serving company bent on growth and further capital investment for its own sake, or a means to more efficient production and marketing—is a question that was hotly debated in the late 1960s and early 1970s. Historically, the advent of the multinational corporation is further proof of the globalization of national economics and the welding of bonds of gold that held Western Europe fast to the United States. Moreover, the primacy of the multinational in the 1960s suggests that the technocrats, as was predicted over a hundred years before by the Utopian Socialists, became as important, perhaps more important, than the politicians.

The Politics of Europe

General Charles de Gaulle (1890–1971), first president of the Fifth French Republic, stood large (6′4″) as a refutation of the previous assertion. The decade of Europe's greatest economic success was also the one in which de Gaulle more than any other man directed, if he did not determine, the destinies of Europe.

Few twentieth-century European personalities seem to have been more heroic in stature. As early as 1934, in the first of his many books, the then Colonel de Gaulle warned of the changing nature of modern warfare and spoke of the need for France to modernize, by mechanizing, its armies. De Gaulle was ignored.

On June 18, 1940, the day after the French armistice with Nazi Germany, General de Gaulle, having fled to England, made a radio announcement in which he announced to the French people that a battle, not a war, had been lost. Again, he was largely ignored. In the ensuing two years, as de Gaulle tried to organize a French fighting force and provisional government, the Allied leaders, notably Churchill and Roosevelt, tried to ignore him. De Gaulle's persistence was initially a bothersome nuisance. But his persistence paid off. Believing deeply in "Eternal France," de Gaulle assumed the responsibility for trying to repair that country's bad fortunes.

His political skills, his administrative ability, and his sheer doggedness eventually won to his side large portions of the French overseas empire, and after 1943, the major part of the resistance forces in France. By 1944, de Gaulle had emerged as France's man of destiny. And when he walked down the Champs-Elysées in liberated Paris in August of 1944, he did so as a minor deity.

After a brief term as prime minister of the new Fourth Republic, de

Gaulle was politically discouraged by constitutional developments, and thereupon retired to his country home where he, like most other war leaders, sat down to compose his war memoirs. He was recalled to high political office by the president of the Fourth Republic in May 1958, when the Algerian war of independence caused deep political dissension.

Once again de Gaulle's career began. Once again he was a figure to be reckoned with.

The Europe of General de Gaulle was a Europe caught up in the Cold War, but in many ways as concerned about the extension of American power as fearful of the intrusion of the Soviets. Through NATO (the North Atlantic Treaty Organization), through capital investment and foreign aid, the United States gained an ascendency in continental politics and assumed a responsibility for Europe's defense that was not always greeted with enthusiasm by European leaders. Moreover, American military strategy for Europe had changed from an earlier concept of immediate massive retaliation against any Soviet invasion of Europe to a new policy of gradual escalation. Europe was thus made more responsible for its own defense—and somewhat less sure of the degree of potential American commitment.

Into this atmosphere of doubt and concern strode Charles de Gaulle. Much has been written about de Gaulle's highly idiosyncratic view of foreign affairs and of the nation-state that directed them. In some ways de Gaulle was an unrepentant nineteenth-century nationalist. Most critics agree that he was a political anachronism who handled foreign affairs with consummate skill.

De Gaulle wished two things: the dominance of France in Europe and the independence of Europe from the United States, both militarily and economically. He advocated as his basic principle a "Europe of States." He considered as absurd the grand notions of political integration proposed by some of the Eurocrats. For him, the nation-state was the highest form of political and social institution. He thus was willing to use the Common Market for his own purposes: to assure France's ascendancy in Europe. And in so doing, he caused many difficulties, not least of which was the refusal of Great Britain's request for entry in 1963.

It was in the military domain that de Gaulle had the most important effect, however. His concept of national independence implied the nation's right and ability to use force. Distrustful of the Americans and convinced that France had a major role to play in world affairs, he pursued an independent military policy which was a nuisance to American strategists. He encouraged already ongoing atomic research so that France became the third Western power to have an atomic bomb (1960). He then fostered a *force de frappe*, a "striking" force of bombers capable of delivering the bomb. Finally, in 1966, he withdrew France from NATO.

The Europe of de Gaulle was a Europe attempting to redefine itself politically. By the middle 1960s Europe was no longer the center of the Cold War and no longer so dependent on the United States. Perhaps the most notable political change was that concerning the "two Germanies." The split of Germany into two at the end of World War II, with Russia dominating East Germany, had been a source of continuing antagonism. The West German Federal Republic, established in 1949, had not recognized the division and had found support in its stand from General de Gaulle. Then in 1969, the new federal chancellor, Willy Brandt, began his *Ostpolitik*, or Eastern policy. Through negotiations with the Soviet Union, Poland, and East Germany, he came to accept the new status quo. In 1973 when both East Germany and West Germany were admitted to the United Nations, the legitimacy of both states was universally recognized and a major obstacle to the settlement of European affairs was removed.

Furthermore, the Cold War itself had passed through several seasons. With the death of Stalin in 1953, a period of "thaw" occurred in which the Soviet leadership under Premier Nikita Khrushchev turned to increased industrial and agricultural production with the intention of outstripping the United States economically. However, in the early 1960s, Khrushchev again took to denouncing the United States, and the Cold War frosted over. By the end of the decade a new policy of *détente*, of an effort at mutual understanding and accommodation, was being pursued by both of the superpowers. The Cold War in Europe was now over.

Thus, the role that General de Gaulle was able to play as France's chief of state was in part a reflection of changed conditions in Europe. Beyond the alteration in Cold War politics, there was the strength of domestic economies. As de Gaulle himself frequently remarked, no nation is able to negotiate from weakness. France could now negotiate because it was strong. The domestic improvement of France therefore enabled that nation to assert itself as it had not since the peace treaties of 1919. However, in de Gaulle's scheme of things, the improvement of the general lot of the French people was not a good in and of itself; it was, rather, the means by which a successful foreign policy could be pursued.

Because his eyes were focused on global affairs, because he did not seriously interest himself in domestic policy beyond how it would help foreign policy, General de Gaulle failed to see or understand many of the internal changes that were taking place in France and in the other nations of Europe. When he left office in 1969, it was because he had failed at home.

Europe at Home

General de Gaulle was sixty-seven years of age when he was recalled to direct France's government. Around him was a new youth culture, symbolized in that transatlantic phenomenon known as the Beatles.

The Beatles were a musical group who popularized, if they did not introduce, the musical idiom of "rock," variously described as reworked Beethoven or a combination of blues and country music. The musical style was less important than the mood it represented.

In a sense the Beatles were modern troubadours; their music was an expression of social consciousness, an astute commentary on the culture of the times. They sang of middle-class loneliness; they sang of drug use; they sang of youth in quest of self and of one another. Parents denounced them; youngsters applauded them; the press covered them.

When they made their first American tour in 1964, the Beatles showed the popular dimensions of youth culture. What was described as "Beatlemania" seemed to seize young people in the United States.

But there was a less pleasant side to the emergence of youth as a cultural and social category in the modern world. The new "generation gap" resulted in generation conflict, one of the most important social disturbances in postwar Europe.

"Youth" as a social category may only have been defined in the postwar era, but the role of youth in European society had been important for some time. One of the leaders of the French Revolution had been a young man of eighteen; the English Romantic poets were all young men; student movements in Germany and France had an impact on politics in the first half of the nineteenth century. And the "Lost Generation" of World War I was essentially a youthful generation.

Nevertheless, the situation of youth in Europe after 1945 was of quite different proportions. The population spurt meant a much more youthful population than before. The total collapse of older aristocratic values which emphasized tradition now meant a new cultural freedom or license, noticeable in manners, fashion, and language. Moreover, new social opportunities, notably the availability of university education, were made possible by the European economic "miracle." Finally, the American presence in the form of university students and the children of members of the armed forces, exercised an influence, perhaps most noticeable in a new casual manner of style and behavior among European youth.

Part of an affluent society and detached from the social values of their elders, many young people became "alienated," positioned in resentful opposition to the world in which they lived. Although there had been some youthful outbursts before 1968, it was in that year that university student movements proliferated, deeply disturbing European society and the world at large. In West Berlin, Paris, Rome, London, Mexico City, Tokyo, and Berkeley, California, students rose in protest. The "student movement" was, perhaps, well named, for it set off in several directions and was comprised of a variety of protestors. But there was one general thrust: the movement was made against the contemporary social order.

All of the rebellious students denounced what was popularly known in the United States and Great Britain as the "establishment," those agencies—notably government, corporation, and university—seen as the holders and manipulators of power.

The growth of state bureaucratization, the intensifying regulation of personal life, the emphasis on a consumer-oriented economy more concerned with goods than humanistic values, and, last—but of great importance—the

Vietnam War, were factors combined in various slogans and hastily contrived ideologies.

The university was selected as the immediate target—with student "take-
overs" and "sit-ins" frequently occurring—because it was seen as closely
allied with the "establishment." In the words of one young French professor
who participated in the student revolution in Paris, "The professors respond
more as guardians of the social order than as managers of a changing order."

Certainly the phenomenal growth in European higher education after
the war was a result of technological improvement and demand. The intensifying concern with public welfare, the new interest in state planning, and
the expansion of industries called for new skills and more personnel. The
extension of older professions, like medicine, and the opening of new professions, like business management, moved the universities away from their older
aristocratic image to a more popular base. Moreover, increasing state subsi-
dies allowed students from different economic backgrounds to continue their
study. Even a limited statistical sample gives some indication of the rapid
increase in the university population:

	1958	1968
Germany	139,555 men 26,155 women	406,831 men 106,612 women
Italy	206,058 men 53,766 women	342,478 men 126,641 women

To its critics—the radical students—the university had become a process-
ing system for the acquisitive society. Their protest was, in effect, against
much of Europe's most recent achievement. And for this reason the students
found little support outside their own community. The efforts of French
students to enlist support from the French workers were short-lived. Indeed,
wages were low as a result of General de Gaulle's policy, and workers' discontent was accordingly high. But the purposes of the students seemed vague
and removed from the workers' real concerns. The alliance between students
and workers was therefore a matter of convenience, ended as quickly as it had
begun. Once the government conceded on wage increases, worker support
for the Parisian student revolution of May 1968 subsided.

Nearly as swiftly as it was generated, the violent activity of the students
in Paris disappeared, swept away by public antagonism or indifference, by
brutal action on the part of the police, and by governmental concessions.
There is an ironic note found in the fact that the major leader of the French
student movement, Daniel Cohn-Bendit, was making a cowboy movie one
year later.

The end of youth protest did not occur in 1968, however. It continued in
virulent form in the university environment of contemporary Italy—and
Japan, half-a-world away—and it recently took on more sinister form in the

terrorism evident in the late 1970s. Even in its most benign expressions, the youth movement was the most important cultural development of the 1960s. From rock music to the use of drugs, it represented dissatisfaction with the social effects of the "economic" miracle, with the seeming materialistic acquisitiveness and governmental manipulation complacently accepted by the older—over thirty—generation.

Conclusion

In 1956 the English scientist and novelist Sir Charles P. Snow introduced the concept of "two cultures," a thought he developed more fully in a major lecture delivered in 1959. The two cultures that Snow saw in opposition were that of science and that of the humanities. Modern intellectuals, so divided by their disciplines of study, could no longer communicate with one another, for they spoke different languages and dealt with different concepts.

Above all, Snow feared the ill effects of scientists unenriched by humanistic concerns and humanists incapable of understanding—and judging—scientific developments. That his "two cultures" was widely and favorably discussed suggests that Snow had described what others believed existent: a new social and cultural division based more on profession than on economic class. The growth of specialization, in part necessitated by technological progress, had done away with what the English used to call the "all-rounder," the individual who did many things well, but none with particular expertise.

Contemporary society, as viewed by many Europeans—and Americans as well—was dividing between the "experts" and the rest of the population. An intellectual and technocratic elite had come into being. Here was the subject of much of the objection registered by the student movement. The radical student emphasis on "spontaneity" and on "participatory democracy" was a statement of rejection of expert management and a demand for a new political equality. Even the Soviet Union and the various national Communist parties were viewed as vast, impersonal bureaucracies, run for the benefit of the officeholders, not for the people at large. As early as 1957, Milovan Djilas, a former vice-president of Communist Yugoslavia, had written an indicting book entitled *The New Class*. The new class in Communist society was, according to Djilas, the "political bureaucracy."

What the new economy of scale seemed to produce was a social order of scale. The vastness of contemporary enterprises, whether the multinational corporation or the welfare state, had reduced the significance of the individual. Radicals frequently used the word "imperialism" to describe this condition, suggesting a new form of domination and regimentation. And yet the efficiency of production and the extent of managerial planning that such large-scale operations had enabled were greatly responsible for Europe's contemporary economic well-being.

Europe of the 1960s, like the United States of the same decade, was a society with well-defined economic achievements and vague, even conflicting, cultural purposes.

The Great Engine Match, from Punch, *July 1847 (London)*.

The Humor of Technology

Punch, the English humor magazine of the middle-class, was founded in 1841 and has since held the foibles of modern European society to the mirror of gentle ridicule. One of the favorite topics of the magazine's many cartoons has been the social implications of technological progress.

NOSCE TEIPSUM.

Lady Cyclist (touring in North Holland). "What a Ridiculous Costume!"

Nosce Teipsum, from Punch, *June 4, 1898 (London).*

Within a few years of its founding, *Punch* found the new railroad a subject worth lampooning. In an 1847 issue the editors announced—in fun, of course—a forthcoming railroad steeplechase, in which the tendency for engines to jump the tracks would be converted into sport. Hurdles should be placed across the tracks, wrote the editors, "for the purpose of testing the metal of the highflyers."

The bicycle, the first popular form of mechanical transportation, appeared in many late nineteenth-century cartoons, where its riders were frequently treated as eccentric or very modern—even outlandishly faddish.

Motor Fiend, "WHY DON'T YOU GET OUT OF THE WAY?"
Victim. "WHAT! ARE YOU COMING BACK?"

Motor Fiend and Victim, from Punch, *December 12, 1900 (London).*

With the turn of the twentieth century, the automobile made its noisy appearance and soon served as a vehicle for much of modern humor in which the machine is described as dominating—or grinding down—mankind.

Even in the dire years of World War I, the editors of *Punch* caused

The British Tank, from Punch, *September 27, 1916 (London).*

their readers to smile at the most horrible of technological developments. The "tank" (an English weapon disguised in official literature as a "water tank" in order to assure its secrecy) made its military entrance in the Battle of the Somme, 1916, and was sketched in several forms in *Punch* of that same year.

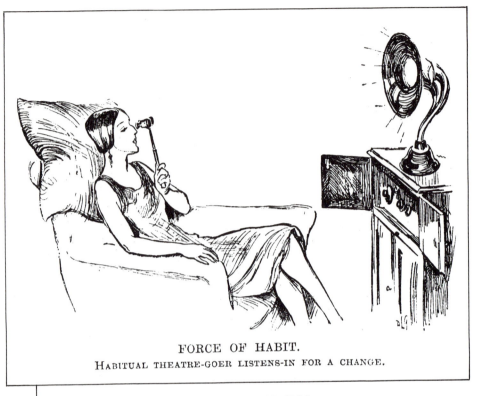

FORCE OF HABIT.

HABITUAL THEATRE-GOER LISTENS-IN FOR A CHANGE.

Force of Habit, from Punch, *October 20, 1926.*
Copyright 1926 by Punch/Rothco. Reproduced by permission.

The interwar period was one in which electronic wonders intruded into the European middle-class household. Although electric lighting had first been used on a grand scale in the Paris Exhibition of 1889 (the one famous for the Eiffel Tower), electrical appliances only became commonplace in the 1920s and 1930s.

The radio set generated a new form of entertainment, one that caused a *Punch* cartoonist to suggest that its use required some cultural adjustment.

The center of the new, energy-consuming European society was the vast central generating plant, which provided electrical energy to satisfy the many needs of citizens who often did not understand even the basic principles of electrical transmission.

"No, Madam, there is nothing wrong at the power station. We are extremely sorry that your little boy's electric train won't go."

"No, Madam, there is nothing wrong . . .", from Punch, February 27, 1935. Copyright 1935 by Punch/Rothco. Reproduced by permission.

Santa swatting TV aerials, from Punch, *December 15, 1948. Copyright 1948 by Punch/Rothco. Reproduced by permission.*

    The telecommunications revolution of the era after World War II was not ignored by *Punch* as the magazine passed its one hundredth anniversary. In 1948 the magazine celebrated Christmas by offering a modern representation of an old seasonal myth.

    Finally, *Punch* anticipated the space age in its traditional way.

"*There won't be any fuss about parking it there, will there?*"

*Entwhistle Lunar Expedition, from Punch, December 5, 1951.
Copyright 1951 by Punch/Rothco. Reproduced by permission.*

16

Contemporary Europe

Man has the fundamental right to freedom, equality, and adequate conditions of life, in an environment of a quality that permits a life of dignity and well-being, and he bears a solemn responsibility to protect and improve the environment for present and future generations.

PRINCIPLE ONE
Stockholm Conference on the Human Environment
June 5–16, 1972

The first transatlantic flight of the supersonic aircraft, the *Concorde,* took place on January 21, 1976. The plane, a joint development of the French and the British, was designed to introduce a new era of swift, intercontinental travel and to serve as proof of Europe's intention to remain in the forefront of technology.

However, environmentalists protested against the *Concorde's* noise level at take-off; politicians criticized the enormous expenditures made for the aircraft's development; and economists complained of the plane's gluttonous consumption of fuel. The *Concorde* thus unintentionally transported across the ocean a small inventory of new global problems. International affairs now included communications, economics, and ecology, as well as traditional interpretations of war and peace.

New European Dimensions and Problems

In the last two decades the world has socially diminished in size to become what the American architect and critic Buckminster Fuller has described as "Spaceship Earth." All of our living space has been bunched together by advanced telecommunications systems, while the condition of the environment has become a common concern.

The world no longer is centered on a single continent, nor does any continent remain in isolation. As a result, contemporary Europe is both more cluttered and more extended. Two of the most obvious indices of modernization, the number of telephones in a region and the frequency of air travel, stand as proof of the recent changes in European social space. In 1970, there were 80,776,000 telephones in Europe; in 1975, that figure increased by nearly one half to become 118,199,000. In 1970, 37,935,000 European passengers were carried on international aircraft flights; that figure rose to 51,-843,000 passengers in 1975.

Beyond the ring of the phone and the roar of the jet are found more impressive telecommunication developments that have silently supported the new social order that has made Western Europe a "neighborhood" of North America. In 1956 the first transatlantic telephone cables were laid, thus allowing for near-instantaneous voice communication of high quality between Europe and America. Then, in 1965, the International Telecommunications and Satellite Consortium (Intelsat), primarily an American and European organization, launched its Early Bird satellite that was designed to carry both telephone and television signals. Since that date, Intelsat has developed more sophisticated satellites, such as the *Intelsat IV* series, first launched in 1971, which are able to carry ten thousand messages simultaneously. The direct intercontinental broadcast of television programs was now possible, while telephonic communication between New York and London is, for instance, as easily and quickly made as a call between London and Manchester.

This new social mobility indicated by telecommunications developments is an expression of Europe's continuing economic growth. With a per capita income that now is approaching that of the United States in general (and which has exceeded the American in a few countries like Sweden and Switzerland), Europe has once again become one of the wealthiest regions of the world. Both trade and investment are of impressive global proportions. European automobile assembly plants have been built in Russia, Romania, Africa, and the United States; while investment in American firms has reached striking proportions, with the Germans alone placing $730 million in the United States in 1977. As simple an indicator of the new prosperity that can be found is the tourist trade. Europeans now spend more abroad annually than do Americans. In 1977 the West German tourists spent $8.9 billion—

more than any other nation in the world.

However, such general economic ascendancy has not been without its downward side. Industrial and technological progress has meant pollution. Tall factory chimneys in England have had their fumes carried by unfavorable winds to Sweden. Overcrowded Parisian roads led the government to the decision in 1967 to build expressways along the picturesque banks of the Seine River. Excessive noise from Heathrow Airport, outside of London, led to such severe complaints from neighboring residents that the government, in 1966, forced the British Airport Authority to allocate special funds for some soundproofing. More spectacular in bad effects has been the breakup of two super oil tankers: the *Torrey Canyon*, which in 1967 spilled over a hundred thousand tons of crude oil on the beaches of Cornwall, England; and the *Amoco Cadiz*, which did even greater damage in 1978 to the beaches of Brittany, France.

These new industrial hazards were first dramatically headlined in 1952, when London endured its worst smog. For four days in early December, the city was ashen with soot, darkened to the point where automobiles were abandoned, and unhealthy to the extent that four thousand Londoners lost their lives. In response to this disaster, the government passed a Clean Air Act in 1956 which attempted to regulate urban smoke emission.

Since then, there has been a variety of European responses to environmental problems. In 1968 the West German government declared a ban on all supersonic civilian flights over the land. In the same year, the British provided more stringent measures on smoke emission with another Clean Air Act. A Ministry of Environment was created in 1971 in France. And in the French elections of 1978, four major ecological movements joined together to form Ecology '78, the first ecological party in Europe.

On the international level, the United Nations has found an area of activity in which its institutional strength can be effectively used. Since 1954 that organization has held a series of conferences on population and pollution control, the most famous of which was the Stockholm Conference on Human Environment, held in 1972. As a result of this particular conference, an Environment Secretariat was set up as a permanent unit of the UN, with its headquarters established in Nairobi, Kenya.

Such expressions of concern with the environment have still not led to a noticeable cleaning-up of the European atmosphere. Although some 125 varieties of birds now reside harmoniously with some 7 million people in clear-sky London, the situation is exceptional. Elsewhere there is continuing tension between the technocrats who speak of growth and the environmentalists who speak of decay.

Economic issues have lately been complicated by the energy problem. The cheap energy that largely fired the "economic miracle" of the 1950s and 1960s is no longer available.

The New Economics of Oil

Petroleum products reordered European life just as they had already done so to the American. Fuel oil replaced coal as the source of industrial energy, while gasoline usage increased rapidly with individual ownership of automobiles. Economically and geographically, Europe now moved on oil.

ESTIMATED CONSUMPTION OF ENERGY IN PETROLEUM-RELATED PRODUCTS (IN KILOGRAMS PER CAPITA)

	1950	1960	1974
Spain	39	133	955
United Kingdom	254	713	1,605
Italy	89	375	1,597
France	214	500	1,889
West Germany	49	504	1,879

Because little of the world's petroleum production takes place in Western Europe, even though off-shore oil rigs in the North Sea are now exploiting new reserves, the region has depended on imported oil for its major energy needs. In the period prior to this last decade, such importation was readily facilitated by low petroleum prices and the advent of "supertankers" capable of cheaply carrying enormous quantities of crude oil to European refineries.

This attractive economic arrangement was disrupted by a new turn in international relations. For the first time in their two-hundred-year history the industrial nations of the world could no longer easily exploit the natural resources of the so-called "underdeveloped" or nonindustrialized portions of the world.

Most of the world's oil reserves are found in the Near East, and the political turbulence of that area upset the favorable oil flow. First, a change in government in Libya in 1969 brought to power a nationalist military dictatorship which initially increased the share of profits the government would receive from foreign oil concessionaires and, then, nationalized oil production. The result was an enormous increase in crude oil prices from that nation. Following Libya's initiative, the Organization of Petroleum Exporting Countries (OPEC), an international marketing consortium in existence since the 1950s, raised the crude oil prices at its wellheads. However, OPEC's major increase was taken in the autumn of 1973, following the Arab-Israeli war of that year. Crude oil, which had cost $1.71 per barrel at its port of origin in Arabia in 1950, rose to $2.48 in 1972; and then rose spectacularly to $11.65 in 1974.

Although the OPEC decisions may have seemed capricious to some observers, and even a form of international blackmail to others, these decisions were reflective not only of Near Eastern political concerns but also of a new spirit of national resentment expressed against the wealthy West and the ever-increasing prices of its industrial products. Since the end of World War II, industrial prices had risen sharply while the price of raw materials remained rather stable. The result was a favorable balance of trade for the industrialized West and severe financial encumbrance for the rest of the world. The OPEC decisions may thus be considered a stratagem by which to bring the "revolution of expectations" to the Near East.

The multiple effects of the increase in oil prices were quickly felt in Europe. "Petrodollars" now moved in great quantity to Saudi Arabia, Kuwait, Iran, and the other oil-producing countries. Suddenly surfeited by new wealth that they could not effectively invest in their own lands, the Arab nations replaced the money in the West. This process, ironically labeled "recyclotron," has led to Arab investment in European firms, to widespread purchase of real estate, and even to lavish vacations that but a century ago seemed only a European prerogative. Perhaps the most striking example of the new disposition of wealth occurred on July 17, 1974, when Iran purchased 25 percent of the stock of Krupp Steel for a sum of $75 million. That venerable old company, manufacturer of weapons for the two world wars, then took on new international importance.

The most obvious effect on European society of the new oil prices was serious inflation. Although inflation was noticeable at the beginning of the decade of 1970, and concomitant in growth with the increased demand for consumer goods and the equal demand for higher wages, the end of the era of cheap energy was the major factor accounting for the rapid rise in the European cost of living.

CONSUMER PRICE INDEX OF ALL GOODS CONSUMED
(1970 = 100%)

	1968	1973	1975
France	89	120	153
West Germany	92	119	135
Italy	93	123	171

Recently intensifying alongside inflation is the problem of unemployment. In 1966 the Common Market countries found 5 percent of their labor force without jobs. That percentage went up to 5.9 in 1977, and then on to 6.9 (some 6.2 million individuals) in early 1978. In April of 1978 the European Trade Unions Confederation called for an Action Day, an international protest of short-lived strikes throughout Europe, to indicate labor's dissatisfaction with current economic policies. Over 15 million workers joined in the brief strikes, most of which were one to four hours in duration.

The contemporary problem of "stagflation," to use the descriptive American term, is a serious one in Europe. Inflation has combined with market stagnation to produce conditions of economic distress, which are particularly disadvantageous to the young, now entering the labor market.

Moreover, governmental concern with "stagflation" has recently been matched by anxiety over political unrest.

Dissent and Disorder

One of the most obvious European developments of the last two decades, but particularly of the 1970s, has been the increase in expression of political unrest. Extending from intellectual dissent in the Soviet Union to violent terror in Italy, this far-ranging dissatisfaction suggests a postwar domestic political turbulence even deeper and more persistent than the student rebellion of 1968.

The outspoken attitude of Soviet intellectuals was a concomitant feature of de-Stalinization. Criticism of the oppression and ineptness of Stalin's rule was first publicly made by Nikita Khrushchev at the Communist Party Congress of 1956. From that date until the official denunciations of the work of the writer Alexander Solzhenitsyn in 1964, the Soviet Union seemed to be entering a period of liberalization, of self-criticism. Poets, novelists, and artists gave expression to this new freedom in what appeared to be an intellectually pluralistic world, where ideas other than those officially promulgated might be tolerated.

However, a sharp turn away from this liberalization was evident shortly after the publication of Solzhenitsyn's first major work, *One Day in the Life of Ivan Denisovich* (1962). A description of political prison life under Stalin, the work was initially praised, but then roundly condemned by 1964. When Solzhenitsyn was awarded the Nobel Prize for Literature in 1970, the decision was officially denounced in the Soviet Union as an expression of anticommunism.

Once again, the Russian leadership had been reorganized, with Khrushchev removed, and Leonid Brezhnev taking his place in late 1964. The change in leadership was the most obvious indication that the brief period of official, political self-examination was terminating, and a reinforcement of older restraints on criticism of the government beginning. Yet intellectual dissent was not silenced. On the contrary, it took on new proportions after the signing of the Helsinki Accords of 1975. Officially entitled the "Conference on Security and Cooperation in Europe," this meeting in Helsinki of representatives from thirty-five nations chiefly resulted in American recognition of the postwar political status quo in Eastern Europe. However, this recognition was given in return for expected Soviet relaxation of restrictions on travel, personal freedom, information, and international commerce. The failure of such a relaxation to occur has, in the last few years, led to increased intellectual protest and this, in turn, has officially been greeted by a series of arrests and trials that in 1978 aroused international concern.

In Western Europe, protest of quite a different sort gained in notoriety, also in 1978, when one of Italy's leading political figures, Aldo Moro, was kidnapped in March and executed in May. Moro, several times premier and foreign minister of Italy, and the leading figure in the Christian Democratic Party, was the victim of a terrorist group, the Red Brigades. Pledged to the overthrow of the state, denouncing Italian society as corrupt, and espousing a rhetoric of violence and radicalism, the Red Brigades have become the most significant of the terrorist groups now operating in Europe.

Postwar terrorism first attracted world attention when a number of hijackings of European civilian aircraft occurred in the early 1960s. Perpetrated by dissatisfied nationalist groups, of which the Palestinian Liberation Organization was the major one, the hijackings were a political tactic designed to alert world opinion to the plight of minorities incapable of changing the political order by their own means and, therefore, seeking support from without, even if by the device of hostages and ransom.

Within Western Europe itself, there was a variety of terrorist organizations operating in more traditionally clandestine and disruptive ways. In Northern Ireland, the Irish Republican Army in 1969 began a series of terrorist attacks, notably bombings and assassinations, in an effort to dislodge the British and the dominant Protestant majority from control of the territory. Although denounced by the Irish government, IRA terrorism has extended to bombings in England and has not yet abated in Northern Ireland. In the Netherlands, South Moluccan refugees from the former Dutch East Indies have, in the late 1970s, seized trains in protest against the lack of support of the Dutch for the freedom of the Moluccan homeland from Indonesia. And in Spain, Basque terrorist forces have assassinated Spanish officials.

Yet the most striking development in terrorism is the emergence of "transnational" groups, those which operate without a regional or nationalist purpose, which often lend support to similar groups in other countries, and which—in contradistinction to "international" terrorists—receive no support from outside nations. The two most important of the European "transnational" groups have been the Baader-Meinhof Gang, named after its two leaders; and the Red Brigades. The former has been active in Germany since 1972, when they were held responsible for the killing of five American soldiers. In 1977 they gained international notoriety with the assassination of a well-known German industrialist and the seizure of a German aircraft, which they forced to fly to East Africa. Although both Baader and Meinhof were imprisoned and subsequently committed suicide, the influence of the group is still considered pervasive.

In 1977 and 1978 the Red Brigades made terrorism the major Italian problem, creating a condition of "civil war," according to one politician. With over two thousand terrorist attacks recorded in 1977 alone, the domestic situation was already precarious when the kidnapping and assassination of Aldo Moro shook the nation.

Critics who have attempted to analyze the new terrorism of the 1970s have frequently seen it as a reflection of the economic conditions of the time. Many of the terrorists come from middle-class families and are or have been university students. They belong to that social segment which Italians call the "marginal ones," those who do not have jobs, or do have jobs that pay poorly. Self-declared victims of the economic system, the terrorists are thus directing their revolt against capitalism and what they consider to be the politically compromised state that supports it. In this interpretation, the terrorism of 1978 may be a newer manifestation of the student rebellion of 1968: general discontent with the present social system and its economic inequities. Certainly, it is evident that a small segment of discontented youth is responding bitterly and viciously to what they interpret ideologically as a corrupt society, or to what they see as a social and economic order in which they cannot find a suitable role.

Whether this modern terrorism will become the "key problem of the so-called liberal societies," as one French critic has suggested, or whether it will eventually be seen as a minor social phenomenon projected by the communications media to undue proportions, as some other critics have asserted, it does remain a serious consideration of the present and an indication of the vulnerability of modern society to violent action by clandestine groups.

It is worth noting that the new form of terrorism has intensified during the same period in which the domestic politics of Western Europe have been changing with the appearance of Eurocommunism, a form that publicly eschewed revolution.

Eurocommunism

The leader of the Spanish Communist party, Santiago Carrillo, remarked in 1976: "For years Moscow was our Rome, the Great October Revolution was our Christmas. Today we have grown up." What he meant was that each national Communist party had matured so that it could enjoy the right to pursue its own policy in light of its own political needs. Eurocommunism has thus come to mean many communisms, each tailored to the nation in which it is situated. But Carillo carried the idea further, insisting in 1978 that communism no longer meant perpetration of revolution, but participation in parliamentary practices. And most Eurocommunists generally agree with him in asserting that their intention is to guide their parties along the lines followed by the more traditional European parties: engaging in elections, supporting foreign policy, and even leaving office if voted out.

This obvious deviation from the former international practice in which Moscow dictated policy is an indication of the further fracturing of the

Communist "bloc." Not only did ideological disputes with China cause initial trouble for the Soviet Union, but also the practices that state followed in attempting to prevent independence within the system of European political satellites had disturbing effects.

Ever since Marshal Tito led Yugoslavia away from Soviet control through his policy of national independence in 1948, Moscow has been concerned with the possibility of other such acts of defiance. When a revolt against Soviet control broke out in Hungary in 1956, following upon de-Stalinization, the Soviet leadership responded quickly and forcefully with tanks and troops.

More significant was the Prague invasion of 1968. In that turbulent year throughout all of Europe, the Czech government, under the new leadership of Alexander Dubček, sought a policy of liberalization, of what Dubček called "socialism with a human face." Dubček's reforms included certain basic freedoms, like those of the press, assembly, and travel. While the response to his efforts was favorable in some Communist countries, notably Yugoslavia and Romania, Leonid Brezhnev of the Soviet Union viewed the reforms with grave displeasure. After efforts at political maneuvering proved unsuccessful, the Russians made a firm decision. In August of 1968, Warsaw Pact troops invaded Czechoslovakia and ended any further "socialism with a human face." Dubček resigned and soon retired to private life.

It was against this background of harsh Soviet interference and in light of their growing belief that parliamentary success might soon be theirs, that many of the Communist party chiefs in Western Europe grew bold. The occasion for their affirmation of independence was a meeting in East Berlin in July 1976 with Brezhnev and the Eastern European heads of state. Despite his efforts to achieve solidarity and his attempt to find acceptance for his concept of "proletarian internationalism" (the official justification for intervention in Czechoslovakia), Brezhnev was unable to prevent a public declaration of the new national policy, which would soon be labeled "Eurocommunism."

Since 1976 the Eurocommunists have refined their ideology and program. They have dropped the term "dictatorship of the proletariat," and, in 1978, Carrillo even called the notion of class warfare outdated for Western Europe. It would appear that the French cry of "socialism decked out in the national colors of France" is a clear description of the new approach.

Yet the sincerity of Communist intentions is still doubted by many people in Europe and warily assessed by the American government. To date, Eurocommunism seems only clearly successful in Italy, where the Communist party has long had a strong following. Elections in France in the spring of 1978 resulted in a stunning defeat for the parties of the Left, with both Socialists and Communists doing poorly.

Whatever its less than successful showings in general elections, Eurocommunism gives further proof of the political fermentation in contemporary Europe.

Conclusion

What was recently called the "postwar era" has already become part of a dimming past for Europe. A new generation that was born after 1945 and introduced to the benefits—and problems—of a materialistically directed and highly regulated society is now taking over. It is confronted with the major issues of inflation and unemployment, but also cannot ignore the equally persistent difficulties of pollution.

Yet even if hampered by these conditions, European economic recovery has brought to a hitherto unimaginable number of citizens a new standard of living and a new style of life which clearly distinguish Europe today from all the Europes of yesterday.

There exists a new Europe, one in which history is a part of tradition, not an active force in daily life.

Epilogue

Photographs taken of the earth during the American space missions to the moon revealed our globe to be a small blue-and-white planet shimmering in a setting of endless darkness. There is no more spectacular proof of the physical oneness of our contemporary world. Yet, present-day technological advancements also confirm the growth of a common global order. Airline systems, telecommunication networks, even individual "hot lines" between world leaders allow for direct, frequent, and even instantaneous contact among peoples whose predecessors and problems of but a few generations ago were considered "foreign."

In such a cultural environment the older, distinctive characteristics of each region are being swept away. However, their disappearance has only revealed other, often more disturbing, global divisions.

Economically, the contemporary world is arranged on a north-south axis. The overwhelming amount of the world's current wealth—measured in gross national product, per capita income, and actuary tables—is found in the northern hemisphere. Europe, the United States, the Soviet Union, and Japan produce most of the world's goods and consume the greatest part of the world's available resources. The vast number of nations outside of this privileged economic zone have populations living in conditions of poverty and want. Even where the rise in the cost of oil importation has upset the balance of payments, the effect has been most severe on the non-industrial importers, those nations of the southern hemisphere who are now endebted in an amount exceeding $200 billion.

Furthermore, there is a severe political division in the ranks of nations. Only a small number of countries now have freely-elected, democratic government. The majority of the peoples of the world are ruled autocratically. More chiefs of state wear military uniforms today than they did at any other time in history. Indeed, in many parts of the world, the military coup has become a common condition of political life. The political instability and intolerance of opposition that military rule so often suggests account for another dire development: the repression or denial of civil rights.

Europe remains on the brighter side of this rather gloomy global picture. The privileged position that that continent has enjoyed in the modern era has been retained. Western Europeans continue to live within a political tradition of representative government, and they benefit from more guaranteed personal liberties than inhabitants of most of the other continents of the world. Although the threat of terrorism is present daily, and urban crime figures are ascending, the average European's domestic life is more secure and comfortable than it ever was. Moreover, despite inflation, the population has never been better off economically.

By most available indications, contemporary Europe is prosperous and peaceful. Its present status, therefore, remains consonant with its historical condition of growth.

It is not too much to argue that the modern era was in large measure European in definition. Industrialization, communications, urban development, technology, even organized leisure-time activities—those characteristics generally associated with modernization—were probably more pronounced in Western Europe during the nineteenth century than anywhere else at the time. In turn, these characteristics were built upon a tradition of commercial development, rational inquiry, and national consolidation. Comparable modernization in the United States, Japan, and Russia was initially an outgrowth of European precedents and justified by European-inspired ideology. The influence of Isaac Watt, Adam Smith, and Karl Marx, by way of obvious examples, extended well beyond their native Europe.

The lead that Europe initially enjoyed was soon lost to the United States, but the continent was never pushed from the forefront of industrial regions. The inventiveness, productive capacity, and organizational ability of its peoples have continued to be impressive. Today, the visitor to Europe will find a cultural mosaic of striking variety: gothic cathedrals and steel skyscrapers, castles on the Rhine and jet aircraft on the runways, folk festivals and rock concerts, museums and shopping malls.

In all of this, Europe seems to have unusual cultural resiliency, a capacity for renewal. Certainly, contemporary Europe is no longer the "Old World."

BIBLIOGRAPHY

The following is a brief bibliography of works that should help the introductory student pursue in some detail issues and problems that have been assessed in this text. Dates for the most recent editions are cited and reference is made to the paperback edition, if there is one currently in print.

General Interpretations

Major issues in modern European history have been concisely reviewed by many authors. Those studies which merit particular attention are Hajo Holborn, *The Political Collapse of Europe* (1951), an assessment of the developments of modern political history in light of World War II; Ludwig Dehio, *The Precarious Balance: Four Centuries of the European Power Struggle* (1962), a brief, rather philosophical treatment of balance-of-power theory as the operating mechanism of European affairs; Raymond F. Betts, *Europe Overseas: Phases of Imperialism* (1968), an interpretive essay explaining the rise and fall of the European colonial empire; L. C. B. Seaman, *From Vienna to Versailles* (1956), an enjoyably written book with a very idiosyncratic approach to international affairs.

In addition to these studies, several of a more particular nature should be considered: Cyril Falls, *The Art of War: From the Age of Napoleon to the Present Day* (1961), and John F. Fuller, *The Conduct of War, 1789–*

1961 (1961), both of which are excellent introductions to military developments in modern Europe. Finally, see Robert L. Heilbronner, *The Making
of Economic Society* (1975), a broad review of economic systems beginning
with ancient Egypt, but with particular attention given to the modern market system.

Part I: The Reordering of Europe, 1789–1871

The period of Early Modern European History has recently attracted
considerable scholarly attention, with the result that a wide variety of good
books is now available. On the political and social system of Europe prior to
the French Revolution, the following are recommended: E. N. Williams,
*The Ancien Régime in Europe: Government and Society in the Major States,
1648–1789* (1970); Max Beloff, *The Age of Absolutism, 1660–1815* (1954);
and Frank Manuel, *The Age of Reason* (1952). On intellectual developments, see Robert Anchor, *The Enlightenment Tradition* (1967), a clear
and concise introductory statement; and Peter Gay, *The Enlightenment: An
Interpretation* (2 vols., 1977), the latter by far the most comprehensive and
challenging interpretation. Scientific thought is given a remarkable overview
in Herbert Butterfield, *The Origins of Modern Science, 1300–1800* (1962).
On the major changes in the seventeenth century, developments now considered by some historians to be as serious as those following 1789, see Trevor
Aston, ed., *The Crisis of the Seventeenth Century* (1965).

The French Revolution and Napeolonic era have generated a rich literature of their own, perhaps only rivaled by the work on the Civil War in
American historical literature. A tightly argued explanation of the immediate
background to the Revolution is Georges Lefebvre's classic, *The Coming of
the French Revolution* (1961). One of the most easily read explanations of
the revolution itself is Albert Goodwin, *The French Revolution* (1962). Of
much more magisterial proportions is Georges Lefebvre's *The French Revolution* (2 vols., 1962 and 1964). For an assessment of crowd behavior, looked at
from a left-of-center position, see Georges Rudé, *The Crowd in the French
Revolution* (1967). Very conservative in its evaluations of the social effects of
the Revolution is Alfred Cobban, *The Social Interpretation of the French
Revolution* (1964).

The selection of works on Napoleon is enormous. Robert E. Holtman's
The Napoleonic Revolution (1967) is an excellent, concise introduction.
Felix Markham, *Napoleon and the Awakening of Europe* (1954) is another
such introduction. For an appreciation of the historiographical debate over
Napoleon, see Pieter Geyl, *Napoleon: For and Against* (1949).

There are a few good analytical surveys of the revolutionary era, 1789–
1848. One of the best is Eric Hobsbawm, *The Age of Revolution: Europe
from 1789 to 1848* (1969), which embraces all of the major subjects affected
by revolutionary activities. More traditional in interpretation is Jacques Droz,
Europe Between Revolutions, 1815–1848 (1968). On the year 1848, see the

very readable, more descriptive than analytical, work by Priscilla Robertson, *The Revolutions of 1848: A Social History* (1950). And Lewis B. Namier, *1848: The Revolution of the Intellectuals* (1946), is a fascinating study of the German revolution. However, the best introduction is to be found in William L. Langer, *Political and Social Upheaval, 1832–1850* (1969).

On the major international activities of the time, see Harold Nicholson, *The Congress of Vienna, A Study in Allied Unity 1812–1822* (1946), and Henry Kissinger, *A World Restored: Metternich, Castlereagh, and the Problem of Peace, 1812–1822* (1973). The growth of nationalism, pronounced in this period, is intelligently explained in Boyd C. Shafer, *Nationalism, Myth and Reality* (1955); a broader sweep through the centuries of Western civilization is found in Hans Kohn, *The Idea of Nationalism: A Study of Its Origins and Background* (1961).

General histories dealing with national problems and development are Gordon Wright, *France in Modern Times: 1760 to the Present* (1974); Hajo Holborn, *A History of Modern Germany*, Volumes II and III (1964 and 1969); David Thompson, *England in the Nineteenth Century, 1815–1914* (1964); and Dennis Mack Smith, *Italy: A Modern History* (1969).

The major economic changes have been given extensive historical treatment. A fine introductory study for the period of the early nineteenth century is Alan S. Milward and S. B. Saul, *The Economic Development of Continental Europe, 1780–1870* (1973). On the industrial process and its effects, see the older work of Thomas S. Ashton, *The Industrial Revolution* (1962), which, while superseded in some of its interpretation, is as good a short introduction as will be found. Much more detailed is Phyllis Deane, *The First Industrial Revolution* (1965). The most praised of recent works is David Landes, *The Prometheus Unbound: Technological Change and Industrial Development in Western Europe from 1750 to the Present* (1969).

Urban change is provocatively and critically assessed in Lewis Mumford, *The City in History* (1961). Studies more directly concerned with the period are Asa Briggs, *Victorian Cities* (1963), an extremely well-written account; Bruce Coleman, *The Idea of the City in Nineteenth Century Britain* (1973); and David Pinkney, *Napoleon III and the Rebuilding of Paris* (1972), a fine analysis of the politics of urban development.

Then, on class and social organization, see Charles Morazé, *The Triumph of the Middle Classes* (1966), a sympathetic study; George Lichtheim, *The Origins of Socialism* (1969); and Guido de Ruggiero, *The History of European Liberalism* (1959), an old study, but a clear introduction to liberal thought.

Part II: Expansion and Explosion, 1871–1918

The best introductory survey of this particular period is the one that concentrates on the last two decades of it: Orin Hale, *The Great Illusion, 1900–1914* (1971). Diplomatic matters are well presented in René Albrecht-

Carrié, A *Diplomatic History of Europe Since the Congress of Vienna* (1958). A recent survey of European empire-building is Raymond F. Betts, *The False Dawn: European Imperialism in the Nineteenth Century* (1975). In addition, Heinz Gollwitzer, *Europe in the Age of Imperialism, 1880–1914* (1969), gives an interesting assessment of the social and intellectual activities that generated an imperialist mood. On Darwin and Darwinian thought, the best-written study, and one marked by the quality of its analysis, is Loren Eiseley, *Darwin's Century: Evolution and the Men Who Discovered It* (1961). On economic activities for the period, again refer to Landes, *The Prometheus Unbound.*

Changing intellectual attitudes in the late century are well considered in Gerhard Masur, *Prophets of Yesterday: Studies in European Culture, 1890–1914* (1969); H. Stuart Hughes, *Consciousness and Society: The Reorientation of European Social Thought, 1890–1930* (1961); and Barbara Tuchman, *The Proud Tower* (1977). A beautifully wrought introduction to French thought and attitudes during *La Belle Epoque* is Roger Shattuck, *The Banquet Years* (1968). For the more dismal thought found on the other side of the Rhine, see Fritz Stern, *The Politics of Cultural Despair: A Study in the Rise of Germanic Ideology* (1974), which carefully traces a growing conservative sentiment, both antimodernist and nationalist in tone.

Of course, beyond all of these issues looms that of the First World War. Since the first months of the war, explanations of—and justifications for—its outbreak have been offered in great array. Two of the most intelligent and crisp introductions to the causes of the war are Laurence Lafore, *The Long Fuse: An Interpretation of the Origins of World War I* (1965), and L. C. F. Turner, *The Origins of the First World War* (1970). A most compelling account of the outbreak of the war, a book illuminated by brilliant descriptions, is Barbara Tuchman's *The Guns of August* (1976), which has, however, met with some criticism because of its failure to consider some of the most recent research on the subject. The most provocative, recent account of the causes of the war is Fritz Fischer, *Germany's Aims in the First World War* (1968), which again places the blame on the Germans.

As for the war itself, the most accessible and concise history is Cyril Falls, *The Great War* (1961). On the activities of the home front, the standard work is Frank P. Chambers, *The War Behind the War, 1914–1918* (1972). The fictional accounts that describe the war experience are many. Two that are regularly cited as best conveying the meaning of the war are Erich Maria Remarque, *All Quiet on the Western Front* (1974), and Jules Romains, *Verdun* (1938), published as Volume 8 of his grandly proportioned narrative of turn-of-the-century life, *Men of Good Will.*

Part III: Reconstruction and New Order, 1918–1945

The interwar period has been dominated by historical considerations of reconstruction in the 1920s and, then, by the rise of dictatorship in the 1930s.

There are few studies that treat both decades well in terms of coverage of European domestic history, but a good introduction to the period is Raymond J. Sontag, *A Broken World, 1919–1939* (1971).

International developments, as should be expected of such a turbulent age of diplomacy, have been given considerable attention. Perhaps the best, recent introduction is Hans Gatske, *European Diplomacy Between Two World Wars, 1918–1939* (1971). But two older books, both appearing when World War II was beginning, remain sound and penetrating: E. H. Carr, *The Twenty Years' Crisis, 1919–1939* (1964), and Arnold Wolfers, *Britain and France Between Two Wars* (1966). Another good, recent introduction is Elizabeth Wiskemann, *Europe of the Dictators, 1919–1945* (1966).

The social and cultural situation of the various countries, while not so extensively treated as that of the United States of the 1920s, has been analyzed in several worthwhile studies. Peter Gay, *Weimar Culture* (1968) is a brilliant essay on changes in German thought and intellectual activities. The early portions of H. Stuart Hughes, *The Obstructed Path: French Social Thought in the Years of Desperation* (1968) are excellent. And Robert Graves and Alan Hodge, *The Long Week-end* (1941), offers biting—and amusing—commentary on interwar Britain.

The Great Depression has not been the subject of the broad syntheses that characterize American treatment of the subject. For a good overview of the American "Crash," see John Kenneth Galbraith, *The Great Crash, 1929* (1972). On a grander scale, but with excellent appraisal of the European situation, is Charles Kindelberger, *The World in Depression, 1929–1933* (1975). On particular responses to the Depression, see John T. Marcus, *French Socialism in the Crisis Years, 1933–1936* (1958), and Robert Skidelsky, *Politicians and the Slump* (1967), an account of British Labour Party reactions.

The history of the interwar period has been dominated by accounts of the rise of fascism. The term as a broad, descriptive one has met with opposition. Some historians have contended that only Mussolini's policies and practices in Italy appropriately fall under "fascism," although it is often inappropriately applied to Hungary, Spain, and Portugal. Much the same criticism has been leveled against "totalitarianism." In the historical debate the question of generalization and conceptualization has been complicated by new social science thought on "dysfunction" in modern, industrial societies, a condition seen in Italy and in Germany.

Thus forewarned, the introductory student will appreciate the following studies, but these are only several from a rich literature. The grand theoretical explanation of totalitarianism remains Hannah Arendt, *The Origins of Totalitarianism* (1973). Other books of broad analysis are Ernst Nolte, *Three Faces of Fascism* (1969), a work arguing that fascism was essentially a response to communism, and Francis Carsten, *The Rise of Fascism* (1967), a comparative study, with a good general introduction.

Particular works on Mussolini's Italy that should be considered are Laura Fermi, *Mussolini* (1966); Ivone Kirkpatrick, *Mussolini: A Study in Power*

(1967); and Dennis Mack Smith, *Mussolini's Roman Empire* (1977).

On Hitler, see Alan J. Bullock, *Hitler: A Study in Tyranny* (1971), still the best biography, and Joachim Fest, *Hitler* (1975). Furthermore, there are David Schoenbaum, *Hitler's Social Revolution* (1967), concerned with the social elements from which Hitler drew his support, and John Wheeler-Bennet, *Nemesis of Power: The German Army in Politics, 1919–1946* (1964), to which ought be added the relevant sections of Gordon Craig, *The Politics of the Prussian Army, 1640–1945* (1964), a splendid volume.

Political changes in Russia may be followed in Robert V. Daniels, *Red October: The Bolshevik Revolution of 1917* (1969); Bertram D. Wolfe, *Three Who Made a Revolution* (1964), now something of a classic; Robert Conquest, *V. I. Lenin* (1972); and Louis Fischer, *The Life and Death of Stalin* (1952).

As with the First World War, the Second World War has been covered by many fine studies. On the coming of the war, see Laurence Lafore, *The End of Glory* (1970), which is of broad scope. A sensitive and profoundly nationalist account of the collapse of France is Marc Bloch, *Strange Defeat* (1968). On English appeasement, see Martin Gilbert and Richard Gott, *The Appeasers* (1963). The full dimensions of the war are very well treated in Gordon Wright, *The Ordeal of Total War, 1939–1945* (1968). On the strategy of the war, see B. H. Liddell-Hart, *The History of the Second World War* (2 vols., 1972).

Internal developments in Europe may be approached historically through the following studies. The Resistance movements are comprehensively reviewed in Henri Michel, *The Shadow War: The European Resistance, 1939–1945* (1962); see also Hans Rothfels, *The German Opposition to Hitler* (1976). On the French Vichy regime, see Robert O. Paxton, *Vichy France: Old Guard and New Order* (1972). For German economic developments, turn to Alan S. Milward, *The German Economy at War* (1975), and the celebrated, self-serving work of the German armaments minister, Albert Speer, *Inside the Third Reich* (1972).

Part IV: Europe in the Contemporary World

The contemporary period of European history may be initially approached through the following studies: Walter Laqueur, *The Rebirth of Europe* (1970); Geoffrey Barraclough, *Introduction to Contemporary History* (1968), which places Europe in a world setting; Maurice Crouzet, *The European Renaissance Since 1945* (1971). An excellent introduction to intellectual developments is Roland N. Stromberg, *After Everything: Western Intellectual History Since 1945* (1971). And the best economic survey is M. M. Postan, *An Economic History of Western Europe, 1945–1966* (1967).

The two major international problems confronting Europe in the immediate postwar decades—the Cold War and decolonization—have been given ample consideration. A good, general survey of Europe's change in world status is F. Roy Willis, *Europe in the Global Age: 1939 to the Present* (1968). On the Cold War, see Norman Graebner, *The Cold War* (1976), an abbreviated version of his outstanding study on the subject; also consult Paul Seabury, *The Rise and Decline of the Cold War* (1967), which has the virtue of compactness; and André Fontaine, *History of the Cold War* (2 vols., 1968, 1969), a very detailed study by the former foreign editor of the prestigious French newspaper *Le Monde*.

Europe's retreat from colonial empire is a subject that still awaits a grand synthesis; however, there are a few good analyses that the introductory student will find very useful. Consult Rupert Emerson, *From Empire to Nation: The Rise of Self-Assertion of Asian and African Peoples* (1962), which offers an excellent assessment of colonial unrest from the Versailles Treaty onward, but which is somewhat outdated. Far more detailed is Rudolph von Albertini, *Decolonization* (1971). Also see Ignacy Sachs, *The Discovery of the Third World* (1976), a pithy and highly critical account of Western overseas involvement.

On particular national developments, the following are suggested: For France, John Ardagh, *The New French Revolution: A Social and Economic Study of France, 1945–1968* (1969), and Philip Williams and Martin Harrison, *Politics and Society in de Gaulle's Republic* (1972). For Germany, see Alfred Grosser, *Germany in Our Time* (1971). For Italy, there is Elizabeth Wiskemann, *Italy Since 1945* (1972). And for Great Britain, consult C. J. Bartlett, *A History of Postwar Britain, 1945–1974* (1977).

On the broader problems of European cooperation and integration, see F. Roy Willis, *France, Germany, and the New Europe* (1958), and A. E. Walsh and John Paxton, *Into Europe: The Structure and Development of the Common Market* (1972).

INDEX